W9-ADT-683

B. F. F.

B. F. F.

A MEMOIR OF FRIENDSHIP
LOST AND FOUND

CHRISTIE TATE

THORNDIKE PRESS
A part of Gale, a Cengage Company

LIBRARY OF CONGRESS CIP DATA ON FILE.
CATALOGUING IN PUBLICATION FOR THIS BOOK
IS AVAILABLE FROM THE LIBRARY OF CONGRESS.

ISBN-13: 979-8-88578-963-9 (hardcover alk. paper)

Published in 2023 by arrangement with Avid Reader Press, an Imprint of Simon & Schuster, Inc.

Printed in Mexico
Print Number: 1   Print Year: 2023

To Meredith — a promise is a promise

"MY DEAD FRIENDS"
by Marie Howe

My friends are dead who were
the arches the pillars of my life
the structural relief when
the world gave none.

My friends who knew me as I knew them
their bodies folded into the ground or
   burnt to ash.
If I got on my knees
might I lift my life as a turtle carries her
   home?

Who if I cried out would hear me?
My friends — with whom I might have
   spoken of this — are gone.

PROLOGUE

When it was my turn to speak, I squeezed the pink heart-shaped rock with my left hand and grabbed my notes with my right. If you looked closely, you'd see my whole body slightly shaking. Halfway up the stairs to the stage, I lost my shoe and had to backtrack to retrieve it.

Slow down. Breathe.

This was my first eulogy. I wanted to honor my friend Meredith — the first friend I'd ever lost like this. To death, that is. I'd lost plenty of friends by other means. During my four-plus decades of life, I'd been in friendships that blew up or dissolved in both inevitable and unexpected ways. I'd withdrawn, drifted away, lost touch; I'd also ghosted and, more than once, watched seemingly close friends vaporize before my eyes. It was a miracle that Meredith and I enjoyed an uninterrupted run of close friendship for more than a decade.

My eulogy could best be described as a collage. A Meredith collage. I'd culled lines from over 1,300 emails she'd sent me over the years. Each snippet highlighted a specific role Meredith played in her life. Most of us gathered in this multipurpose room of the Ebenezer Lutheran Church on Chicago's North Side knew Meredith as a pillar of recovery in twelve-step meetings, because she attended roughly one zillion meetings in church basements, elementary school classrooms, and hospital atria during her too-short life. But she was also a striving graduate student, an earnest wife, a jealous sister, spiritual seeker, an exhausted employee, a faithful daughter, and an anxious friend. She, like all of us, contained multitudes, and I arranged her words to celebrate her in all of her complicated realness.

From the stage, I gripped the microphone in the hand that held the heart rock Meredith had given me months earlier, the day before one of her scary scans. Since her death, I'd carried it with me everywhere. I'd read that quartz not only enhanced spiritual growth and wisdom but also clarified thought processes and emotions — all of which I needed now more than ever as I stood in front of a hundred people memorializing the life of our friend.

As I spoke the first few lines, my voice echoed off the stained-glass windows and bounced back to me sounding tentative, shaky. I took a quick pause to center myself, and then read Meredith's thoughts on her lifelong struggle with loneliness in friendships. Several of the women in the audience chuckled. They knew. Friendship is hard. For many of us, friendship has been almost as tricky to navigate as romance. In some ways, more so.

A minute or two into my speech, my muscles relaxed, and my shoulders sank back into my body. My hands steadied, my voice stabilized. I slid into a good rhythm. Every few lines, I made eye contact with audience members as I'd learned in high school speech class. When I looked up, I met the gazes of women in the audience. Their smiles beamed love and tenderness toward me, and I received it. Another miracle.

It was with Meredith's help that I'd learned how to be a friend. A bona fide, true-blue, long-term, steady friend. Through her, I learned to tolerate the vagaries of friendship, address the pain of competition with and envy of other women, and confront the lie of my own unworthiness. Without the work I'd done with Meredith, I would have looked out into the audience and seen threats, competition, and frenemies. But as I spoke Meredith's words out loud, I saw loving allies. I felt suffused with tenderness, even for those women over whom my inner demons of envy, resentment, bitterness, and scarcity had taken me to very dark places. Standing on that stage, I could feel it: I'd changed.

After I read the last line, I made my way back to my seat, relieved to be done with the public-speaking portion of my mourning. Through the remaining speeches and songs, I sat squarely inside the bull's-eye of grief, running my fingers over the cool surface of the rock in my palm. I missed Meredith. Every day, I craved conversation with her. I longed to text her about everything: my new meditation app, whether my dress made my breasts look lumpy, Adele lyrics, complaints about my husband, a question about what to get my dad for his birthday, a recipe for no-bake cookies. I felt bereft and understood that I would for a long, long time.

But there was also the faint drumbeat of anxiety. Sure, I felt bighearted and magnanimous toward every female soul at Meredith's memorial service, but what about in the weeks and months to come? Would I revert to my old ways? Slip into the version of Christie who ghosts when conflicts and tension arise? Without the scaffolding of Meredith's presence, could I remain the steady, solid friend she'd encouraged me to become in all my friendships?

Not so long ago, Meredith and I both believed that we simply weren't cut out for go-the-distance friendships with women. We joked that we were too damaged by our history of addiction, too twisted by our petty jealousies, and too wounded from growing up alongside golden sisters with luminous hair, radiant complexions, and all-around upright lives. But we decided — actually it was her idea and I went along with it — to focus on friendships. "Let's do the work to get better at them," she said, her cobalt-blue eyes boring directly into mine. We excavated our pasts and appraised where we'd done wrong by our friends and where we'd been led astray by toxic ideas that no longer served us. We did it in conversations over breakfast sandwiches, on coffee dates, on walks down the sidewalk after twelve-step meetings, and over the phone.

What happened was simple: we changed.

About ten months before she died, Meredith called me early on a Saturday morning when I was out walking in my neighborhood. That fall morning, the sun fell through the trees, dappling the leaves on the sidewalk under my feet. All that glorious light and color. *We have plenty of time,* I thought. In those days, I swaddled myself in denial; I rarely thought of Meredith as my dying friend; she was just sleepier than everyone else I knew.

"I want to write about you," I blurted right before we hung up.

"Make me sound smart," she said. "Use big words."

"Of course. And footnotes."

The jovial tone soothed me. We were simply two friends on the phone before the quotidian demands of our lives overtook the day. I walked north along the Metra tracks between 59th and 60th Streets. One hundred blocks away in Andersonville, she sat in her comfiest chair next to her cat and her husband's dog.

"Oh, and do me a favor, will you?" she said brightly. I expected *Can I pick my pseudonym?* or *Don't mention my dentures.*

"Sure. Anything." Yes, I was still in denial about her illness, but lately, I couldn't help but notice her whittled face and her jutting cheekbones, now sharp enough to slice an Easter ham. Somewhere inside me I knew she was slipping away. I would grant any goddamn wish she had.

"Please be sure it has a happy ending."

I stood still on the sidewalk in a pile of yellow leaves, nodding and swallowing a cry. I didn't like the word *ending,* and I didn't understand the word *happy* in this context. How could I honor that promise if she ended up, you know, not making it? What kind of happy ending could I give her?

"Of course, a happy ending," I chirped, and instantly hated the false, shrill tone of my voice — that wasn't what we needed right now. We needed the firm, solid notes of honesty. "Mere, I'm not exactly sure how to do that."

"Oh, honey. You do. Tell the truth. Tell how we helped each other let go of being so brittle and scared and unable to connect with so many women because of our own hang-ups. Tell them how we learned friendship. Together. Tell them how we changed by holding each other's hand as we looked honestly at ourselves. Tell how one life can alter another."

■ ■ ■ ■

PART I
WHAT IT WAS LIKE

■ ■ ■ ■

1

I met Meredith in December 1998, and I still remember her outfit. A red blazer, multicolored silk scarf, gold pin. Black leather shoes with a kitten heel. A pencil skirt. Boniest ankles you ever saw. Her hair was blond with a few gray streaks, and her manicured nails were a pale pink that today I could identify as Essie's Ballet Slippers. She stacked multiple rings on several fingers of both hands, which clacked softly when she gestured. Later, I told her she'd looked like a meteorologist from the eighties with that scarf and pin. "I was jealous of how put together you were — the outfit, the manicure." At the time, I was twenty-five years old; Meredith was in her mid-forties.

We met at a recovery meeting held in the back booth of a Swedish diner on the North Side of Chicago. The purpose of the meeting was to help the friends and family members of alcoholics — anyone who loved a drunk, basically — reclaim their lives from the chaos of being intimately involved with someone who drinks too much. People had been recommending this recovery program to me for many years — starting with a biology teacher in high school who knew I was dating a basketball player who liked to party — and I'd refused, even though I spent half a dozen biology classes crying over the basketball player's infidelity and nonstop pot smoking. *No, not for me.* Sophomore year of college, I found my way to a different twelve-step program, one for people with eating disorders, and it helped me address the bulimia that had dogged me since I was thirteen. One recovery program was enough, thank you very much.

I'd finally decided to walk through the doors of the weird Swedish diner meeting when Liam, my boyfriend at the time, came home yet again from the bar and puked in the toilet, too blitzed to say his name, much less *Goodnight, Christie,* or *I love you.* Sex was most certainly out of the question. In those days, I spent my waking hours perseverating over the question of why Liam would pick a six-pack of Schlitz over hanging out with me, wonderful me, who was turning into an emotionally bankrupt shrew whose primary job was to tally how much he was drinking and how little we were fucking. I'd become an abacus: all I could do was count how much he drank and all the ways he disappointed me. The night before my first meeting at that Swedish diner, I'd decided there was no harm in checking out another twelve-step meeting. Meetings typically last sixty minutes, and I wasn't terribly busy with my secretarial day job and my nighttime job of waiting for Liam to tap into some desire for me. Maybe the people at this meeting could teach me how to get my beloved to stop drinking until he blacked out.

At the time, I lived and worked on the South Side of Chicago, in Hyde Park, one hundred blocks away from the Swedish diner in Andersonville. The morning of the meeting, I woke up before six to shower, dress for work, and pack food for the day, because as soon as the meeting was over, I'd have to bolt to my Honda and book it one hundred blocks back to Hyde Park, where I worked as an administrative assistant to a prominent social sciences professor at the University of Chicago. My job entailed sending faxes, answering the phone, and tracking down my boss's speaking fees — tasks an average sixth grader could have executed. The boss wanted me there by 9:00

a.m. sharp in case the president called at 9:01 a.m. inviting him to discuss his research at an upcoming U.N. conference.

When the diner meeting started, only five other people huddled around the table in the back corner. "Hi, I'm Meredith. Welcome. We're a small meeting," said a smartly dressed woman when she saw me looking around for more people. My recovery meetings for bulimia took place in hospitals and churches — solemn institutions that smelled like antibacterial soap, mold, or incense — where we sat in folding chairs or on lumpy couches. Meeting in public at a table beneath stenciled images of old-timey Swedish townspeople, I felt exposed. What if I burst into tears? What if a member of the public overheard me talking about my boyfriend's beer tab? What if someone I knew walked in for lingonberry pancakes before work? If Meredith hadn't spoken to me, I would have turned around and walked out.

The person in charge, seated to the right of Meredith, had short, spiky brown hair and brick red lipstick. She introduced herself as Sherri and read from pages in a blue binder. At some point, she asked if there were any newcomers. I raised my hand and said my name. Around the table, each

22

person said "Welcome" and smiled at me. My eyes filled with tears without my permission. These people — four women and one guy — were already paying more attention to me than Liam had over the past week. Underneath the table, I picked my cuticles, a terrible habit that left my skin tender and blood-streaked. I worried that after the meeting, one of these people would pull me aside and tell me I had to break up with him, or corner me and insist I stay. I blinked and blinked, trying to keep the tears from falling.

Throughout the hour, I bobbed along the bottom of my pain, pining for the early, blissful days of my relationship with Liam when we dated long-distance: I had lived in D.C., he in Chicago. He wrote me a letter every single day, and during our monthly visits, we'd spend the weekend in bed, laughing, dozing, and getting to know each other. In our long-distance year, I rarely saw him drink, and never once saw him drunk. But since I'd moved to Chicago to be with him, he changed jobs and began working sixty-hour weeks at a consulting firm. The drinking surely relieved the pressure of his job, as well as the strain of my constant surveillance of his alcohol consumption. A few beers took the edge off my weekly reminders about how long it had been since he'd bothered to fuck me.

I prayed one of the people who'd welcomed me to the meeting would tell me how to make the drinking stop. No one offered anything close to a quick tip; there were no hacks, only suggestions that we look at our own lives. *Take the focus off the alcoholic,* more than one person said, which I thought was dumb because my only problem was Liam's drinking. There were, of course, several items in my own life I was ignoring every time I fastened my laser focus on Liam's affinity for beverages in brown bottles, such as my dead-end job that didn't cover my mountain of student debt; my dusty-ass apartment that lacked central air and a single free inch of kitchen counter space; and my distant relationships with every other human being on the planet. I sure as hell couldn't see that this consuming "romance" with my boyfriend had crowded out my friendships. Every single friend had gone blurry in my peripheral vision. One minute they were there, and then: vanished.

When I met Liam, I was part of a trio of friends in the same master's program in humanities at the University of Chicago. Amy, Saren, and I ate lunch together every day on campus, discussed the readings we did for our classes, planned dinner parties, and piled in Saren's car for shopping trips to the suburbs. We had inside jokes about our professors and the eccentric characters in our graduate program, like the woman who could not have a conversation without quoting Bertolt Brecht. We'd met each other's parents, and when we talked about the future beyond graduate school, we assumed our friendship would remain in the center of our lives. But when I started dating Liam right after graduation, I let the friendships wither, quickly and fatally. And it wasn't because I was too busy and blissed out from the hot sex to join my friends for Thursday-night must-see TV or sushi downtown. Liam was in our graduate program; we could have all hung out together. But I was threatened by Amy and Saren — I didn't drink and they did, so they were livelier and looser than I was. I couldn't have admitted it at the time, but I feared Liam would compare me to them and realize he'd mistakenly chosen the uptight teetotaler who liked to go to bed by nine thirty after spending the day battling low self-esteem and anxiety. They were a better match for him, especially Saren. She'd read *every*thing, drove a red Bronco, and wore trendy, belted outfits. She also had an impressive job lined up with a Chicago magazine. The one time we went out as a group, she and Liam had a long, heated conversation about Studs Turkel and post-capitalism poverty in Chicago. From their reddened cheeks and loud voices, I could tell they were buzzed, energized. They looked like they wanted to mash their lips together. My sole contribution to the forty-five-minute conversation was "I heard they're tearing down Cabrini-Green." To me, the vibe between them was unmistakable, but instead of having an honest conversation with them or asking Amy for a reality check, I withdrew from the friendships, backing Liam and myself into an isolated corner so no one could see how mismatched we were.

I cut Amy and Saren out of my life with little remorse. I cared only about my faltering relationship with Liam. And it was a vicious cycle: I dumped my friends and became more isolated, which made me hold on to the unhealthy romance even tighter, because there was no else around. I lost my friends and myself, as Liam became the subject of most of my sentences. *He's under so much pressure at work. He screamed at me the other night about a coffeepot that he left on. He likes to drink at the dive bar on Oakley.*

Maybe if I'd held on to the friendships, Amy and Saren could have helped me sort out my relationship. If I'd let them, they could have had a close-up view of what was happening to me and asked questions. *Are you happy in this relationship? Is this working? Why are you holding on so tightly?* They could have pointed out that I had no plan for the future and less than $30 in savings. They could have helped me find an apartment that didn't make me want to die in my sweaty sleep when the temperature rose above 85 degrees.

If I'd had close friends, I would have turned to them instead of this random collection of people sitting at a diner talking about alcoholism.

During the meeting, I watched Meredith. And I listened. She talked about her mother and her sister, and I tried to figure out which one drank too much. She leaned forward when she talked, making eye contact with everyone. In her three-minute share, she mentioned having a sponsor, working the steps, and surrendering to a Higher Power. The holy trifecta of recovery meetings. By the end, I sized her up as a wise elder. She slid out of the booth five

27

minutes before the meeting ended. "Work meeting," she whispered to the woman sitting next to me. Her heels *click-click-click*ed against the diner's tiled floor.

In Meredith, I didn't see a friend, a confidante, a sponsor, or a sister. I didn't have that kind of imagination. I saw a wise middle-aged woman who liked gold rings and spent her days at an important day job, where she wore blazers and managed a staff. I never dreamed we'd talk on the phone, cry on each other's shoulders, or become each other's family. I saw no common ground between her pain with her mother and sister and my devastation over my boyfriend's drinking.

Anyway, I wasn't looking for friends. I had my hands full trying to get Liam to cork the bottle and pay attention to me. He was my first great love, and I couldn't bear the thought of living without him. If only I could get him sober, I'd have the perfect life.

2

After driving those hundred blocks north and then the hundred blocks south every Tuesday morning for six months, I learned something about myself. The meetings didn't confirm whether Liam was an alcoholic, but the moment he took a sip of alcohol — actually before the sip, when I heard the clink of the bottle as he eased it out of the fridge — I wanted to pull out my hair and scream my throat raw. To me, his drinking meant we slipped away from each other, and I couldn't stand it. My body wouldn't let me stay in the relationship — I slept in fits and starts, cried at the fax machine at work, and picked my nails into bloody stubs.

On the night that would be our last, he rented *The Days of Wine and Roses* from the hipster video store on Milwaukee Avenue, and as soon as I realized the movie depicted the near ruin of an alcoholic husband and wife, I popped off the couch and stood in front of him, my whole body shaking.

"I have a really hard time with your drinking," I said, my voice wobbling as I pushed the words out. "I don't think I can handle it. I can't, I just can't."

He pointed the remote control at the screen and clicked Pause.

"We have vastly different ideas about how to relax," he said, shaking his head.

"I think we're not a match," I said.

"I think you're right," he said.

We both cried. It was the first honest conversation we'd had since I'd moved back to Chicago one year earlier to be with him. I stayed the night — waking every ninety minutes to sob anew — and the next morning I slipped out of his bed and drove home, totally unsure of what came next on this drizzly, ash-colored Sunday morning. I knew that other women survived breakups by joining their girlfriends for $1-shot nights or trips to Vegas. I wished I had a friend on whose doorstep I could land so she could scoop me up and let me fall apart on her futon.

I did have Tony, my roommate who was a graduate student in the Divinity School at the University of Chicago. I leaned on him after the breakup, borrowing his cigarettes and tagging along with him to his regular twelve-step meetings and outings for Thai food. He'd recently broken up with a boyfriend — his first after a marriage to a woman — and felt as lost romantically as I did. We were a pair, holed up in our stifling apartment, crying into our pillows and wishing for more counter space.

"I dropped everything for this relationship, and now it's over. What's going to happen?" I whispered to Tony as we sat in traffic on I-94 one night, blowing our cigarette smoke out the window. "I'm serious. What's going to happen to me?" I was so bereft I could not picture anything positive in my future.

"You're going to find out who you're supposed to be."

"What, like my destiny? Is that what they teach you in Divinity School? I thought you studied medieval nuns?" I didn't believe in destiny any more than I believed in myself. I couldn't process the obvious truth that without an alcoholic relationship to suck up all the oxygen in my life, I was likely to build better relationships with lots of other people, including myself.

There were a handful of women I was friendly with from my original twelve-step program for my eating disorder. We talked on the phone outside of meetings, and sometimes we went for dinner in a big group, each of us ordering food that wouldn't trigger our bulimia/anorexia/binge-eating. Sauce on the side. No butter. Substitute fresh fruit for potatoes. We left big tips because we were pains in the ass.

Several of those women called to check on me right after the breakup. One Sunday, after I cried through a meeting in a second-floor hospital multipurpose room, seven women left messages. "Thinking of you and wondering how you are." I wrote each of their names on the back flap of my journal as I listened to their voices.

Trish
Lisa
Laura
Amanda
Colleen
Maya
Sharon

During that long, sad summer, I'd lie in my bed, filling my journal with my existential dread until my hand cramped. When I got sick of that, I'd flip the book over and read the women's names over and over. The list turned into a poem. I'd called a few of them back, but not all of them. Sharon and Maya intimidated me with their put-together lives. I wasn't scared to call Laura because she was going through a breakup, too; Trish and Colleen always smiled warmly when I walked into a meeting and seemed available for the minimal amount of friendship I could provide between crying jags. As the weeks went on, I kept crying through meetings, while the other women of recovery reported to their jobs, shuttled their children to soccer, and planned trips with their partners. They lived in the fullness of recovery, as I wandered, lost in heartache. My aloneness and sorrow felt pathetic.

A few weeks before the breakup, I'd asked a woman named Chloe from the diner meeting to be my sponsor. A sponsor is someone who leads you through the steps. Typically, they've been in the program longer than you have, and you picked them because they have something you want. A light in their eyes. A sense of joy and gratitude that prevents them from crying through every meeting. Self-acceptance. A life.

"Lean into your female friendships," Chloe said one morning when I arrived a few minutes early to the diner meeting after the breakup. "You're going to need them."

"So they can set me up with a new boy-friend?" I'd read that 28 to 39 percent of people met their partners through their friendship network.

Chloe, an elementary school teacher who took zero shit from her fourth graders or from me, bopped me on the head with a menu. "No, you ding-dong! To help you find *yourself*. They are your net. Let their hands catch you. Call them up and ask if you can cry on their couches and watch *Thelma and Louise.*"

Chloe's words made sense, but they didn't match my life. She had no idea that my life was a friendship graveyard. That my obsession with my most recent boyfriend's drinking had crowded out my relationships with my grad school friends; that in graduate school, I'd ghosted my college friends because I'd been freaked out to land in Chicago after a lifetime in Texas — the bitter winters socked me in the face and the intense graduate school courses full of references to Derrida and Cixous left me feeling like a backwater hick; that through graduate school, I stuck my head down, read for hours in the library, and went to recovery meetings — and soon enough, my college friends, busy in their new careers in Houston, Austin, and Dallas, stopped chasing me; that in college, I'd let go of my high school friends, the few souls still reaching toward me after I spent senior year chasing — surprise, surprise — a budding alcoholic.

"I don't have a ton of girlfriends," I said.

Talking to Chloe about my anemic friendship skills highlighted one of my great personal failures: an inability to hold on to friendships, not only when I was diving into an alcoholic romance but also in times of transition. How come I never called my college roommates or any of the girls I'd loved during the five years I spent on the campus of Texas A&M? It horrified me, though only slightly, that I had no idea how to answer that question.

"Get some," Chloe said. "Quick."

3

When I was in grade school, I pined for a best friend. I pictured a cherub-faced girl with bangs and freckles who shared her Hostess treats with me and held my secrets close to her heart. This fictitious B.F.F. would find me endlessly fascinating — our inside jokes would leave us belly-laughing, and our mutual adoration would be as secure as a swaddle. We would share an emotional shorthand like that between twins or old married couples. Our moms would be friends, and we'd be so close people would stop us at the mall and ask, "Are y'all sisters?" When I looked around the playground, I saw friendships that looked like the one I dreamed of. Maria and Ginger. Ann and Robin. Carrie and Moira. If I couldn't have a singular B.F.F. all to myself, then I wanted to be part of a defined group of friends that moved through the world of recess, lunch, P.E., sleepovers, and the birthday party circuit as a unit. A unit that I was clearly a part of. If three of these girls showed up somewhere without me, I wanted them to field the question, "Hey, where's Christie?" That these friends would know my whereabouts was a given.

The only thing standing in the way of my friendship dreams was my personality.

"Let's play ballet," I urged the girls standing around during recess in first and second grade at Christ the King School, where we wore green-plaid jumpers and obeyed the nuns who taught us how to spell words like *communion, crucifixion, reconciliation.* "I'll be the ballet master." Obsessed with every aspect of ballet — barre work, Balanchine, Baryshnikov — I could not imagine how this invitation failed to entice my classmates. Sometimes I had takers. A few times Hattie and Kate joined me under the covered walkway between the school and the convent.

"Let's work on *tendus.* Point your toes." I tapped on Kate's knee, urging her to straighten it. Like my French ballet teacher, I demanded precision. Didn't everyone want to be perfect? Why do anything unless you were striving to be the best? It was only recess, sure, but why not pretend it was an audition for *Swan Lake*? "Like this," I'd say as I showed them my own board-straight leg.

Soon enough, Kate and Hattie were plenty bored and ran off to jump rope. I stood there, confused. Sharing my obsession with ballet and bodily perfection was my best guess on how to connect. If they were real friends, they would join my obsessions and match my intensity. How could I find someone like me?

I wandered from the swings to the merry-go-round over to the jump ropes, always hopeful that I'd stumble upon someone whose longing matched my own.

Where was she?

"Let's all stand in a circle," I said to the handful of fourth-grade girls gathered on the bleachers of the newly designed soccer field at Christ the King. On the cusp of middle school, we were allowed to wear plaid skirts instead of jumpers, and I took the wardrobe evolution as a sign that this would be my year to draw toward that circle of friends I'd dreamed of. "Here's my idea for a game. One person stands in the middle and everyone else will take turns saying one thing they don't like about her."

Poor Kate and Hattie signed up for this terrible game. At least I wasn't impersonating a tyrannical French ballet master.

Melissa and Nicole joined us. Did Kate volunteer to go first or did I cajole her into the middle?

Kate took her spot in the middle and smoothed out her skirt. The look of expectation on her face proved she believed in my genius.

"I'll go first," Nicole said. "You never invite me over, and you've been to my house ten times."

"Your lunch smells funny," Melissa said, looking down at her saddle shoes. "Egg salad is gross."

"You cry too much," Hattie offered, chest puffed out with the illicit thrill of tearing Kate down. "Like a baby," she spat.

"Isn't this fun?" I said, as I watched the emotion collapse Kate's smile and twist Hattie's smirk.

"You haven't gone yet," Hattie said to me, crossing her arms.

I looked again at Kate and for the first time noticed the tears pooling, ready to spill down her cheeks. My sadism now seemed shameful. I hadn't pictured crying. My body suddenly felt hot and too big. What I'd been after was something meaty and genuine that might build a deep connection between us, but my best idea now made me feel sick to my stomach.

"Come on," Hattie said, annoyed. I'd enticed them to cruelty, and now I had to ante up. I looked from Hattie to Kate, stalling for time to think of something I didn't like about her that wouldn't sting.

"I don't like how you always do well in spelling." I smiled at Kate, letting her see my tender feelings. *I'm not a monster.*

"That's not real," Hattie said. "Unless you mean you don't like how Kate acts like she's better than us."

Kate looked at me, her expression a plea for me to stand by my first statement, but Hattie wanted more. I hated how dirty I felt for setting this up. I had to make it stop. "Maybe we should switch to saying what we like about the person. I'll go first. Kate, I like the way you share your snack with me." Kate brought plump raisins in the small red boxes and homemade cookies.

Hattie was already climbing down from the bleachers. "This is stupid," she said. "I'm not playing."

Everyone else dispersed. I hung back with Kate as she regained her composure.

"I don't think you cry too much," I told her, churning with guilt.

"Hattie does."

"Sorry."

Back in the classroom, my stomach roiled;

I couldn't concentrate on the lesson about solving word problems involving fractions. Why had I suggested such a mean game? What did I think would happen? I should have volunteered to go first. What would they have said about me — I burned to know.

Christie has a big stomach and greasy hair.
Christie is no fun.
Christie is an awkward black hole of neediness.

Kate's crumpled face haunted me. Years later, I would remember that afternoon so vividly. I'd been gunning for expressions of displeasure and the chaos of resentment, which was my idea of intimacy. I have no other memory of fourth-grade recess, just that single day marred by my sick feeling of shame as I watched Kate slump over her desk all afternoon. Somewhere beneath my white uniform blouse and my little kid ribs, I knew I was going about things all wrong. When the bell rang at three and everyone poured out of the classroom, Hattie and Kate piled into Hattie's wood-paneled station wagon and would hang out at Hattie's until Kate's mom picked her up. Ann and Robin, sporty girls, scarfed their snacks and then headed to soccer practice. Behind me, Maria and Ginger talked about a weekend

sleepover. In every girl, I heard the easy, effortless syllables of friendship, like a secret
language I couldn't decode. How could I
learn it? How come I didn't know it already?

4

Chloe had advised me to huddle up with my best friends, but I didn't have friendships like that and had no idea where to get them.

Instead, I searched online for a new job, one that would require something more than manning a phone and faxing expense reports to the procurement office every few weeks. I signed up for the Law School Admissions Test, since I had no clue what to do with my graduate degree in humanities. I put together a version of the future that hardly seemed perfect, but it was an improvement on my present.

I spent my free time in recovery meetings, hoping to keep my eating disorder in check and to steer my heart away from active alcoholics.

Eventually, I discovered there were roughly thirty meetings for friends and families of alcoholics closer to my house than the Swedish diner one, and I started attending those. I lost track of Meredith for a few years, but then we both popped up in the same Saturday-morning meeting held in a kindergarten classroom of a Catholic grammar school in Lincoln Park. Gone was the smell of powdered-sugared pancakes and the public crying from the diner meeting days. We smiled at each other and nodded during meetings; we chatted in the parking lot before climbing in our cars and launching into the rest of our weekends. There was no deep connection. She still had those manicured nails, those gold rings, and an impressive array of scarves, and I spent most of my effort trying to sort out my romantic life. I focused on boyfriends and love interests almost exclusively because of societal pressure, loneliness, and a desire to have a family.

The word *spinster* hounded me as I celebrated my twenty-seventh and twenty-eighth birthdays. My chief fear was dying alone and unloved in the carnal sense, and the pressure I felt to sort myself out romantically grew to lethal proportions — one day I found myself wishing for death. Everyone I knew was coupled up. From TV, I knew it was acceptable to be single only if you were as glamorous or promiscuous as the characters on *Sex and the City,* and as someone who wore ill-fitting sweater sets from Marshall's and repressed my sexuality, I felt round-the-clock shame about my single status. Soon I added intensive group therapy to my mental health regimen.

I also landed in law school and made friends: brilliant, hilarious women with whom I studied and on one occasion joined for a bar crawl. I kept a distance between myself and them, though, hiding behind giant property textbooks while I chased A's and a high class ranking, hoping those external achievements would compensate for my unsatisfying personal life. In March of our first year of law school, Clare, Kiley, and Amma planned to attend the St. Patrick's Day Parade in downtown Chicago.

"Come with us, Christie," they said during the break between civil procedure and legal writing.

"Totally. I'll meet you there."

And I did. I put on my most festive black jeans and a cream-colored sweater — I hadn't even searched my closet for something Kelly green. I stood next to them on Columbus and Balbo for almost ninety minutes, and then slipped away to work on a criminal law outline, even though finals were two months away. I ran to the Red

Line train like Cinderella trying to outrun midnight. All my bluster about having to study on a Saturday afternoon was a thin cover for the shame I felt about being a few years older than each of them, yet still sadly single while they were all in serious relationships, and I was the only one of us in need of intensive therapy and recovery meetings to cope with basic life functions.

I'd lugged so much baggage to law school: shitty romantic résumé, eating disorder, and a pervasive insistence on my own alienation and apartness. At law school "prom" one month later, we all showed up with full-length dresses and smoky eyes, but I felt like a different species because they all brought dates, and I was, as always, the seventh wheel. I saw myself as "the problem child," grimy next to their shiny potential and fresh-cheeked luminance.

During these messy years of law school and my first few years of practice, Meredith sat on the periphery of my consciousness as a pleasant professional woman with a solid spiritual foundation whom everyone seemed to know. She sponsored several young women in my orbit, and she volunteered to chair meetings and serve as the treasurer. When I didn't see her around for a few months in 2006, I asked one of her friends at the meeting where she was.

"Treatment for breast cancer, but she'll be back."

The C-word struck me as sad and scary, but I didn't feel close enough to reach out to her or offer to deliver a meal. I didn't even know her last name. I only knew it started with a *D.*

She returned to meetings with short cropped hair and a slightly thinner frame about six months later, and I felt relieved to see her.

"I missed you," I told her after a Saturday meeting in the kindergarten classroom. This admission felt like a big leap — I'd never really talked to her, yet I was admitting I noticed and cared that she'd been away. "Hope you're okay."

"I'm glad to be back," she said. "I missed you, too. Sounds like you're making progress."

I was. I no longer cried through meetings for weeks on end. I sponsored a few women, and I had a new job working for a federal judge. I was doing well, and I reveled in her noticing. A compliment from Meredith D. on spiritual progress felt like a blessing from the Dalai Lama. Even through a cancer scare and treatment, she continued to share in meetings about "trusting God's plan for her, one day at a time." She regularly shared how grateful she was, not for cancer but for all the support she received from her community. Meredith radiated spiritual seeking and spiritual finding. And I really had missed her.

St. Patrick's Day, March 2007 — eight and a half years after I first met Meredith and six years after I bailed early on the parade with my law school friends — I signed up to tell my story at the meeting held in the kindergarten classroom.

For years, when I spoke in a meeting, I sounded like this: *Why can't I find a decent sober guy to date?* And on some raw mornings, my pitch was shrill: *WHERE IS MY BOYFRIEND?*

But on that Saturday in March 2007, I had something new to share. Meredith sat across the room in her Saturday casual clothes: jeans, sweatshirt, monochrome scarf, no pin. For the past few weeks, I'd been gliding into the room, beaming about my new boyfriend, John. "He doesn't drink, y'all. Like ever. Just doesn't like it. He's sober, and I like him!" In fact, I'd signed up to share my story because my new relationship with this smart, kind, sober man made me feel like the wisest person on the planet.

48

Who wouldn't want to hear my gems of wisdom? I'd wriggled my way out of the alcoholic pattern that had ensnared me for years.

"I'm so grateful I can be honest with John just like I'm honest with all of you," I said. "I told John on our first date that I don't drink and would prefer that he didn't either." I shared how I felt comfortable in my skin with this new wonderful man, and then I tossed off a final comment.

"I used to hate holidays, especially the minor ones. Who cared about national days of celebration when the guy you love is drinking until he pukes every weekend?" I pointed at the Kelly green sweater from J. Crew I'd dug through my closet to wear on this chilly March morning. "But now that I'm not in permanent relationship-crisis mode, I'm ready to celebrate. Happy St. Patrick's Day, everyone!" Had there ever been a more spiritual person to walk the streets of Chicago?

The following week, I arrived at the Saturday meeting early to help set up the folding chairs around the room. I felt a tap on my shoulder.

"Thank you for sharing your story last week." Meredith's glacier-blue eyes met my gaze, and she smiled warmly. "I loved your green sweater."

"I wanted to be festive." I'd lost so much joy in the past chasing alcoholic men or obsessing about who didn't call or who had dumped me for a sporty intern in his office that it felt like recovery to have simply acknowledged the holiday by selecting a green sweater to wear for the day.

She held out a box to me. "This is for you."

It was a gift box — twice the width of a shoebox, but only a quarter as deep.

"Should I open it now?"

She nodded.

I lifted the top, nervous because we were friendly in meetings, but not at the gift-giving level. By then, I'd learned her last name, but I couldn't imagine wrapping a gift for her. I peeled back the white tissue paper and saw five colorful silk scarves rolled up like scrolls, each with a different holiday print. Pumpkins for Halloween, red and green presents for Christmas, shamrocks for St. Paddy's Day, hearts for Valentine's Day, and painted eggs for Easter.

"Meredith, these are fantastic!" I ran my hand along the edges of each. Who was this Meredith, a woman I'd never really talked to who'd just given me a lovely, if slightly random, present?

"You said you were ready to start celebrating holidays, and you're always talking about my scarves. Celebration looks good on you," she said, squeezing my arm.

I wasn't a scarf person, and I couldn't quite picture myself walking around the courthouse with a pumpkin sash tied around my neck next October, but the gesture was so generous and unexpected that I set the box on the teacher's desk and wrapped Meredith in a hug.

"I can't believe you did this for me. It's so thoughtful." I unfurled the Valentine's Day scarf and tied it behind my neck. "How's this? Do I look like you?"

"You look like yourself, and it's perfect." She winked, and I felt the warm rush of pleasure of being seen. I hadn't pictured Meredith thinking of me outside of meetings. And as I stood next to the bulletin board with the cut-out letters with the words of the day — Red. Go. Stop. Park. Dog. — I saw that Meredith could be a friend. She already was. Why hadn't I seen it before? Was it our age difference? Now, I could see that just because she was twenty years my senior didn't mean we couldn't be friends.

"We should hang out, Meredith. We should be friends."

She laughed. "Right on time," she said.

"On time?" I looked at the elementary school clock above the door, the one that ticked so loudly you could hear it whenever a hush fell across the meeting.

She laughed, eyes twinkling. "You're in a stable relationship with John." I smiled and my cheeks reddened to hear my new boyfriend's name. "So now you can look at other relationships."

Blank stare.

Other relationships?

My relationship with John began less than two months ago. Straightening myself out romantically had taken nine years of weekly meetings and six years of group therapy. She'd watched me sulk through meetings, bawling about this guy or that one, pulling aside women who showed up with new engagement rings begging them to tell me: *How'd you do it? How'd you find your way to partnership?* My relationship with John was the Holy Grail. The Ark. The pot of gold at the end of the rainbow that had been strewn with pieces of my pulpy heart and guys who liked beer and/or work more than they liked me, and guys who didn't want to look at my face when we had sex, and guys who were married to other women. Couldn't I enjoy a few months of peace before embarking on more emotional work in "other relationships"? My God, bite your tongue, Meredith, you freaky scarf chick!

She saw my blank stare harden into offense. She touched my arm. "Sweetie, I'm only suggesting that if John sticks around, then you can start focusing on other kinds relationships that give you trouble."

I gripped the box of scarves with both hands and shifted my weight from my left foot to my right.

She pointed at herself. "Friends. You may find that now you want to look at your friendships. That's how it's been for me, anyway. I'm doing some work on my friendships and with my two sisters now that I'm in a committed relationship with Gage. The work never ends, right?" She winked again like a fairy godmother and soon fell into conversation with someone else.

I was happy to see her go. Her words felt like something sharp piercing my bubble of happiness. She was the character in a fairy tale who arrives to warn the other characters, in mysterious rhyming couplets, that there is danger ahead. Pitfalls, a broken bridge, a troll, flying monkeys, murderous rocks, lotus-eaters. Real *something wicked this way comes*–level shit. By the time I got to my car, I decided Meredith was a witch.

Kind and generous with the scarves but still.
A witch.

5

In fifth grade, my parents liberated me from dogma and the green-plaid uniforms of Catholic school and enrolled me in the local public school, where I dreamed of social success. Twice the size of my small parochial school, Preston Hollow Elementary teemed with noisy kids in colorful clothes. On my first day, I watched students pour out of yellow school buses and their parents' cars and head into the one-story redbrick building that spanned half a block. My B.F.F. had to be there somewhere.

In preparation for my public-school debut, I grew my dark brown hair long and slept in pink foam rollers to make corkscrew curls, which would fall by third period. I listened to Cyndi Lauper and Duran Duran and stayed up late watching *Friday Night Videos* so I could learn the *Thriller* dance. My mom bought me dark-wash jeans and madras tops in pastel colors.

On this foundation, my fifth-grade year started off strong. The popular girls invited me to sit at their lunch table on day one. The queen bee Brittney gave out candy to her loyal subjects, and the moment that sour green apple puckered my lips, I was hooked on the promise of Brittney's friendship. The girls who didn't get a Jolly Rancher slinked off to the edges of the lunch room with their brown paper sacks and cartons of milk. Those of us who did smiled at each other, smug and safe. We belonged in the center, not on the fringes. We'd been chosen. I wanted that Jolly Rancher every single day, and I'd do anything to get it.

Brittney twirled the golden beads of her necklace. "Do you have one of these? It's called an add-a-bead necklace, because you can add on to them. I like the solid gold balls best." Was this really our first conversation? I remember that I shook my head, and when I got into my mom's station wagon after school, I told her I had to have that necklace. Immediately. And the Tretorn tennis shoes Brittney wore. My mom held up her hands, like whoa, whoa, whoa. I'd never pushed for anything before — presents came at Christmastime and at my birthday in July. When my mom hesitated, I told her I'd pay for it myself, but could she please take me to the mall this weekend.

I watched Brittney. I laughed at her jokes. I complimented her school supplies. I hinted I wanted to be invited to her house for a sleepover. I shamelessly adopted her slight speech impediment.

"Why are you talking like that?" my mom asked, when I pronounced the word *Clinton* as I'd heard Brittney at school: *Clinn-EN*. Friendship demanded my sycophancy and my allegiance to all things Brittney.

"What?" I said, ashamed that she'd busted me. I thereafter confined my speech affectation to school hours.

The first time I spent the night at her house, Brittney's mom made us brownies and then took us to see *Footloose* the next day. I knew my mother would object to the violence and racy content, so I didn't tell her about the movie until we'd already seen it. "I wish you would have called first," my mom said when she picked me up. No way, Mom. I wasn't about to let parental discretion stand in the way of my friendship with the great and powerful Brittney.

In a pattern I would repeat with guys a few years down the road, I narrowed my focus to a single person. I could have joined the circle that surrounded Brittney, but the other seven girls at the lunch table hardly registered with me; they were blurry figures with no faces or voices. I never invited them over or wrote notes to them in class. I never adopted their unique speech patterns. I can't recall a single conversation with any of them. My energy in fifth grade was that of the asshole you meet at a party who is always looking over your shoulder to see if there was someone better to talk to. My whole body attuned to Brittney. I dreamed of ways to insinuate myself closer, closer, closer.

I wanted no part of a friendship circle — I wanted only a short, unbroken line from Brittney to me.

"I'm concerned that you only seem to focus on Brittney," my mom said one winter night. "What about the other girls? Rachel, Ashley, Nahila, Allison, Stacy, Carrie, or April?"

"What about them?"

I refused to settle for B-squad friendship. Those girls weren't potential friends; they were threats to my relationship with Brittney. At any point, they could overtake Brittney's affection, and then where would I be? I didn't want their friendship because they didn't have as much power as Brittney. They never gave out candy. Their moms didn't drive a Mercedes. No one copied their style as we all did when Brittney started wearing Guess jeans. As a new kid in middle school, I couldn't fuck around with Ashley or Stacy. My mom didn't understand. She had gone to St. Joseph's Academy, an all-girls school, from first through twelfth grade, and then her whole group of friends had attended the same university down the street in Baton Rouge, where they'd pledged Kappa Delta and lived happily ever after. What did she know about surviving at a suburban public school in Texas?

"What if you and Brittney have a falling-out?"

I shook my head, refusing that nightmarish image. I would never let that happen. Never. I doubled down on inviting Brittney to my house, writing her notes, stoking our inside jokes. Each gesture let the world know: *we are B.F.F.s.*

In February, there was a change in the school schedule. Now half our class went to art while the other half went to history, which separated me from Brittney and all the other girls. I had no one to talk to in history class except a smiley kid named Cole who styled his hair into a modified mullet. We were the only two kids who paid attention, so we stuck together through Mr. Connely's lectures on the western frontier.

A few weeks in, I noticed that for three days in a row, Brittney, Stacy, and Nahila took turns getting out of art class, walking slowly by our classroom, and staring at Cole and me. I twitched slightly with fear. Was I in trouble? When any of them caught my eye, I smiled and rolled my eyes at the teacher so they would see how disaffected and cool I was and how I was definitely not enjoying the manifest destiny lecture in history class.

We don't want you at our table anymore. This was the main takeaway of the note someone dropped on the lunch table in front of me a few weeks after the schedule change. Brittney and all the other girls signed it. After I read it, a hand snatched it back. My vision went blurry from tears and shame; I felt all of their eyes on me, but I couldn't look up at any of them. Eyes down, I gathered my lunch and hid in the bathroom, legs shaking from the fear of having to see some of them in music class next period. No more Jolly Ranchers for me.

My mom had been right, and I held in the cry until I sank into her station wagon after the last bell.

I received my eviction-from-the-popular-table notice on February 20, and I never returned. Brittney and I never spoke again. I accepted my ouster and endured the waves of shame every time I passed her in the halls or when she would direct other girls to prank call my house on Friday nights.

Is Christie there?

This is she.

No one likes you.

For years, the shame of this story meant I never told it. When the shame burned off, I shared the story here and there after college, downplaying my obsessive focus on Brittney and playing up my victimhood. I found I rather enjoyed the sympathy it elicited. Christie, the innocent victim of middle school cruelty among girls. I left out the part about how I'd been a ruthless social climber who sought emotional security by elbowing out all the girls who might stand between Brittney and me. In my half telling, I glowed with the light of innocence. When one acquaintance called Brittney "a bully," I nodded my head. Yes, she was a bully! I'd been bullied.

Slowly, after many years, I began to widen the lens and include the part of the story highlighting my contributions to my social isolation. I became less sympathetic but more honest.

And I've never told this part of the story:

The only girl willing to fraternize with me after Brittney dumped me was Dani, an affable girl with a wide-open smile who lived three blocks away and seemed oblivious to the social hierarchies that had ruled my every decision since I walked through the doors of Preston Hollow. Dani did her own thing — talked to everyone who sat around her, laughed with abandon during class, and wore Levi jeans because she thought the inverted triangle of Guess jeans looked silly. She paid no mind to Brittney and her crew.

"You want to come over after school? My parents are buying me a new bike," Dani said about a week after I started eating lunch in the bathroom.

I stared at her, wondering what the catch was. Every other girl at school steered clear of me in the lunchroom and the halls. I studied Dani's smile for a hidden motive but saw only curiosity. I stepped back toward my locker and slowly she came into focus: blond hair, a beauty mark on her left cheek, and a red-striped shirt. We'd had most of our classes together, but I'd paid her little attention given how far removed she was from the blinding strobe light of popularity. I saw her now, though. And I realized with quiet joy: she could be a friend!

"Sure, I have to ask my mom, but she'll say yes."

At the bike store, Dani asked me if I liked

the yellow or the blue bike (yellow) and whether she should get a basket for the front (of course). Her mom took us to Luby's Cafeteria, where we ate little bowls of kernel corn and green beans with slivers of bacon and white rice we slathered with butter. At one point, I wondered how I was having such a good time when eight girls at school actively disliked me. Didn't Dani know that I was on the outs with all of the popular girls?

After she got her bike, we rode to school together every day. I felt relaxed with Dani — all the striving and breath-holding I did around Brittney dissolved. I didn't feel compelled to copy Dani's style or grasp for her affection. It was there for the taking.

Dani had no social power, no following, and her mother drove a nondescript American car, but in my friendship with Dani my stomach unclenched. I said what was on my mind; I ate more than my share of tortilla chips her mom offered when I went to her house after school. It was friendship, as pure and simple as any I'd ever known. Dani's loyalty was a straight line running between us, the line I'd longed for between me and Brittney. She didn't care who did or didn't like me; she just wanted to know what time we were going bike riding. Every day after school she waited for me by the bike racks; every day at lunch we pooled our money to buy the hot, starchy rolls we stuffed in our mouths like two girls who didn't know pubescent weight gain was zooming straight for us. Her dad took us to Six Flags, and my dad took us to visit my grandma's farm.

And it should have been enough. One true friend — a best friend — after the public humiliation I'd endured. But my scrambled brain and heart still pined for the power and popularity represented by Brittney and her coven. Dani offered friendship and emotional safety, but we were also socially invisible, and I wanted to be on the map. While we laughed as we pedaled around the neighborhood, the easy companionship felt like a consolation prize. At ten, I wanted more than to be loved and accepted by someone kind and faithful.

Every time I think back to fifth grade, I zero in on Brittney and the golden crew of popular girls who sat at her table and snatched up her candy. I rarely consider Dani, without whose friendship I would have eaten lunch alone for the rest of the year. It's ugly but true that the friendship Dani extended to me made the rest of the year bearable, and often joyful, and yet I never fully took my eyes off the real prize —

popularity — which I wanted more than true friendship.

In mid-May of fifth grade, as the cotton-wood trees cried puffs of white fuzz all over the city, I held my head high in the halls of Preston Hollow because I now had an exit strategy. My parents declared the public-school experiment a failure. For sixth grade, I would attend St. Rita's, a Catholic school a few neighborhoods over.

"You never paid any attention to us. It was all about Brittney for you," Allison said to me in music class during the last week of school. It had been months since I'd been dumped, and this was the first conversation I'd had with any of the girls involved. "None of us wanted to stick up for you because you didn't care about us," she said, not unkindly.

I don't remember what I said, but we walked to P.E. together, and she invited me to her house the next weekend. As I sat in her bedroom that smelled like rose-scented room spray, listening to Boy George, I felt surprised to be there after all that had happened. My time at Preston Hollow could have been different if I had been different. I believed I understood the lesson and planned to carry it with me to St. Rita's,

which would offer a whole new buffet of
B.F.F. options and a fresh start.

6

Less than a year after Meredith gifted me the holiday scarves and made her witchy prediction about my friendships, John and I decided to get married. He gave me a ring, and I gave him a set of fancy golf clubs because I thought we should both get something shiny to signal our upcoming nuptials. (Feminism in action!) Then we launched into the things you do when it's time to plan a wedding: we announced our news to friends and family, picked a date, made a budget. Our announcement spurred my law school gang to get together for dinner. *It's been too long! Let's celebrate!*

On a Friday night in late March, John and I walked from my place in River North to De Cero for dinner with Clare, Amma, Kiley, and their husbands. These were the women — friends — with whom I studied for countless law school exams and attended parades (or portions thereof), for whom I crossed state lines to witness their marriage vows, and by whom I'd measured my own success. Over the years, I'd shown up at their weddings in various states of romantic distress: sadly single but involved with a married man (Amma's); on a blind date with a guy who didn't understand why I refused to go to third base in a hotel room where two of my friends were sleeping four feet away (Kiley's); and with a boyfriend who wore an ill-fitting olive green suit and bailed before dessert so he could go home to play video games (Clare's). I loved these women, but my pervasive, sinking feeling that my messy romantic life and extensive mental health regimen made me inferior to them impeded my ability to fully inhabit the circle of friendship; I always pushed myself to the outside.

It shouldn't have mattered — these arbitrary timelines I made up — but I was fixated on my view of life as a race I was losing. I quietly kept tabs on our ages; I was the oldest of the crew by a few years and the last to get married and start a family. I tabulated this data in the service of measuring not them but myself. Each calculation showed me how far off I was. *Clare and Stephen got married in 2004, when I was five years older than they were and still dating a guy who wanted to be alone in his apartment all weekend.* How far was I from the mean? How much more fucked up was I than each of them who met and married great men years before I learned how to date a solvent, hygienic man who wanted a committed relationship with me? It was a dis-eased thought process that I was powerless to shut down. I could see that the competition, envy, and being-behind-ness I brought to these friendships was unhealthy; in the back of my mind, part of me was always whisper-ing: *You're not like them. You're lagging. They are one thing, and you are another.*

But that would be over now! I was en-gaged! No more dragging guys with mullets and overdrawn bank accounts to our re-unions and get-togethers. No more crying on their couches when my latest romantic adventure crashed into Lake Michigan.

This night was part of our new era. Next to me was John, not some random guy who would never love me.

John and I stepped into the darkened restaurant, and I spotted Clare, Kiley, and Amma huddled in the back by the brightly lit kitchen. Their husbands leaned against the bar, watching an NCAA basketball game on TV. Kiley spotted me first and rushed over to hug me. From the corner of my eye, I saw Amma turn around and smile at me and John. When Kiley stepped aside, I saw Amma's belly taut and round. We held our arms out toward each other, and I took in her gorgeous baby bump.

"You!" I screamed. "You beautiful mother-to-be!" Amma, gorgeous as ever, looked like a brunette Cameron Diaz: long legs, stylish jeans, three-inch heels, flawless skin. "Of course you found the only stylish maternity top that exists," I said, admiring her turquoise silk tank and her glowing skin.

When our table was ready, I took a seat at one end. John took the chair to my right, and Kiley's husband sat to my left. Kiley, Clare, and Amma ended up on the opposite end from me, and their husbands filled the seats between us. I didn't think to rearrange the seating because I imagined the table would engage in one conversation, each of us chiming in with stories about work, kids, and travel, interspersed with the requisite frolics into our shared law school memories.

After we ordered, John and I fielded questions about our wedding. The group raised a glass to our future. I felt joyful, bright as a flame. I excused myself to the restroom, and inside the stall decorated with shiny Mexican tiles, a Coldplay song about the color yellow piped in, and I had the impulse to fall on my knees to say a prayer of gratitude. In this exact stall, years earlier, I'd been on a date with a man I met online who was kind, smart, and sweet, but for whom I felt zero attraction. I'd called someone from my therapy group, bawling, not because the date was going badly but because he was objectively great and I still didn't like him. My voice breaking, I told Emily, "I should like this guy. On paper, he's exactly what I want. But I feel nothing." I called him The Bird because he seemed delicate and bony, which was a strong clue that I did not see him as a sexual prospect.

I'd always been so dramatic and tragic about my love life — the stakes at every single date were life and death, not simply an inquiry about whether I would like to go on a second date. I called group therapy pals from the bathroom on every date I went on from 2002 through 2007. In the middle of tapas, sushi, Argentine steak, Irish pub fare, Italian pasta, Bulgarian rice dishes, Middle Eastern kabobs, Kung Pao chicken, smoothies, spanakopita — I excused myself, slid out of the booth, and hid in a stall, phone in hand. The calls, which were my therapist's idea, grounded me in reality, and without the anchor of those supportive voices on the other end, I would have left

71

the evening either monogramming towels with my date's initials intertwined with mine or claiming near-suicidal depression because I felt no attraction and thus would die alone. More than half the time, the voice on the other end of my phone calls belonged to Emily.

I dialed her number for old times' sake.

"Guess what — I'm in the stall where I once cried to you over The Bird —"

"I remember him! You were inconsolable that night."

"After all the calls you took when I was bawling my eyes out, I wanted to report that I feel happy and whole, and I'm so grateful. Whatever I went through was worth it, because it allowed me to be here now."

"You deserve to be happy. Now go enjoy your tacos. Order the carnitas, they're the best."

When I returned to the table, the conversation among the women had turned to babies. Kiley had a son in preschool, and Clare's daughter recently turned one. Over the din, I heard Kiley and Clare offering Amma advice on professional-looking maternity clothes, breast pumps, and after-birth pads. Between me and the women, the men at the table discussed March Madness brackets, and I had to strain to hear my friends' conversation. As a familiar sinking feeling of apartness came over me, I realized that this seating arrangement served as a self-fulfilling prophecy: I *was* apart from my friends, and therefore, I *felt* apart from them. My shoulders tensed as I weighed my options. I was a thirty-four-year-old woman with a fully formed prefrontal cortex and years of therapy and recovery under her belt. I knew what it meant to play the victim, and I had all the tools in the world to speak up and get what I needed.

Before I could find the right words, Amma's husband stepped away to find the men's room, and I took it as a sign. I squeezed John's arm, *I'll be back,* and made my way to the empty spot next to Kiley and across from Clare. My body relaxed into the chair. I knew how to take care of myself. When Amma's husband returned, he nodded at me and smiled as he took his new seat next to John and Kiley's husband.

"You have to get the Medela pump," Kiley said, pointing a tortilla chip in the air for emphasis. "It's insanely powerful."

"Actually, if you can swing it, get a pump for home and one for the office. Dragging that thing on the train is a pain," Clare said.

From breast pumps, the conversation

73

flowed to the various ways to keep breast milk from leaking onto your blouse when you returned to work after maternity leave. I'd never heard of putting cabbage leaves in a bra.

"We aren't sure when to do the christening," Amma said, lowering her voice to tell us about her in-laws and their rigid religious expectations without her husband overhearing.

"I'm glad my husband is an atheist," Kiley said, taking a long pull of her beer.

"In-laws," Clare said, rolling her eyes. "Those relationships get much more intense once there's a baby."

I'd moved closer to my friends to kick my insecurities in the balls, but the familiar shame hovered like an unwelcome houseguest. How had I returned to this emotional place, convinced I was behind and not quite as worthy as my friends because my life milestones didn't match up to theirs?

The waiter placed plates of tacos in the center of the table, and I could hardly taste the mahi-mahi, the lime, or the homemade corn tortilla. I made a few feeble attempts to join the conversation but lost my enthusiasm. Why would Amma want my advice about doulas? And I'd never given two seconds of thought to postbirth undergarments, had never heard of special salves for when your baby sucked the skin right off your nipple.

I held out a smidge of hope that the subject would change from pregnancy and babies to a topic about which I had some knowledge or proficiency. Travel? Spanx? Mariah Carey's seventeenth number one hit? But there were miles of terrain to cover about becoming a lawyer-mother, and it would be years before I understood that or knew firsthand how valuable it was for a lawyer on the cusp of motherhood to talk to other lawyer-moms who were making it all work.

I kept a smile on my face but withdrew into the shame cave I thought I'd never see again once I found John.

I didn't use the word at the time, but Kiley and Clare were *sistering* Amma. Telling her what to expect, sharing their experience, creating a space right there among the tortilla crumbs and drained lime wedges to sister her. Sacred space. I didn't know how to invite myself into it, nor could I imagine there was room for me. I sat next to them — my shoulder inches from Kiley's — but still apart, ruminating like I had for years when they described their fulfilling sex lives and Valentine's Day plans, while I, ever the spinster, mapped out a study schedule for finals still months away.

Was that me who'd called Emily less than an hour ago ecstatic with prayers of thanksgiving? Where did that Christie go? *Come back!*

The evening wound down, and we said our goodbyes on the sidewalk, hugging one another and promising to schedule something again soon.

"You guys want a ride?" Stephen and Clare asked John and me when the valet pulled their car around.

"No, we'll walk," I said before John could answer. "It's a beautiful night." My hand found John's, but I couldn't look at him because I was afraid of bursting into tears.

From the outside, it was a perfect evening. Longtime friends sharing a spring night on one of the liveliest streets in Chicago. The temperature held steady at 70 degrees, and above, both a full moon and a smattering of stars lit up the night sky. I held the hand of a man I loved, a man who loved me back.

And yet my body twitched. I wanted to move my legs and dispel the dark energy that had gathered in me during the meal. When I'd felt this energy before — mostly shame mixed with anger at myself and my toxic way of seeing the world — I'd go for a run. Miles on the lake or on a treadmill. I joked about pounding the pain out, a practice that kept me from being carried away by my intense emotions.

But it was ten o'clock, I'd just eaten dinner, and my black espadrilles were not suitable for jogging a few miles. And John wasn't much of a runner.

We turned toward Lake Street, and I picked up the pace. "Let's walk under the el tracks," I said. I suspected I would start crying, and the el tracks seemed like a good place to lose my shit. The roar of the trains overhead and the creaky steel beams crying above us meant that, if necessary, I could sob without drawing any attention to myself.

"What is it?" John asked.

"It's just that —" My throat constricted, and words evaporated. Honestly, what was the big deal? Amma was pregnant, and it generated more excitement than my engagement? Of course it did! She carried new life in her body; I'd gotten a new piece of jewelry. What was my problem? I slowed down and dropped John's hand. The apartness from my friends, which I'd always attributed to my singlehood, was something bigger than being the only one without a steady plus-one. This evening had shown me that my apartness had nothing to do with my relationship status; it was something inside of me. Now that I'd seen it, the part of me that kept myself from joining the tight inner circle of female friendship — had always kept me from joining friend circles — I couldn't unsee it.

"All through my friendships with Kiley, Amma, and Clare, I've been sad and ashamed of being a hot mess in my romantic relationships, the sad girl running off to a recovery meeting or group therapy. My big problem was my terrible taste in men! My romantic fuckups. My struggles with addiction. All these years, they had boyfriends and then husbands, while I had" — I waved my hands in front of my face — "whatever it was that I had. Broken, failed, flawed relationships. Tonight was supposed to be a triumph. A leveling. A chance to stand right next to them without, without —" My throat closed up again. "I don't know what's happening," I whispered.

Above, the Green Line train rumbled toward us from downtown, and the Pink Line rolled in from the west. The trains overlapped, and the sound was deafening. The rush of air blew my hair back. My whole body shook from the vibration.

I put my head down, encouraging the tears to fall. Just fall, already. But nothing.

John grabbed my hand again, and we walked in silence. I felt grateful that John knew to give me space until I was able to find the words.

In my darkened bedroom, we crawled into bed, and I rolled toward him. Still no tears. I had some words, though they didn't yet carry the full meaning of what I'd come to understand about myself. I buried my head into the spot between his shoulder and his heart. I don't think he could hear my muffled words; I wasn't ready to say them clearly to another person.

I thought having a partner would fix my apartness from my friends.

I thought the shame attacks would be gone for good once I got engaged.

I thought the big work of my life was learning to find a healthy partner.

I thought the problem was my singleness.

I thought the hard work was over.

The next morning, I caught Meredith's eye at the end of the meeting in the first-grade classroom. Now she no longer seemed like a witch; she was a prophet. As we put away the chairs, I told her how I engineered my own separation by choosing the seat at the far end of the table, and how even after I moved, I got stuck in a story of my own not-like-them-ness.

"Why is apartness more comfortable for you?" she asked.

"It's not. I hate it." This apartness from other women, the ones who were doing their lives right and succeeding at being women/ wives/ mothers, while I was hopelessly behind, felt old. It felt like a pattern so entrenched and encompassing that I couldn't quite see it and didn't know how to shake myself out of it.

"Then why did you choose it?"

"That's the question, and I don't know. I slid into my seat as if that's where I belonged: apart. Then I moved to be near them and crawled into my shame cave."

Meredith's blue eyes blazed. "There's more to this story."

I nodded. Sure, of course. Isn't that always the case? She hugged me and tossed off a random comment about her sisters and mother shopping together without her while they were growing up and how she felt left out.

"Feeling left out is how I started in the world," she said. As she spoke, her rings made that comforting, soft clicking sound. "It's not a surprise that part of me is always trying to get back there, to the place where I felt left out. It's terrible, but familiar.

Don't forget the power of the familiar."

"I want to stop doing that, you know, setting myself apart."

"Me, too."

"How?"

"Maybe you could do some writing about apartness — how it's operated in your life and interfered with your friendships. I'll do it, too, and then we can share it with each other."

I hadn't expected a homework assignment, but I shouldn't have been surprised. Lots of recovery people believed in the power of picking up the pen to take an inventory or to make a list of people you harmed or to write an amends letter. Recovering from addiction — as an addict or someone who loves addicts — takes more work than passing AP calculus. You need paper, a pen, patience, and time. And you need a tutor.

That morning was the first time I saw what Meredith could be to me: a friendship tutor. Also known as a sponsor. I wasn't ready to ask, but I could imagine it.

7

Apartness I wrote at the top of a page of legal paper during a lull between projects at work the next week. Nothing came to me. I heard someone down the hall ask her assistant for a file and listened to the traffic below me on Wacker Drive. I closed my eyes.

Still nothing.

My email pinged, and I put the pad away. But on the bus ride home that night, as we crossed the Chicago River gleaming at dusk, an image appeared in my mind: my childhood home in Texas.

My household consisted of my parents, my older brother, Dirk, and my younger sister, Virginia. Virginia's bedroom stood across the hall from my parents' room in the section of the house they added a few years after she was born. Virginia shared the master bathroom with my mom. Because my parents believed that the secret to a strong marriage was maintaining separate bathrooms, my dad set up camp in the bathroom down the hall, next to the bedrooms belonging to Dirk and me. Growing up, the "girls" bathroom belonged to Virginia and my mom. It smelled like Ysatis perfume and floral hairspray. The walls were covered in bright cream and golden striped wallpaper, and the shower tiles glowed bright white — no hair, no wear and tear, no weird stains. That bathroom represented the heart of femininity in our house. It smelled sweet, shined brightly, and no boys were allowed.

And I never went in there, either.

I showered in the "boys" bathroom every morning, where the tiles were pale gray and a dark brown shower curtain lined the tub. When I was old enough for makeup, hot rollers, curling irons, and contact lenses, I commandeered the powder room adjacent to the boys' bathroom for my after-shower primping.

This childhood geography reinforced my sense of apartness and fueled my idea that I was not a bona fide girl or the right kind of girl the way my sister and mother were. If I had been, wouldn't I have shared a shower with them, instead of with my brother and father? Wouldn't I have been entitled to their sweet-smelling bathroom? I drew my own conclusion: I wasn't fully a girl by the definitions in my family, and my deficient femininity was both unspeakable and best relegated to the boys' bathroom.

In retrospect, I imagine it's entirely possible that I insisted on using the boys' bathroom because it was close to my bedroom, but, tellingly, I have no memory of that. The story that stayed with me was that there was something missing from me that made me different from the "real" girls in the family. The proof was in the bathroom.

I wrote this all down at the kitchen table in Chicago when John was working late, and then tucked it into my briefcase. I'd never thought about the bathroom arrangement when I was growing up, but I could see a line from my childhood bathroom to the night at the tapas place. Part of me believed I had no place next to my friends; they, like my mother and sister, were the "real" females. I wasn't totally sure how or what to do about it, but Meredith's suggestion to write about apartness shook something loose.

The next morning, as I brushed my teeth before work, I thought of the geography of the kitchen table where my family ate dinner when I was growing up. Most nights my mom prepared homemade meals for us — hamburgers, lasagna, chicken with rice, macaroni and cheese with a bread-crumb topping — and all five of us sat around the sunflower-yellow Formica built-in table shaped like a flat tire. The flat end was attached to the wall under a picture window that looked out over our suburban street. We sat in a semicircle: Mom closest to the stove, my sister next to her, then my brother, my dad, and finally me. I sat farthest away from Mom and my sister. I could reach out and easily touch my dad's arm, and if I leaned, I could touch my brother's left hand or swipe a dinner roll off his plate. In this seating arrangement, my parents did not serve as bookends for us kids, as I imagined they did at other family dinner tables. And once I knew how to divide the world by gender, I noticed that our table, starting with my mom, proceeded: girl, girl, boy, boy, and then me. I interpreted that order as further proof that I didn't quite fit into my family as I should. My apartness from my mom and my sister signaled I was something different from them, and that something different added up to something less than or not quite right.

And that lonely powder room where I stored my curling iron and contact lens solution? That was where I perfected the messy art of bulimia. From ages thirteen to nineteen, I defiled that bathroom with secret vomiting that left me momentarily dizzy and weak-kneed; I'd have to grab the counter to catch my breath. The toilet bowl held the foul evidence that seemed to prove, every night, that I didn't belong in the pristine girls' bathroom with its floral mists and beautifying potions. I was gross, I did gross things, and I had a gross body that was the wrong shape and size. I belonged far, far away from my mom and sister, who were truly beautiful, precious, and feminine.

By my mid-twenties, I understood that my beliefs that I was dirty and wrong kept leading me to self-destructive romantic relationships. Of course they did. How could someone with those beliefs pick a loving partner?

Until Meredith suggested this writing assignment, I'd never truly considered what these beliefs did to my *friend*ships. I'd never considered how my isolation from my mother and my sister long before I started purging might have complicated my relationships with girls and then later with women. Of course my secret eating disorder created a substantial barrier between other people and me, though I dropped hints to friends in high school and college. During those years, I also chased boys who were deep in their own burgeoning addictions to alcohol and drugs. How could I be available for any close friendships when I was occupied chasing drunk frat boys and hiding my bulimia?

I wrote all my insights down in brief snatches during lulls in my workday. Then I called Meredith on the phone for the first time and read it to her in one go. I told her about the peculiar geography of my childhood home and all the meaning I made from it. She listened, and I could picture her nodding on the other end of the phone. I told her I didn't know why I felt like crying.

"It doesn't matter why. Let yourself cry. It's how we get well."

Then she told me about a terrible afternoon when she was a little girl and a group of older boys led her to a secluded spot and violated her body. Her voice was low and thin, as if it might evaporate.

"That afternoon, what those boys did to me, it made me feel ruined. Something like that would fuck anyone up. And in my little world, it meant that I was dirty, bad, rotten. And guess who wasn't ruined like me?" Meredith paused, and I held my breath, unsure of what to say. "My two sisters."

"How awful. All of it. How terrible." I can't remember if I insisted that sharing a bathroom with your brother and father was nowhere near as traumatizing as a sexual assault, but I'm sure I did. Meredith pressed on, determined to expose the connections between our thinking and our ways of moving through the world.

"It's so painful to be the bad sister. The failure. The faulty version. And those beliefs bleed into all my relationships with women. They always have. Every single day of my life."

I knew what she meant. I believed I was "the bad one," too. From my childhood through my early adulthood, I regularly recited these lies to myself: *My body is disgusting; I'm all wrong; There is something wrong with me.* Those lies were built on the foundational belief that I was a misfit in my family. I cried too much, ate too much, needed too much. From the belief that I was a faulty version of a girl — missing something essential and elusive that my mother and sister possessed — I built a whole personality on compensation. Perfect grades. Chronic people pleasing. Anxiety, depression, and shame that I hid beneath achievement. I'd been addressing this in recovery and therapy since the age of nineteen. I knew all about this part of myself.

"I have a sinking feeling in my stomach right now," I said.

"What do you mean?"

"I can't believe I'm going to have to do as much work on my relationships with women as I did with men." A few years earlier, Dr. Rosen, my therapist, told me I actually had *more* work to do in my relationships with women than I did with men. At the time, I told him to bite his fucking tongue, but his words had stuck with me, and now I realized he might have been right.

Meredith laughed for the first time during the call. "Maybe more."

" 'Et tu, Brute?' "

"All I'm saying is that there's definitely more to the story."

Yes, Meredith, there was more to the story, but how would my sense of apartness — the I'm-less-than-and-not-as-good-as-other-women — ever change? Was it something I could overcome? The thought made me laugh out loud. Of course I thought my friendship issues were intractable; that was exactly what I said when I was dating all the wrong men and people would say, "Just wait, Christie! You'll find your person. Be patient." And I never once believed them. I sank my teeth into the juicy lie that I was different, that my commitment/intimacy problems were extra-special and extra-hard to treat. I ignored the hundreds (thousands?) of books and articles describing how some women are attracted to emotionally unavailable men. I pretended that all the stories I'd heard in thousands of therapy sessions and recovery meetings were about miracles that were reserved for other people. Not for me. I believed you had to be a miracle to get a miracle. And one thing I knew for sure: I was no miracle.

I no longer believed that about romantic relationships, but part of me was still holding on to old ideas about miracles in friendships.

"My friendships come to life — or fail to thrive — in the shadow of my sisterhood," Meredith said. "And it sounds like it's time to write about yourself as a sister."

I hung up the phone, dread thudding through my chest and out to my limbs. My sister story came in a tidy package I carried around for years, never revising, only adding support to my long-standing thesis that I was the bad one, and my sister was the good one. Meredith had invited me to unpack it. If I accepted the invitation, I would have to examine the history and narratives I'd come to believe about myself as a sister, how they tripped me up and turned me sideways, draining energy that might be better used to connect with the women in my life. I wanted that connection.

But I wasn't sure I was ready to face the work.

8

Four-and-a-half years younger.
Lives three states away.
We aren't close.
We were never really close.
I don't know why.
Is it my fault? I'm pretty sure it's my fault. I'm the older one.
For thirteen and a half years we shared parents, a brother, an address, a last name.

At Meredith's suggestion, I wrote about my sisterhood, my handwriting scrawling across a legal pad that turned into a three-page list of all the things I never did with or for my sister, the girl born into my family when I was four and a half years old.

In the space where there should have been a deep, singular relationship, there was a series of missed connections.

I never shared a secret with her; I never coaxed her secret crushes out of her; I never made her a mixtape; I never sat on her bed and played with her hair; we never shared clothes until I was a freshman in college; I never visited her at college; we didn't attend each other's college graduations; we never double-dated; we never drove around in a car blasting "our" favorite song; we never shared shampoo, a curling iron, a phone line, a hobby, a favorite teacher, a joke, or a novel with dog-eared pages; I never attended a single one of her swim meets; I never helped her with her homework; I never gave her advice; I never loaned her money; I never lobbied our parents on her behalf; I never gave her a ride to a boy's house; I never helped her create an alibi so she could do something against our parents' wishes; I never helped her sneak out of the house; I never discussed who she wanted to become, what she wanted to study, who she wanted to love; I never asked if her friends loved her well or if she had any regrets; I never knew what mattered to her or what the stakes were.

I never knew her.

As I wrote about my sister, I felt a tightness in my chest. I'd thought about our distant relationship before. In high school, I envied my friend Lia's close relationship with her sister — they were each other's best friend. For them, sisterhood looked like an actual place of company and comfort, a tight huddle of two. When I applied that paradigm to my sister and me, I had a lot of excuses why our relationship wasn't like that, mostly because of our age difference and my inherent deficiencies. Our lifetime of distance felt like a personal failure. While I'd thought about it before, I'd never focused my attention on it for too long. It was too painful, and there was always a romantic crisis to pull my attention away.

But once Meredith shared the secrets of her childhood, I felt more willing to look at parts of my own life I'd long ignored. My God, if Meredith could do it, so could I.

When I learned my mother had a baby in her belly, I was standing in the backyard of our redbrick house next to the green garage door. In my memory, Mom's thick brown hair was pulled back into a low ponytail and a floral maternity top covered her roundness. I was four years old, and I was going to become a big sister.

My memory next cuts to my dad turning on the light in the bedroom where my brother and I slept in bunk beds. "Wake up, the baby's coming!" The early-morning streets were quiet, empty, and dark as Dad drove us to Lana's house. Lana, my mom's

94

best friend, would watch us while our parents went to the hospital. I remember stopping for doughnuts, and that mine, as always, was chocolate.

Did I want a baby sister? It seems impossible I would have wished for another brother, when the one I already had bested me all day long. He ran faster, jumped higher, and claimed the last cookie before I even realized we were running low on Oreos. I loved my baby dolls — Allison, the one with the silky blond hair and white pinafore over her pink dress; Blue Baby, my favorite doll with the blue gingham dress and brown hair cut in the shape of a bowl. During the day I fed them and read to them, and at night I clutched them to my chest. I must have been excited about the new baby, a doll come to life.

Lana opened her big wooden front door and welcomed Dirk and me. I was mesmerized by her thick blond hair and dazzling white teeth. She also had the high energy and lean physique of a woman who ran five miles every day; she won our affection by letting us watch *The Price Is Right* and taking us to the park. I'd never been around Lana without my parents, but I don't remember feeling scared because she smiled easily and seemed relaxed and happy to have us around. It was out of the ordinary, but everything should be extraordinary on the day a new baby arrives. At some point, Lana told us we had a new baby sister.

The next day, Dad took us to the hospital, but my brother and I were too young to visit Mom's room. We played in the day-care center with a friendly lady who taught me to play hopscotch on the patterned carpet. She gave us hard peppermint candy when it was time to go.

Dad steered the car around the side of Presbyterian Hospital and pointed up at Mom's room. Her face appeared in the window, and she waved down at us. We screamed, "Hi, Mom!" even though she couldn't hear us four floors up. Mom looked just like herself, smiling wide, excited to see us.

They named her Virginia Alexandra. When she arrived at home, swaddled in hospital blankets, I touched her soft head with the tips of my fingers. In those first few weeks, I was surprised at how floppy and boring she was with her cycle of eating and sleeping. She didn't *do* anything. And her umbilical stump offended me. Why did my perfect little sister have something so crusty and unappealing on her belly? I remember feeling relieved when it fell off one morning as

Dad changed her diaper. I spent so much of her first few months peeking into her crib, watching her tiny nose, pink lips, and round cheeks as she slept. She was so beautiful! More beautiful than any doll I'd ever seen. Her tiny beauty overwhelmed me; it felt like an ache, a stronger version of the one I felt when I reached for Blue Baby in the middle of the night, so glad she was there, so glad she was mine.

When did I turn all that achy love and adoration against myself?

One day in second grade, I climbed into my mom's idling station wagon after school. While we waited for Dirk to file out of his third-grade classroom, I sat in the back next to my sister, who, at four, wasn't yet old enough to join us at Christ the King School. I'm sure Mom asked me about my day — the spelling tests, the times tables, the preparation for First Holy Communion — and I'm sure I offered the standard answers. What I remember is watching uniformed Catholic grammar schoolers marching to their mothers' sedans while I repeated my sister's name over and over — *Virginia Alexandra* — like a mantra. All those syllables. A mouthful of letters. The exotic *V* at the start and the very rare *X* in the center of her middle name. Those *I*'s popping up in her first name like sunflowers in a field. Was this the first time I thought with some bitterness, *Why did she get the better name? Were they saving the best girl's name for her?* I knew Virginia was the name of a state, because Dirk was studying the capitals and Mom would coach him at dinner: "The capital of Virginia is Richmond. Remember it like this: Virginia married a rich man."

It also stung that Virginia shared her middle name with my mother. *Alexandra* was a name fit for a queen. It was fancy, European-sounding. A stately bond between her and my mom, like the gleaming bathroom they shared down the hall.

By this time, I already hated my name. *Christie* sounded like the name of a girl who didn't wash her hair regularly and whose best friend was a horse. Neither elegant nor sophisticated. At a slumber party that year, I asked the other girls to start calling me *Margo,* a name I believed inched me closer to the gravitas in *Virginia.* It didn't stick. Literally no one ever called me Margo.

I can't fully explain why I was committed to seeing Virginia as so much shinier and beloved than I was. All siblings have to adjust when a new baby arrives, but why did I lock down my feelings of inferiority with steel bolts? And while I was hung up on the luminescence of Virginia's name, both first and middle, why is it that I never considered that I also shared a middle name with my mother? My mother gave me the middle name *O'Brien,* her maiden name — the name she was born into, the one that sat next to her first name until she married my dad and O'Brien became her new middle name. None of that mattered to me because Virginia got the name Alexandra, objectively more feminine and more regal than O'Brien. My older sister reasoning lacked logic.

By the age of ten, I still ached with love for my adorable little sister, but right next to the adoration ran the jaundiced river of my jealousy from which not-so-loving thoughts sprang. Thoughts like, *Hey this adorable little bitch sprang into our family and lapped me. I hate her stupid blond hair that looks perfect in the pink plastic clip with a baby lamb on it. Why does she get to be the one with a small appetite and no sweet tooth? Why does Cuddles, our little gray cat, love to snuggle with her and not me?*

I wrote all these memories down. Pages about names, first, middle, and last. Pages about luscious blond hair versus flat brown hair. I'd write in my notebook for three days in a row, and then drop it for a week or two. When I saw Meredith at a meeting, I'd share snippets with her out on the sidewalk on the way to our cars.

"I'm fucked up around names," I said, falling into step beside her. "Why my sister got the better name."

Meredith laughed. "Right, but if you had your sister's name, you would hate it and wish your name was Christie. What is your sister's name by the way?"

"Virginia."

Meredith guffawed. "You know my sister is Ginny, right? As in Virginia?"

"I thought it was J-E-N-N-Y! Short for Jennifer."

"Nope. GINNY!"

We laughed so hard on the sidewalk, each gripping the other's arm. Two guys from the meeting passed us with raised eyebrows.

"Were you jealous she got that name?" I asked.

Meredith shrugged. "No, I wasn't hung up on the name. Ginny was always my mother's favorite — perfect grades, popular at school, good at everything. I was jealous of that, but I didn't pin it on her name."

In her own excavation, Meredith realized that she drove back and forth to Rockford to visit her elderly mother every few weeks

— no matter how busy she was with school and work — trying to win her love. "She's always rude to me — comparing me to my sisters, saying weird shit about how I'm not good enough for Gage. The whole thing is so dysfunctional. When I leave, I feel miserable, filled with self-hate. On the way home, I drink a half liter of chocolate milk just to calm down. I tell Gage I'm never going back. But then I do, because in the back of my mind, I'm thinking: maybe this time will be different; maybe this time she will see me, really see me. I want her to see Meredith, the good stuff about me that Gage and my friends in recovery see."

I nodded and realized that I really wanted that for Meredith, too. Her mother recently celebrated her eighty-fourth birthday, and her health was far from robust. I wanted to shoot down I-90, storm into her assisted-living facility, and beg her to recognize her daughter before it was too late.

"Do you have to keep going there?" I asked, feeling protective.

"You sound like my therapist with that leading question."

That's never a compliment. Oops.

When I apologized, she shrugged and said, "She's my mom. She's all alone."

We walked a few more steps toward Meredith's car, and she suddenly grabbed my arm and gave it a little shake. "You want to hear my biggest insight? I don't know if I can explain it exactly. Part of me knows that if my sisters lived in town and visited her every few weeks, she'd most likely be rude to them, too. She might even compare them to me. Highly likely that she'd insult their hair, their housekeeping, their hem length. Negative and critical — that might be how my mom is with everyone. I've taken it all so personally all these years. You know" — she brought her face so close to mine that I could smell the coffee on her breath and count her eyelashes — "it might not be personal at all!"

Meredith's words cracked open a door in my mind. I'd dreamed up a million fantasies about the intimacy between my mother and my sister. I imagined they talked on the phone every day. Called each other for advice on matters ranging from the purchase of a new house or what kind of panini to order at Corner Bakery. Traded recipes for dishes involving meat and potatoes. Discussed gossip from the church and the neighborhood. When I actually talked to my mother or my sister, I didn't hear any proof of this intimacy my imagination spun for them, but no matter. A fictitious version of my mother and sister haunted me, ever highlighting my deficiencies as both a sister and a daughter and etching out an intimacy that never included me.

Now it was my turn to shake Meredith's arm with my own realization. "Meredith! Me, too! Everything from my childhood has always felt so deeply personal. The story in my head has always been that my parents wanted another baby girl because I'd been such a disappointment. In my twisted child logic, my sister's purpose was to make up for all that I wasn't. But that doesn't hold up, right?" I waved my keys around, energized. "For one thing, in 1977, my parents couldn't control the gender of their baby; Virginia could have easily been a boy named William or Joshua. And when they conceived my sister, I was not yet overweight or bulimic. My hair was decidedly dark — brown as coffee with a teaspoon of cream — but it was too soon to pronounce it chronically limp and outside the realm of Texan acceptability. We didn't know then that my permanent teeth would arrive in a haphazard pattern full of gaps and odd angles that would require years of orthodontics. Virginia wasn't meant to be an upgrade; my parents simply wanted to grow our family. I made the whole story all about me, and year after year I added more chapters to support my central thesis: Virginia was the best girl, and I was something else entirely."

"That's so fucked up," Meredith said, eyes twinkling. "And I totally get it. There is something so precious and untouchable about baby sisters. Older sisters can't compete —"

"Oh yes we can!"

"Well, we can't win, unless you count Pyrrhic victories, which I don't."

"Maybe the paradigm of 'winning' is fucked from the start."

"You think?"

"It's embarrassing — the things I was so undone by. My parents checking her car seat, fixing the locks on the cabinets where we kept the bleach and the Drano. In my little-kid brain, those actions, which all parents should take to protect their children — and my parents took to protect me — were an elaborate demonstration of how much more precious Virginia was. Even if my parents knew what I was thinking and pulled me aside to set me straight, I wouldn't have believed them. I wouldn't have been able to hear them."

"Exactly. That's why we have to do the work now."

104

I rolled my eyes. Work, work, work. Always more work.

"We do the work, we get the miracles," Meredith said, squeezing me tight. I rolled my eyes again. "Actually, I think we do the work so we can see the miracles all around us."

More eye rolls. I didn't believe like she did. Maybe one day I would be like her, pointing out miracles in everyday life, but I was not there yet.

Meredith put both hands on my shoulders and squared off so she could look directly into my eyes. "Christie, you know what I think all this work is for?" I shook my head, but the possessed look in her eye convinced me she had a grand answer to her own question. "This is so we can understand that we *are* the miracles. You and I. Our lives. We are living, breathing miracles."

I nodded my head as if I understood and agreed, but the sole thought in my head was: *Bridge too far, Meredith. Settle down.*

On the way home, I laughed to myself thinking that Meredith and I both had a Virginia to contend with. I saw us on the sidewalk outside of the meeting, not as the grown women we were but as the girls we had been, our hair in pigtails and our little minds full of delusions and half-spun lies. I had to admit that it felt like a small miracle that I'd bonded with Meredith. Twelve-step meetings in Chicago were filled with women of all ages interested in untangling their lives from the grips of addiction and unhealthy patterns. I could have allied with Cheryl, Diane, Karyn, Jess, Alana, Elise, or a dozen other women, but somehow it became Meredith and me working on sisterhood and friendship, becoming better versions of ourselves.

When I walked into my first twelve-step program at nineteen and stopped bingeing and purging, the only word that accurately described that experience was *miracle*. My early recovery convinced me that miracles could happen *to* me. But there was no way I could *be* the miracle. That was something reserved for extra-special people.

People like my little sister.

9

In the years before we welcomed Virginia, our family of four faced a crisis.

Dad's drinking cast him into the darkest of places, where he was forced to answer a single question: Live or die? I was two years old at the time, and therefore too young to remember this period, but I've heard many stories about how I contributed to that darkness.

"Oh, you cried all the time," my mom told me. "You just cried and cried and cried."

Mom makes it sound like I was a baby in a demented Dr. Seuss book: she cried on a plane, on a train, with a bee, and in a tree. The pictures in my parents' photo albums confirm the stories. The albums that include pictures of me from birth to age five most typically show my lips downturned, my eyes brimming with tears, a cry visibly moving across my face or having already arrived. There are pictures of me crying at the beach, in the snow, at my grandparents' house, in the front yard, in the living room, in the kitchen.

"We were afraid your face would get stuck in the expression you made when you were about to start crying, the one where your lips are turned down and your lower one was sticking out," my mom once said, pulling her lips downward in a perfect imitation of the pouty face that I wore nonstop in my earliest years.

When a family member sinks into alcoholism, his family slides down with him. There are financial, emotional, and spiritual stresses squeezing the adults' hearts into shriveled, barely beating organs, and the kids, even the babies, feel it in their bones and in their still-developing nervous systems. There are happy hours after work that lead to long, lonely, terrifying nights of wondering what happened, when he'll be home, is he okay? There are mornings marked by pounding headaches, unbidden retching, quiet devastation. In such cases, guess what's not helpful: an infant crying for hours every day, who also cannot do one single thing for herself.

It was 1973, and my mom stayed home to take care of me and Dirk, who was fourteen months older. We had food in the fridge and ample clothing. We had a plastic kiddie pool in the backyard. Both my parents had fully functioning cars. We had afghans my mom's mother made for us and two oak trees in the front yard. The pictures from that period show my brother and me as clean-faced, well-fed, our hair brushed and parted just so. For my first birthday, Mom baked a double-decker cake — chocolate inside with white frosting — and the always-smiling Lana arrived with presents and her two kids, who splashed around in our kiddie pool. *Happy Birthday!* There's a picture of me in my high chair, cake stationed within arm's reach, Dirk cheesing at the camera beside me with his blond bowl haircut. I know it was Mom who snapped the picture. When I pointed at the image years later in a photo album, she told me Dad had been too sick to join us after a rough night out with friends. He stayed in the bedroom, huddled under the covers with the shades drawn.

When I first heard the word *hungover,* I was probably in middle school, and I pictured a sleeping person whose body was flung over a shower curtain rod like a damp, used towel. A body folded over itself, head knocking into knees. But I didn't have that word on my first birthday. I only knew *Mama, Dada, milk,* and *cake.* The basics for a girl with a bright future in disordered eating. I couldn't have discussed what it meant to celebrate a year of staying alive while my dad was too sick to celebrate, but my cells knew how off-kilter we were, how much slack my mom had to pick up, how very ill Dad was. A daughter knows when her dad is trying to die, even if she's too young to have the language for how sad and scared she feels.

No wonder I cried.

There was a happy ending for that dark chapter in my family. Dad decided to get help. He crawled out of the darkened bedroom away from the sickness and desperation. He found his way to recovery meetings. He lived. As my family stepped back from the edge, my parents extinguished the fires burning around them, and for the first time in many years they could see something new and promising on the horizon: the future. A few years later, with the blessing of sobriety, my parents decided to have another child. Virginia was the child who existed because of sobriety, the one who would never know the quiet desperation of her sick father or that of her mother stuck at home alone caring for two kids under the age of two with an incapacitated husband.

When I was six or seven, all five of us went

to a party on a Sunday night. We wore the same clothes we'd worn to Mass earlier in the day, but now we climbed the steps to a second-story room that smelled like smoke and burned coffee. Rows of brown folding chairs sat facing a podium with a microphone. Behind the podium hung a chalkboard with a list of first names and last initials followed by a number of months or years. After we found our seats in the middle of the room, I spotted my dad's name halfway down: *Peter T., 5 years.*

Dad called this gathering a "birthday celebration," even though his real birthday wasn't for another month. This was the place where Dad came for his meetings every night after dinner. I knew the meetings were important because they kept him from drinking so he could coach my soccer team and make our school lunches. And I knew that drinking was bad because it made Dad very sick — sick enough to miss my birthday parties and make Mom's smile slide off her face. By the time we attended this sobriety celebration for my dad, I thought I had the timeline straight in my head: Dad took his first drink shortly after I was born, and he drank because I was a baby who cried all the time and wouldn't stop for anything. This timeline turned out to be totally wrong, but I wouldn't know until I was twenty-seven years old that my crying wasn't the cause of his drinking, which had started long before my birth.

Before the official "birthday" celebration began, we sat in a row of folding chairs arranged in lines from the front to the back of the room. People milled about, shaking my dad's hand and refilling their coffee cups. My tailbone ached in that hard metal chair, so I swiveled around to check out the room. At a table in the back, a guy with a ponytail stirred powdered creamer into a Styrofoam cup of coffee. I spied a half-empty box of Entenmann's cookies next to the coffeepot. I could tell they were chocolate chip, and I wanted one. I liked the satisfying crunch of a cookie, the way the chocolate slicked the front of my teeth. Already, I found cookies more comforting than anything people could offer.

"Look." My brother elbowed me and pointed to a second room on the other side of the stairs. The walls were made of windows so we could see through. "Cake and punch."

I saw it, too! A woman placed a giant sheet cake with thick ridges of white icing decorated with blue and red rosettes on a table. She dipped a ladle into a crystal punch bowl filled with frothy lime-green juice. I hoped the cake was chocolate inside and that I could get a corner piece with extra icing.

A man stepped up to a mic at the front of the room. The rumble of chatter slowly quieted. The guy at the podium welcomed everyone and introduced himself as Gerald R.

"Hi, Gerald," the entire room responded. Their voices erupted like thunder. Gerald then called each person celebrating an anniversary to the podium, gave them a chip commemorating their sobriety, and allowed them to say a few words.

I hooked the heels of my sandals on the low metal bar on the back of the chair in front of me and let my body slouch. Might as well get comfortable.

When Gerald called out a name, the birthday celebrant — most of them men — would weave through the aisles, take his new coin, and introduce himself. I knew I was supposed to say, "Hi, Rick," or "Hi, Jared," or "Hi, Burt," when they introduced themselves, but I couldn't do it. Neither did Dirk.

Eventually, Gerald called my dad's name, and he rose from his aisle seat, buttoning his sports coat as he walked to the podium. He stepped up to the mic and said he was grateful for all of the people, many of whom were in the audience, who helped him. He praised my mom as a wonderful wife and mother. He mentioned my brother and me by name, and I ducked my head low, scared to see all the eyes turned toward me. I let my hair fall over my face.

"And then there's our youngest, Virginia. She's our sobriety baby. She's our miracle."

I didn't hear a single word after *miracle*. I felt a shiver of satisfaction in finally hearing someone say it, *Virginia is a miracle*, but it flickered and disappeared. Thanks to my first-grade teacher, Sister Mary Margaret, I was well versed in miracles — the tomb, the loaves and fishes, the lame man who stood up and walked. Miracles were extraordinary. They were inexplicable. They were straight from the heart of God. Virginia was a miracle; I was a reason to get drunk. I swung my feet back and forth hard, hard enough that my chair scooted forward. Mom set her hand on my thigh to still my legs.

The meeting finally ended, and I got that corner piece of cake. The flowers felt greasy on the roof of my mouth and the sweetness clung to my tongue. I slipped away from my family's huddle and snagged a second piece. I considered lunging for a third, but Mom was onto me. She warned me about a stomachache from all the sugar, but she was wrong. Sugar made it possible to live in my body and carry the blame I was sure belonged on my shoulders.

I shared this miracle story with Meredith a few days after she called us *miracles.*

"See why that word fucks with my head?" I said.

For a split second, I thought she was going to scold me for latching on to this tiny moment — *Get over it, already.* If she had, I would have spat back, defensively, *I'm trying!* I felt shame about how fiercely I clung to this line my dad said when I was seven or eight years old. Or at least that's the line I remember him saying. We all know that memory is faulty. In law school, our torts professor set up an experiment where one of the administrators knocked on the door of our classroom, talked to her for a few minutes, and then handed her a file. After the incident, our professor told us to write down a description of the administrator. When we shared our descriptions, the answers varied widely — some reported brown hair and khaki pants; others insisted her hair was blond and her pants were gray. Some said the interruption lasted for thirty seconds; two people insisted it was over three minutes. Intellectually, I understood the malleability of memory and the ways that perception shifts over time, and for God's sake I was in grammar school when I heard the line on which I hung so much of my identity. My dad's words proved that my little sister was divinely perfect, and I held that truth close to my bones.

"Oh, I relate to so much of that," she said. "Both of my sisters were perfect in ways that I wasn't. All I wanted was to be someone's favorite. It really messed me up. I drank and starved because I'm an addict, and I fell in love with addicts because I'm deeply codependent and terrified of intimacy, but my perfect sisters were good excuses. I blamed my misery on their perfection." She shook her head and pressed her lips together. "All that's made me skittish as a friend. Once I decide a friend is better than I am, she becomes one of my perfect sisters, and I withdraw. I've missed out on a lot."

Obviously, I used food and bulimia to cope with my feelings of jealousy, envy, and inferiority. I hadn't binged or purged in years, but I remembered how soothing it felt to chew and swallow more food than my body needed. It took the edge off my roiling feelings for a spell, but then the inevitable shame about my appetites and horror at the calories I'd consumed telescoped my life to the size and shape of the toilet bowl. I'd binged and purged over crushes who didn't like me back, academic pressure, ballet solos I wanted and didn't get chosen for, friendships that crashed, and over and over because of my shame at being a failure as a girl, a sister, a daughter, a friend, an eater, a human in the world.

Every time I talked to Meredith, I felt amazed we had so much in common. It seemed improbable. On the day I was born in 1973, she was twenty-three years old and well on her way to drinking herself to death. Maybe the night I was born was the same night she fell asleep drunk with a lit cigarette that started a house fire in which she would have perished if her cat hadn't roused her. I didn't know drunk, self-destructive Meredith — she got sober long before I met her at the Swedish diner. The Meredith I knew from meetings sounded strong, full of faith in her Higher Power.

In our one-on-one conversations, though, I heard someone different. Someone more like me. Searching. Seeking. Unsure. Willing, but not always strong enough to undo bad habits or create new ones. Up close, I could see that she often deprived herself.

117

Once after a meeting, we walked to a coffee shop, and when she ordered tap water, I offered to get her a bottle of the good stuff (San Pellegrino). "No, no, no," she'd said, and I could tell she was uncomfortable with my offer. And she'd recently told me that she drove three neighborhoods away to shop at a discount grocery store, even though the sketchy location scared her and the traffic made the trek a hassle. When I asked her why all the effort to save a few bucks, she waved her hands and said, "I'm working on it in therapy," with enough edge that I understood further questions were not welcome. She dreamed of a vacation in Italy but spoke as if such an extravagance was as unlikely as booking a private jet to circumnavigate the globe. I noticed her deprivation, but I didn't press because it didn't seem like my place. Up close, she was as messy and "in progress" as anyone — as I certainly was — and it comforted me to know she wasn't nearly as perfect as I once imagined.

10

Catholic school was a balm for my soul after the social bruising I took in fifth grade. In sixth grade, I returned to nuns, plaid uniforms, and religion classes. Now I saw my classmates on the weekends at Mass, and the world felt less hostile than it had in the godless quarters of public school. I started St. Rita's with the humbling knowledge that I could be dumped on my ass at any time, so I should be kind and attentive to everyone, even if their lunch sacks didn't double as tiny piñatas for their chosen friends and followers. In these calm waters, I entered my first best-friendship at the tender age of eleven.

Tara lived across the street from St. Rita's and earned A's with little effort. We had all of our classes together. We both wrote poetry — hers was insightful and showed a sophisticated grasp of metaphor; mine less so. We flirted with dieting. Tara said we should say the Apostles Creed, a long, complicated prayer from Mass, between every bite of food. My method was to drink lots of Kool-Aid and ask God for skinnier thighs after eating a row of Nutter Butters. We talked on the phone, passed notes in class, and gave each other filthy nicknames. Tara was Asswipe; I was Buttface. For the first time in my life, I stepped into the buoyancy and joy of comfortable, compatible friendship without wishing I could be with someone else.

Once when we were in the bathroom after recess, Tara asked me to turn to the wall so she could sing "Don't Cry for Me, Argentina." She'd recently seen the New York production of *Evita* and longed to sing Perón's anthem with abandon. Tara's rendition gave me chills and almost made me cry, but I couldn't weep or we'd be late to class. After she hit that final note, we hurried back to class, and I remember thinking, *Tara is the best friend in the whole world.* I admired her voice, but also the bravery it took to share it with me and only me. The first time she signed the note she passed me in science class, *Your B.F.F.,* my head grew light. The thrill of being claimed! It was all I ever wanted. But instead of simply enjoying that we had so very much in common — musical theater, a hatred of our math teacher, nascent eating disorders — I felt afraid of losing her. I gripped tightly. I finally found my B.F.F., a good and true friend, and I wanted it to be official.

"We should get friendship rings," I said. I had my eye on a James Avery sterling silver ring; the design was two hands clasping. In the catalog, it was called "the friendship ring." If we had this ring, we'd have proof we belonged to each other. We couldn't break up if we had jewelry. When Tara agreed, I buzzed with joy.

I hadn't picked Tara because she was the queen of sixth grade; I picked her because we laughed so hard together and being with her made time fly by. It felt like we picked each other. The magic of friendship no longer seemed mystifying, unattainable. With Tara, I had the free, unclenched feeling I had with Dani, but there was no longer the sidecar of longing for more.

At the start of seventh grade, my second year at St. Rita's, I gathered my school supplies into my new backpack and floated to school, grateful not to be the new kid. Tara and I picked lockers next to each other. We still despised our math teacher, Mrs. Kramer, and one time our snickers caught her attention, which earned us a trip into the hallway. Mrs. Kramer leaned against the radiator. "What's the problem, girls?" We feigned innocence and copped to nothing, and then went right back to making fun of her for reasons I no longer remember. Mrs. Kramer wasn't soft and kind, but she was fair and gave a reasonable amount of homework. I felt a twinge of shame for being rude to her, but I had no intention of stopping because it was essential to bonding with Tara. I would have snickered and rolled my eyes at Jesus himself if it kept Tara laughing.

At the end of September, we all paired up for cheerleading tryouts, which wouldn't take place until late spring. Tara picked Angie as her tryout partner, and my heart nearly stopped with anxiety when I heard them talking about getting together to work on their routine. The pairing made sense: Angie was tall and strong; she could be the base on whose shoulders Tara would stand to execute the stunts required to make the squad. Tara and I were the same height — neither of us was strong enough to be the other's base. I paired up with a generous, happy girl named Jenni, who was tall, lean, and mighty enough to hold me.

Everyone had a partner who suited her needs, but I fretted about losing Tara to Angie. I was convinced that the pressure of tryouts and hours of practice would bond Tara and Angie, leaving me bereft of my beloved B.F.F. When I looked into the future, I imagined Tara and Angie making the cheerleading squad, and Tara asking me to slip my friendship ring off my finger and onto Angie's.

All fall and winter, I burned with jealousy every time I heard Tara and Angie scheduling a practice session. I didn't picture them solely working on their spread eagles and herkeys; surely they were also learning to smelt iron so they could design their own friendship rings. I felt fear and as the tryouts loomed, it consumed me.

It was Texas in the eighties, after all, and cheerleading was as important for girls as brain-battering sports were for the boys. The prospect of Angie and Tara making the squad without me terrorized me.

The morning of tryouts, I hardly touched my breakfast or lunch. I didn't tell anyone that I'd snuck a full bottle of Tylenol into my bag and planned to swallow every last red pill if the judges didn't pick me. In my mind, I would lose everything. If I didn't die of sadness when Tara reported for three-day cheer camp at SMU in August, I would have to endure the torture of watching Tara and Angie cheering for the football team every Sunday afternoon. I would shrivel into nothingness, while all the cheerleaders grew more lively and colorful.

The bottle of pills gave me a way out of the future I feared.

For tryouts, Jenni and I fastened matching green and white bows as big as pinwheels on our heads. When it was our turn, we cheered our throats raw. "Go Spartans," we hollered as we jumped and clapped across the gym, hyping up an imaginary audience. Afterward, we huddled in the bathroom with everyone else, waiting for the verdict. When we were called into the gym for the announcements, each pair clung to each other like baby monkeys. I squeezed my eyes shut and prayed to hear my number called.

"Number Fifteen! And Number Sixteen!"

Jenni and I sprang to our feet, squealing with joy. The current cheerleaders pulled us to the front of the room. I would live! I survived my own private Hunger Games. When all the numbers had been called, I looked around for Tara and Angie, who remained on the other side of the gym, still clinging to each other, except now they were sobbing. Their numbers weren't called. They would not be part of the 1986–1987 Spartan cheerleading squad. I never once considered how it would feel if Tara didn't make it and I did.

The cheerleading coach ushered each new squad member to a van that whisked us to Crystal's Pizza Parlor for a celebration. A new worry consumed me: Would Tara and Angie become best friends over their shared devastation? Worse, what if Tara resented me for making the squad and that was the wedge that drove us apart?

"Have some pizza, Christie!" Jenni said, once we spilled into the loud parlor where a giant screen broadcast airplanes stunting in midair to Kenny Loggins's *Top Gun* anthem, "Danger Zone." All around us the sounds of happy cheerleaders, Skeeball machines, and pop music invited me into a raucous joy. I felt none of it. My mind was back in the gym where Tara and Angie huddled up, no doubt making plans for a B.F.F.-ship that would be way better than short green cheerleading skirts and rah-rah-rahing at a football game.

"I can't stop thinking about Tara," I said to Jenni. "She must be so sad."

I thought of that bottle of pills rattling in my bag under my chair. It didn't feel right to swallow them after making the squad. But I felt as bad about Tara's loss as if it had been my own. I took one bite of pizza, and my stomach heaved. I left it on my plate until it was cold and limp.

Tara and I weathered the cheerleading season. We didn't talk about it much; over the summer I kept mum about the nights at cheerleading camp, and in the fall, I excised all discussion of cheerleading from our conversation. My official squad duties wrapped up in early November, which relieved me of the burden of pretending I did anything other than go to ballet, study for math tests, and polish my friendship ring. Christmas of eighth grade, Tara invited me to join her family on a ski trip to Lake Tahoe. We took our friendship and our poetry notebooks out west, where she patiently waited for me to snowplow my way down easy slopes. In the back of her family's van, we declared the Survivor ballad "The Search Is Over" as the theme song — not of a mature love between two adults who wanted to fuck each other forever but for our teenage friendship.

When the radio played "our" song, I wept real tears, because the end of our bliss loomed on the horizon. Tara wasn't headed to the all-girls' Catholic high school with me — she was bound for an East Coast boarding school. From there, I understood she'd catapult to a school like Harvard or

Princeton, and we'd never share a zip code again. Once she was fully ensconced in the East Coast Ivied world, she'd hardly remember her junior high B.F.F. from Texas.

Tara and I talked a few times in high school, but I found myself twisting the phone cord around my finger, embarrassed that my provincial stories involved algebra quizzes and school dances with boys we'd known for years, while hers revolved around dining halls, weekend ski trips, and seminar classes among Kennedys and Rockefellers. Our conversations petered out by Christmas of ninth grade. I didn't know how to stay in touch or how to be curious about her boarding school life, while also holding on to a sense that my life wasn't lame and second rate because, at age fourteen, I still lived at home and went to school a mile from my house.

Maybe I could make a friend, a best friend with whom I shared sterling silver jewelry after all; but I couldn't keep her once she crossed state lines. If you didn't go to school together, you couldn't be best friends anymore. That seemed like a truth too obvious to state.

11

I didn't avoid Meredith, but it was easy to become too busy for the emotional labor of "becoming a better friend." I was working full-time as a lawyer at a huge firm with a steep billable hours' requirement, while also planning a wedding. When I wasn't flying across the country visiting manufacturing sites for one client or trying to settle a fraud case for another, John and I squeezed in visits to wedding venues, bakeries, and florists. Underneath the busyness, I had other reasons to delay. I was exhausted. I wanted a few months off from working on myself. For this season, I wanted to be carefree and a little frivolous — a bride preparing for her wedding, not someone constantly excavating her past transgressions.

Couldn't I cruise into marriage and address my friendship issues down the road — after the blur of the wedding and honey-

moon? My friendship issues weren't fatal —
they'd never driven me to suicidal ideation,
like my relationships with men had. Friendship could wait. I deserved this time off.

My plan to flit to the altar with no greater
worries than how to deal with water reten-
tion and how to store leftover wedding cake
did not come to pass. A friendship conflict
blemished my untroubled horizon. Nothing
I couldn't manage, just a little bump or two
in my friendship with Callie.

Callie and I met in recovery meetings
when I was a second-year law student and
she was in school for physical therapy. Both
of us were smart and poised for successful
careers, but we were also single and quite
unhappy about our attraction to men who
were alcoholic, emotionally enmeshed with
their mothers, or otherwise unavailable. Our
friendship had begun when we bonded at
breakfast one morning after a meeting in
December.

"I'm running three miles tomorrow,"
Callie had said to someone at the far end of
the table. Outside the window, three-foot
snowdrifts studded the sidewalks. I didn't
know anyone who ran in the dead of Chicago winter. Except for me.

"You run year-round?" I asked, and she
nodded vigorously.

"I don't really understand people who take the whole winter off."

"Me neither."

I'd given up on finding someone to run with me when the snow made the branches droop and ice slicked the streets. It was hard enough to find a running pal on Chicago's glorious June mornings when the lake is luminous and the flowers are in full bloom. My law school friends liked sleeping in, and my recovery friends liked yoga. When Callie invited me to join her for a run, I felt something novel and exciting click into place: a friend who runs! I knew from what she shared in meetings that Callie was smart, driven, wise, and humble. The prospect of a strong friendship gleamed on the horizon.

The very next day, I drove to her house during a snowstorm, bundled head to toe in purple fleece. We ran three miles as snow pelted our faces. We talked the entire way, covering topics ranging from our careers, our families, and our dating woes to our therapists and our favorite bands.

Callie was my kind of person: she was hard-core about working out (master's swimmer, marathon runner, avid cyclist), going to therapy, and showing up in recovery meetings. She was eight years older than

I was, so I naturally fell into the role of little sister, which I relished. Soon she was on my speed dial, had joined one of Dr. Rosen's groups, and got promoted to the rank of someone I'd call from the bathroom when out on a date. "Callie, he put his elbows on the table, and I just can't," I'd groan into my cell phone from a crepe café in Lincoln Park. "Don't miss a great guy because of table manners," she'd advise. On long, lonely Saturday afternoons when I lamented having no plans and "feeling like a loser," she'd say, "meet me at Target." Together, we'd roll our carts through the skin-care aisles, the clothes, the snacks. When we needed new running shoes, we jumped in the car and drove thirty miles to the Nike outlet near Joliet. The night before my law school graduation, Callie invited all the women from our Saturday meeting to her house to shower me with affirmations — she'd asked each woman to write a message to me.

Christie, you are a bright light and will be a brilliant lawyer!

Christie, You goddess, you warrior, you hero! I will be cheering you on when you argue your first case before the Supreme Court.

Christie, you have worked so hard through

law school — I hope you prosecute assholes who hurt women and children and send them to prison for life!

And when Callie found her match in her sweet, lanky husband, Grant, the guy who captured her heart and married her on a Hawaiian beach about a year after their first date, she helped me keep the faith in romance when I was still eating tapas with dudes to whom I'd given avian nicknames. Callie and I had run hundreds of miles together on Lake Michigan dissecting every relationship in our lives. By the time I met John, she was part sister and part dating coach. She was in the number two position on my speed dial after the esteemed Dr. R.

But once John and I became engaged, the ground underneath Callie and me shifted. In high school and college, I'd dumped my friends for boys, but I was determined never to make that mistake again. I kept up our weekly running dates without fail, but my sad-sack little sister role no longer fit. Now I was someone who spent Sunday afternoons with her future mother-in-law cheering at White Sox games or cruising open houses with her fiancé and a real estate agent. Callie was happy for me, but she also missed how much I'd needed her when I was single and bumping from one romantic crisis to the next. We'd built our friendship on a dynamic where I sobbed to her about this guy or that one, and she coached me on how to demand more than crumbs from the men in my life. When I met John, we tumbled into a space of unfamiliarity.

One Monday evening a few months after my engagement, I called Callie to confirm we were running the next morning.

"See you at six?" I asked.

"That works. I'll come to you this time."

"Perfect. How was the weekend?"

"The usual. We took Grant's parents to church and out to breakfast. I called you on the way."

"Oh, I saw that. John and I were at brunch with his friends from business school at Mia Francesca's."

Silence.

"Hello?" I said. "Are you still there?"

A few more seconds, and then, "I'm here."

All joy leached out of her voice.

"What's wrong?" I asked. Even after years of recovery meetings and therapy, I hated it when people were upset with me. My heart hammered. Sweat formed along my hairline.

"Nothing."

"You sure?"

"I'm just tired."

We'd been here before. Callie had a tell

133

when she was hurt: deafening silence. It always scrambled my mind. Find out what's wrong! Make her happy! Make her smile! I struggled to give her space to have her feelings and trust that she would discuss them when she was ready. Once, a few years earlier, I'd signed up to do a sprint distance triathlon with my friend Emily, and Callie was hurt I hadn't invited her, the consummate athlete, to join us. When I called Callie to debrief the race, she hardly said a word. I hadn't realized that each detail I recounted felt like a jab to her bruised feelings — I never thought she'd be interested in doing the dinky little sprint triathlon in Pleasant Prairie, Wisconsin. Twenty-four hours later, she collected herself and told me she felt hurt to be excluded from the athletic adventure she would have loved to join.

I had to give her space.

"So I'll see you in the morning?" I said, my voice trailing off. I knew better than to beg her to tell me what was wrong, but every part of me wanted to hash it all out, there and then.

"Sure."

That night, I slept in fits, seeing the glowing numbers on the alarm clock at two, three, and four o'clock. My pillow felt too hot, but when I flipped it, the cold side

134

against my cheek made me shiver. Was she mad about the brunch at Mia Francesca's? But why would she want to hang out with John's business school friends?

During the first mile of our run the next morning, Callie offered one-word answers to my questions. She kept her gaze straight ahead, never glancing over at me. I still didn't know if she was pissed or hurt. I searched for a way in.

"You working a full day?"

"Yeah."

"Do you think John and I should do a two-week honeymoon?"

"Yep."

"Do you think Eminem is the best white rapper to come out of Detroit?"

Block after block, I peppered her with banal inquiries, trying to break her focus on the horizon. I wanted her to look at me and be direct, but of course I was doing a terrible job of being direct with her.

When we hit Ohio Street beach, I couldn't take any more. "You're going to freeze me out this whole run or should I ask you some more questions about rappers who grew up on Eight Mile?"

After a few more strides she said, "I felt really hurt when I heard about your weekend plans. You have this whole big new life with John, and I don't know any of his friends."

"It was just one brunch with two other couples." Defensiveness rose in me before I could pause or form a clear thought.

"I'm not saying you did anything wrong, but I felt hurt. Maybe afraid. I got up at the ass crack of dawn to take my in-laws to a lame church service followed by runny eggs at the Pancake House, and you were brunching in the city with John's friends. I feel like we are going in different directions."

Ah. Now I understood. When she and Grant got engaged, they'd talked briefly about moving to the suburbs. We'd gone on a run much like this one, except I was the one feeling hurt and afraid of being left behind. I sulked and withdrew. During those few weeks when I thought she'd decamp for suburbia, I mourned our weekly runs, our Target meetups, and our city-life closeness. My hurt looked like anger, much like hers did now.

"I'm not going anywhere," I said, more gruffly than I meant to. "I'm right here." I couldn't shake the sense that she was blaming me for her discomfort or that it was my job to take care of her feelings, which was not actually what she was saying.

We ran half a mile in silence, our footfalls matching stride for stride. The sunlight shined off the lake, the waves shimmering with silver light — the best of Chicago's summer weather — but I was too agitated to savor the view. I was scared, too. I didn't know how to balance my relationship with John and my friendship with Callie. I'd failed here before and couldn't bring myself to admit my own fears.

"This is just a transition. We will survive and be stronger for it," I said when we headed up the ramp at Ohio Street. "Like when you and Grant got together — there was a weird period and then we settled. We'll settle again."

"I hope so," she said, sounding unconvinced.

See? Nothing but a little blip. Not worth mentioning to Meredith or discussing in therapy or meetings. I handled it, internally, by promising myself I wouldn't let go no matter what happened between us. That's all it took to be this improved version of myself, the Good Friend Christie, and not the seventeen-year-old Ditching Her Friends for a Boy Christie.

Just hold on tightly.

Had this tense conversation taken place between John and me, I would have called my therapist in a panic and spent the next few sessions analyzing all aspects of the relationship. I would have mentioned the interaction in my recovery meetings. I'd learned that my precious romantic relationships deserved all the tools I had at my disposal — recovery and gobs of mental health treatment.

But with friends? I thought those gardens could and should tend themselves. I took a decidedly laissez-faire approach to browning leaves and weeds crowding out the blooms. Friendship, I believed, was supposed to be automatic, natural, effortless. If it failed, well, then maybe it just wasn't meant to be. Or worse, if it failed, maybe it meant I simply wasn't a person capable of holding on to a friendship no matter how hard I tried.

12

In ninth grade, when I put on my uniform — red-plaid skirt, flimsy white shirt, and saddle shoes — for the first day of high school, my heart longed for a new home-girl. I dreamed of a best friend who liked the same jokes, snacks, and music that I did. Like Tara, but someone with whom I was an intellectual equal. I wanted a friendship where we laughed until we cried, borrowed each other's clothes, and spent not only Friday nights at each other's house but also sometimes Saturday.

Lia was smart, sensitive, and hilarious. I knew she was the B.F.F. for me when she referred to areolas as "brown patches." As in, "These uniform shirts are so see-through you can see everyone's brown patches." She knew how to dance like Milli Vanilli and imitate our teachers, especially the nuns, with uncanny precision. We became friends on freshman retreat, when our class was bussed out to a bucolic lakeside rec center to spend the day crying about our zits and our longing for boys we wanted to slow dance with, while hopefully learning to give glory to God.

Lia and I had endless inside jokes about movies we saw, the assigned summer reading list, the boys we liked, and the girls we didn't. Her skin glowed a golden tan color, and her honeyed hair flowed down her back like a lush curtain. Naturally, the boys at our brother school loved her. More than one boy called me for information. "Hey, Christie, is Lia dating anyone? Do you know who she likes? Do you think she'd go out with me?" I willingly managed her dating overflow, which distracted me from my protracted awkward stage: braces, ten extra pounds, lots of electric-blue eyeliner, and a total inability to connect with the boys. My strategy to lure guys into adoring me involved playing really sad Depeche Mode songs in the background of our phone conversations, followed by reading my poetry about young girls who died before enjoying a proper French kiss. I definitely played up my role as chatty sidekick to Lia's golden homecoming queen, but there were enough laughs and prayer retreats along the way to keep me buoyed. I envied that she was effortlessly radiant and beloved, but the envy never choked out my love or our friendship.

When Lia and I spent sophomore spring break at my grandparents' farm in rural Texas, I glowed, too — with gratitude for having a friend who could make my grandma's farmhouse feel as exciting as Cancún or Crested Butte. We slathered our bodies with Crisco, punched a screen out of a second-floor window, and sunbathed in our bras and underwear on the flat part of the roof.

We signed all of our notes to each other, *Your B.F.F.* In my yearbook, her message to me took up a whole blank page in the back. *You bring so much joy to my life . . . I think back at all of our good times . . . and just the times that we sit and laugh our asses off together for no apparent reason — and these good times I wouldn't trade off for anything, not a thing . . . Hell, Christie, I don't know what I'd do without you — you are my touchstone. When you get to feeling down . . . don't you ever hesitate to call me because I am always here for you . . . If I wanted to wish someone the world, I would wish them you, Christie. Thanks for being my friend.*

I would never take this for granted. Ever.

Except, of course, I did.

Because I fell in love with my first alcoholic. My "ur-addict," as I like to refer to Kal. The summer before senior year, I joined Weight Watchers at 142.2 pounds, and followed its program until my body was whittled down to 110 pounds, at my lowest. I also availed myself of a three-month unlimited tanning package from a salon in a strip mall and started senior year looking like a shrunken, bronze-orange version of myself. My new sleek look attracted male attention. A few nice guys reached out to me: a Pat, a Derek, and a Matthew, but I chose Kal, who transferred to the boys' school from Long Island. Kal's exotic vowels and basketball player physique piqued my interest. In our very first conversation, standing on my friend Erin's circular driveway, Kal told me three things: 1. He loved basketball more than anything else in the world; 2. He liked to smoke pot; and 3. He got laid all the time back in Long Island. In our second conversation, he called me on the phone, drunk, after midnight on a Friday. "Christie, if you want to date me, you need to sneak out of your house and come over right now. If you don't, then I'm going to date Sasha, because she said she could be in here in ten minutes."

I didn't pause at any of the red flags Kal

waved in front of my face. Instead, I brushed my teeth, listened down the hall to be sure my parents were sound asleep, grabbed my keys, and walked out the front door. I drove my 1978 two-toned brown Cutlass Supreme — nicknamed "The Dookie" — three miles to Kal's house, where he greeted me at the door and led me upstairs to his room, only a few yards away from a closed bedroom door, behind which his parents were sleeping. I'd never done anything so brazen, so patently wrong, so reckless. The shock of it was almost as exciting as the day I showed up for my weekly Weight Watchers weigh-in and had dropped four pounds in one week. Kal had picked me! The thrill made me stupid and bold. I had no idea what my parents would do if they found out I'd waltzed out of the house after midnight to visit a boy's bedroom. I didn't let myself imagine that Kal's parents might wake up and discover me under Kal's comforter.

I'd been waiting my entire adolescence for a boy to pick me. Why else had I been measuring shredded cheese with a tablespoon before adding it to my lean chicken tacos and drinking eighty ounces of water every day?

On my first official date with Kal, we got tickets to see James Taylor. Actually, I bought the tickets, and I'm sure he meant to pay me back. The night of the concert, basketball practice ran late, so when Kal pulled up in front of my house, he didn't stop his car, walk up the redbrick sidewalk, and ring the doorbell. He beeped his horn twice. As I ran out the front door, I heard my dad's voice, pitched with concern. "He's not coming to the door to get you? That's not very respect —"

"We're late," I said, shutting the door behind me. *Dating has nothing to do with respect, Dad!*

At the concert, Kal helped himself to some beers and then some more beers, which he drank from giant plastic cups. When his eyes went glassy and his lids drooped, I worried about him driving on the highway after the concert. I didn't drink because Weight Watchers taught me to choose: Beer or bread? And I really liked bread. At the time, I was pleased that I'd found a commercial weight-loss program that kept me from bingeing and purging, at least for a while. It would be several months before I returned to bingeing on a box of cinnamon Teddy Grahams and once again found my reflection in the toilet, but the night of the concert, I thought Weight Watchers had cured my eating disorder.

After James Taylor's standing ovation, we filed into the parking lot, and Kal pulled my arm toward another kid's car. "Follow me," he slurred. We climbed into a Suburban with a guy Kal knew from basketball named Will, who didn't acknowledge me when I said hello. Will screeched through the parking lot, blasting INXS's "Suicide Blonde," which felt like a terrible omen and was acoustically jarring after our night with Sweet Baby James. The wind rushed at me from all the open windows. I held my breath as I watched the speedometer tick to the right. Seventy mph. Eighty. Ninety. One hundred. When the needle passed one hundred, I grabbed Kal's arm and told him I was scared.

"What? I can't hear you," he said.

I tried several more times. The wind was too loud; he was too drunk; the INXS was too deafening.

I stared out the window as north Dallas rushed by in a blur and prayed. God, if you get me out of this alive, I will do community service for the rest of the year. I thought I would die in that dumb Suburban on my way to a house party with a guy who'd made a terrible first impression on my parents (Kal) and a guy who made a terrible impression on me (Will). But I tucked all of that

145

terror, confusion, and danger under the novel thrill of having a boyfriend. If this was the cost, I'd pay.

Our weekend nights were like that — Kal would drink, often excessively, and I would grip the door handle and promise God hundreds of hours of community service in exchange for survival. By week two of our relationship, I already wished that Kal drank less, and when I discovered that he smoked pot several times a week, I wished he'd stop that, too. My dream of dating a nice, sweet guy who made me mixtapes and played with my hair as we watched rom-coms dissolved as I spent time with Kal and bargained for my life. From the beginning, I kept my feelings about his drug and alcohol use a secret — from him, my parents, and Lia — because it scared me. I didn't want people to judge him. I walked around loaded up with secrets and full of schemes to get him clean. All of the secret keeping and hiding took a toll on the other parts of my life.

My mom tried to engage me in conversation about my college applications, but I couldn't focus. *I was in love!*

"Christie, what about your application to Loyola Marymount or Creighton?"

"What about them, Mom? Kal loves me." He told me every weeknight when we talked

146

on the phone past midnight. Everything else grew hazy. College applications sat on my desk underneath my schoolwork and the paper I was writing for Kal on *The Great Santini.* My mom and I eventually agreed I would apply to colleges that didn't require essays because I was too distracted to compose 750 words about how I would use my college degree to improve the world.

My friendships took the greatest hit as my center of social gravity shifted from Lia to Kal, but I was the last to notice the change.

Right before Christmas break senior year, Lia organized a small group of friends to go to dinner, exchange gifts, and take pictures in front of a holiday light display. Of course I would be there. This outing would commemorate our last Christmas together before we all scattered to college.

Hours before I was supposed to be at Lia's, Kal and I got into a fight. He'd been flirting with another girl — a freckle-faced junior cheerleader — and I found out that they'd gone to the Dallas Museum of Art together the previous weekend while I was studying for finals. Humiliated and outraged, I went over to Kal's house to demand that he stop going on dates with other girls. He didn't answer the door, so I screamed and sobbed at him from his driveway — like a hysterical Lloyd Dobler minus the boom box. Eventually, he answered the door, and we hashed it out for hours in his bedroom. It was either a credit to Kal's rhetorical skills or to my deep codependence, but the fight ended with me apologizing for getting so angry about his extracurricular dating. "I'll work harder to be more easygoing."

Across town, Lia and the other girls were snapping pictures of themselves in funny poses with a blow-up Santa and his reindeer. Guilt tensed my shoulders when I found them at the park where all the high school kids met up to underage drink. I'd missed the special festivities that Lia had planned.

"Hi, y'all," I said, approaching Lia and three other girls. She offered a weak smile, which I knew I deserved. The others avoided my eyes.

"What's up?" I said twice to no answer.

In the silence, I could see how far I'd fallen away from Lia. The other girls seemed to circle her, protecting her from me, the one who kept disappointing her. This wasn't the first time I'd flounced: I'd backed out of trips to the mall, hanging out after football games, riding together to parties. I flaked or no-showed, and when I did show up, I was distracted. Lia hardly knew Kal, whom I treated as a secret boyfriend because I was embarrassed about how I let him treat me and how often he was fucked-up from alcohol or pot.

My prized and precious friendship with Lia lay in tatters. How did this happen? Standing in the park aware of how I'd hurt her, I realized that I didn't know where she'd applied to college or what she planned to major in; I had no idea how her sister was doing in her first year at school in California, or whether she liked the new Prince album. I knew to say I was sorry, and I did because I was. I wanted to get back to her, but I didn't know how. The shame I suddenly felt for screwing up the friendship made me want to avert my eyes and run away.

I knew this: I'd disappoint her again. Kal and I were on a sick ride, and I didn't know how to get off. I knew I'd choose him and his chaos over Lia next time. And the time after that. I hated that it was true, but I couldn't yet imagine being any other kind of girl. The innocent days of Lia and me skipping Ms. Wallace's algebra class to get Madonna concert tickets or helping each other with student council speeches were long gone. My relationship with Kal tangled me in something dark and sticky.

My instinct was to flee from Lia. She was

a good girl in a good relationship with a sweet boy who didn't drink too much and was devoted to her. Lia would have a good life, and she'd move on without me. At the park, I mumbled something about having to head home and walked back toward my car.

Bree, one of the girls standing with Lia, followed me. Feisty and whip-smart, Bree was one of the only girls in our class headed to an Ivy League college. By no accident, she was our student body president and took all AP classes. She and Lia both made the varsity cheerleading squad, were selected for the Homecoming Court, and suffered through calculus and physics senior year together. When we were out of earshot from everyone else, Bree let me have it.

"Lia made us wait for you for almost an hour. She was sure you would show up, but you never did. Do you understand how hurt she is? How could you do that to her?"

I absorbed Bree's words, knowing I deserved every single one. My body trembled, and I stuffed my hands in my coat pockets. I flashed to scenes at school: Bree and Lia walking down the hall after calculus, leaving together at the end of the day for cheerleading practice, laughing at the lockers just like Lia and I used to. They were one kind of girl — studious, happy, well-adjusted — and

I'd suddenly become a different kind. I was the kind of girl who could get a boyfriend, sure, but he was dangerous and unkind and not that into me. And worse, I was the kind of girl who dumped her friends to chase a destructive relationship.

"I'm sorry," I whispered. Too ashamed to say anything else, I ducked into my coat and jogged back to my car. I couldn't imagine how to fix my friendship with Lia or find my way back to it. I could only put Lia, Bree, and friendship out of my mind and drive home to sit in my bedroom and wait for Kal to call me.

13

In September, two months before my wedding, I found myself standing before a full-length mirror shimmying to Amy Winehouse's "Rehab." Welcome to my bachelorette party. My friends joined me for a dance lesson led by a perky nineteen-year-old with zero body fat and stunning muscle elasticity. I wrapped a white boa around my neck and tried to keep up with the swivels and turns in the routine. I'd hoped we'd learn a routine to a whole song to showcase at my wedding in November, but after an hour we'd mastered only sixteen counts, which I promptly forgot twelve hours later.

At one point during the lesson, the teacher stopped the music to help Emily and Jolie with a complicated pivot-squat-slap-the-floor move, and I glanced at all of us in the mirror. We stood in three horizontal lines across the room. My law school friends, Amma, Kylie, and Clare, along with women

I knew from meetings, including Callie, Jolie, Nina, Megan, and Emily. My friend Rachel from work gamely put on yoga pants and kept the beat. I'd invited Meredith, but she just laughed and said she wasn't a dancer.

These women gave up their Saturday evening to learn dance moves with me. They gifted me silky lingerie wrapped in pale-colored paper. Megan made a piñata out of an old hatbox, and we ended the night with pizza at the new townhome John and I had recently purchased in an up-and-coming neighborhood on the Near West Side of Chicago. All night long, I felt wrapped in the friendship and laughter of the women who had watched me transform from single law student into a lawyer with a fiancé. I didn't feel any apartness that night, maybe because the night was all about me. I let my friends celebrate me, and I let all the ways I'd failed in friendship sit where they belonged: in the past. Mostly. There was one moment during the dancing when I felt a pang of longing for Lia. I hadn't seen her in years, but I remembered us dancing to New Order in high school, and I still carried a wish to be close to her, even though I didn't know how.

At the end of the night, Emily, Jolie, and I

stood around the island in my kitchen, drinking sparkling water and telling stories. My lovely friends. As I rested my elbows on the marble counter, I'd told them that John and I had started trying.

"To have a baby?" Jolie asked, smiling and clapping her hands under her chin.

I nodded and blushed, suddenly feeling shy about saying out loud that I wanted to be a mother. At age thirty-four, I wasn't elderly, but my OB had encouraged me to get going because thirty-five was the dividing line between "old" and "young," gynecologically speaking.

Emily smiled wide, beaming love at me. "You'll be a great mom," she said.

These friends held me close. It felt easy and natural. It felt like they'd always be there and that it would always be as easy as this: celebrating life, whispering my dreams, and letting them hold me as I stepped into a new future.

I could be a friend and keep my friends close.

About six weeks later, I sat in the Saturday-morning meeting next to a box of crayons and scrap paper, craning my neck to see if Meredith was parking her car or walking down the sidewalk. She was rarely late, but

I held out hope she was coming because I wanted to see her. Needed to see her. I'd had another blip with Callie, and suddenly Meredith seemed like the only person who could place an oxygen mask over my face so I could breathe again.

Thirty minutes into the meeting, Meredith showed up, and my whole body relaxed into the tiny first-grade chair I was perched on. I nodded at her when she walked in and mouthed, *Can I talk to you after the meeting?*

When the meeting ended, she folded her chair, and I stood next to her. She scanned my face and noticed the defeated slope of my shoulders.

"Whoa, kiddo, what is it?"

"I'm in the middle of a shitstorm."

She took my hand and led me to a nearly bald tree outside the school.

"I'm pregnant." On our first try, John and I had made a fetus with a 175 bpm heart rate as confirmed by my OB. Our wedding date was three weeks away, and suddenly all I wanted to do was eat salty carbs and buy onesies for my baby.

"I'm so happy, honey!" She wrapped her arm around me and squeezed tight.

"I know. I know. Me, too. It's a blessing I didn't expect to arrive so easily." Ever since the ultrasound tech showed us the heartbeat of our baby, I'd felt a buoyancy I'd never known. Throughout the day, I would spontaneously burst into full-throated laughter — I was so lucky, I loved this baby so much, and I was so surprised to be pregnant. I'd assumed I'd have as much trouble getting pregnant as I'd had finding a suitable partner. When John and I started trying two months before our wedding, I visualized several rounds of Clomid and enrollment in the fertility clinic where many women I knew sought treatment. "I'm so grateful to be pregnant. I really want this baby."

"I hear nothing but miracles." She looked confused.

"Callie." Meredith knew that Callie had been trying to get pregnant for almost two years. I knew she'd understand how guilty I felt for getting pregnant so easily — guilty like I'd stolen her joy for myself. "We had a very tense conversation when I called to tell her the news."

Meredith raised her eyebrows, listening.

"She was silent for a long time. So long I had to ask, 'Are you still there?' "

Callie had endured the heartbreaking slog of shots and visits to the fertility clinic, and disappointment had dogged her month after month. She'd called me on those sad mornings when she got her period or the IVF clinic called with bad news, and I'd sistered her the best way I knew how: by listening, holding her hand, and dropping off a gift basket when she had to stay off her feet after implantation. Callie would be a great mother, and I couldn't wait to be an aunt to her child. But now it was awkward. It was patently unfair. I understood that Callie felt like her woe stacked against my stupid luck looked like betrayal.

"Then, she said something I can't shake."

"What?" Meredith shivered into her coat.

"She said, 'Well, we don't even know if this will stick.' "

"Oof."

"Yeah, it's a fetus — my baby — not a piece of Scotch tape. She wasn't trying to be cruel, but it felt like a punch, like she wanted to remind me that I could still lose the baby to miscarriage. I understand why she said it, but it hurt." I wrapped my arms around my midsection and started to cry. "I want Callie to be pregnant as much I want to be pregnant. If I could fix it for her, I would. But I can't." Now I thought of the time I made cheerleader and felt terrified of losing Tara over it, and recounted the story to Meredith.

"It's hard to hold joy when a friend is suffering," Meredith said. She told me about one of her friends who was struggling to make ends meet with freelance work. "It feels like she's mad at me because I'm on a career path and have no debt."

"I can't fucking believe how close I am to wishing I wasn't pregnant so Callie won't be mad at me."

"We can't use them as excuses to ignore or push away our own joy. That's not what our friends are asking of us. They are hurting, afraid, and want to be seen in their distress."

I felt desperate to make it right with Callie. I needed her and wanted to be there for her. She helped me find my way to John. Now I needed her help being a wife and a mother. I was willing to let go of my anger over what she said, but that might not fix this awkwardness between us.

"Should I call her or give her space?"

"What feels right in your gut?"

I took a deep breath and closed my eyes. What came to mind was simple: run. Callie and I were already struggling with my transition from angst-filled single woman to attached woman with a wedding date. Now this? I did not have the skills to weather the inevitable discomfort my easy path to pregnancy caused between us.

"Well?" Meredith nudged my shoulder

with hers.

"You won't like this, but my gut says to run, withdraw, get the fuck out because it's going to be excruciating —"

"It already is."

I nodded my head, grateful to have this woman next to me who understood every word out of my mouth, even though she'd never been pregnant and had never had this particular situation in her own life.

"I think," Meredith said, "the trick is learning how to show up with all of our joy and light, while also being compassionate for our friends' suffering." She pointed a gloved finger at me. "You couldn't do that in junior high with the cheerleaders, but you *can* do it with Callie. You can and you will. Maybe there's a reason this situation is coming around again."

"Do you want to run from your freelancer friend?"

"Of course! More than anything! I'm scared of her rage and scared of saying the wrong thing. All of it scares me. Relationships are terrifying when they are this real. I feel it, too. But I believe in your strength, and I also believe in Callie's. How'd you leave it with her?"

"Not good. We both clammed up — she in her sorrow and rage and me in my shame for having jumped the line and stolen a blessing not yet due to me. She got off the phone pretty quickly. That was two days ago. We haven't spoken since."

Low clouds dropped light snowflakes on our heads. Meredith pulled her hat over her ears.

"It's very painful to want something with all your heart and work really hard for it and not know if you'll ever get it."

I touched my belly. "I really want us both to have babies."

"Of course you do."

"All those years I was jealous of her relationship with Grant. They had the wedding in Hawaii, their cute apartment with the California king bed, their bike rides on the lake. I was constantly jealous or envious, whatever."

"Envy. That's when you want something someone else has. Jealousy is when there's a triangle — like if Callie was flirting with John, you'd feel jealous."

We were both shivering now, and the snow fell harder. We turned toward the side street where our cars were parked.

"I always wanted a baby, too," she said slowly. "I'm happy for you, really, and you deserve your joy. I want to be honest that it brings up a lot of pain for me. Lives not lived, and all of that."

We held each other's gaze as we both teared up. I'd never heard Meredith say she'd wanted children — I thought of her as mildly disdainful of all of us who were rushing to motherhood. With Meredith, I didn't feel like I had to do anything to fix her sadness. I could let it be there between us, swirling with the light snowfall. I loved her, and I understood under my shivering skin that loving her meant standing next to her and her feelings of loss without making it about me at all. Why couldn't I do that with Callie?

14

"It's a girl," I blurted out to Meredith when we met for breakfast shortly after my twenty-week ultrasound.

"Amazing!" Her eyes filled with tears, and she grabbed my hand. "You're going to have so much fun."

I cocked my head at her and squinted my eyes. "You're the first person to say that."

"That it'll be fun?"

"Yes."

In the weeks I'd found out I was having a girl, I'd mentioned it in almost every conversation. In turn, I'd discovered that people had strong feelings about baby girls, even before the babies were born. I recounted some for Meredith:

A girl? Congratulations and buckle up. So much drama!

Are you worried she'll have an eating disorder like you?

Girls are so expensive!

I'm so glad I had boys — less work and way less drama.

A girl is good because she'll take care of you when you get older, but she'll make you earn it during her childhood.

Good luck with the teenage years.

Wow! You'll be going through menopause when she gets her first period.

"What the hell is wrong with people?" I asked Meredith.

"So much. So much is wrong with people. As if it's not dramatic to get into fights and beat the shit out of other boys on the football field or hockey rink or to knock around a girlfriend. No drama there."

Now that I was carrying a baby girl and listening to strangers, colleagues, friends, and family members project their fantasies of difficulty and drama onto her tiny fetal head, I felt compassion for all of us. Before we take our first breath, we are written into a script about our difficult personalities, our emotional volatility, our fraught relationships, our propensity for so-called drama.

"What chance do we have when the world tells us this crap about our relationships all our lives?" I shook my head and looked out the window. Early-morning commuters streamed west from Millennium Park to their offices across the Loop. "That's my

163

rant. Tell me about you."

"I had an argument with my friend Julia over the weekend," Meredith said. I knew Julia was her oldest friend in Chicago, and that they sometimes had heated arguments over Julia's flakiness. This time, Julia had stood her up for lunch on Saturday because she double-booked. Meredith had called her from the restaurant and screamed at her for being so disrespectful. "It's so painful. I keep doing the same thing over and over. She can't show up for me."

"So what'd you do?"

Meredith shook her head. "Nothing yet. Not sure what there is to do. I'm recognizing the pattern in our relationship. I keep expecting her to be different. She's not going to change. I need to accept her." She wadded up her napkin and threw it on her plate. "You should have seen me. I was that person sitting in my car screaming into my cell; people passing by could hear me shouting, 'Julia, why do you always do this? I'm never making plans with you again!' We've been having this fight for twenty years. I really need to change."

"Change is super easy. Just become a totally different person" — I snapped my fingers — "like that."

"Ha. I wish. You know what I want?

164

Friends who show up for me. On time. Consistently."

A tour bus pulled over on the corner of Madison and Michigan Avenue, and a crowd of tourists with lanyards and maps spilled out onto the sidewalk. I silently prayed they'd already eaten and wouldn't descend on the mostly empty café. I thought about everything Meredith had just said and agreed with every word. I often found myself nodding vigorously when Meredith spoke.

Which was partly why, over the past few weeks, I had been thinking about asking her to be my sponsor.

"I need to change, too," I said, and then found the courage to be direct. "Will you be my sponsor? I mean, you sort of already are, but can we make it official?" For a while, I'd been feeling guilty for not having a sponsor — it felt like I wasn't doing my recovery the "right" way. If Meredith became my sponsor, I could check that box.

She shook her head.

Wait, what? I sat back and blinked at her. She had to know I would work hard on my homework and put my best efforts into addressing whatever was broken inside me. Now, I felt ashamed. I wished I was at my office, scrolling through emails and prep-

165

ping for a noon conference call.

Meredith grabbed both of my hands.

"We have to do it together. I'm not above you or ahead of you, so I can't sponsor you." She squeezed my hands. "I'm surprised you asked. The timing is a little" — she looked away for a second, bobbing her head as she searched for the right word — "strange."

She was right. This sponsorship conversation was a swerve. A way to Band-Aid my still-churning anxiety about my relationship with Callie, which had renewed my fears about my ability to stick with friendships long term. As I headed into motherhood, I wanted to convert my relationship with Meredith from a friendship to a sponsor-sponsee relationship to protect us both.

"If you're my sponsor, you can't leave me. I'm three months into marriage, pregnant with a baby girl, and more than a little overwhelmed. I'm afraid friendship won't be enough to keep you" — I pulled my hands from hers and tapped on the table — "right here, where I need you."

Meredith laughed. "Oh, I see. You'd rather have a hierarchical relationship — I'll be the authority, the sponsor, and you'll be the sponsee taking notes as you learn at my feet."

"You'll have to stick around if you're my sponsor. Your recovery will depend on it." Recovery programs were big on service, and I knew that Meredith took her service commitments, including sponsorship, quite seriously.

"Of course. You want to feel safe, and you don't believe that friendship can offer that kind of security. But you're going to have to trust me that it really will be better if we stay on the same footing — as friends. And, anyway, I have as many friendship issues as you do. Have you ever noticed I never go out for breakfast after the meeting on Saturday?"

I assumed it was because she was exhausted from her night shifts — a few months earlier she'd secured an internship at Hazelden, the nationally famous treatment center where she hoped to one day be hired as a full-time spiritual counselor. For now, she worked overnight shifts on the weekends.

Meredith shook her head. "But I didn't join you even before my schedule changed. It's because I'm scared. You're all younger than I am. You're dating, getting married, having babies, and you have your whole lives ahead of you." Her eyes started to well up. "You all got into recovery years before I did, and it hurts so much to see in you all that I lost. My twenties. My thirties. A lot of my forties. You have no idea how jealous I am of you."

"Me?"

"Yes, of course." She squeezed my hands. "You, Callie, Jolie, Emily, all of you."

My heart seized with an emotion I couldn't name. Sadness? Shame? Fear? I never dreamed Meredith was jealous of me and the breakfast crew. I liked my routine, but I always secretly wished I had something more exciting planned, like boating on Lake Michigan or jetting off to a day concert in the park. I could never shake the feeling that there was something shinier and brighter that "normal" people did on Saturday mornings. In those greener pastures of my imagination, I pictured a woman — very self-contained and graceful, like Carolyn Bessette-Kennedy or Penelope Cruz — wearing a big straw hat, white linen shirt, gauzy latte-colored skirt, and buttery leather sandals strolling through a farmers market, wicker basket in the crook of her arm filled with fresh wildflowers and sourdough bread. I certainly never imagined anyone looking at my Saturday mornings — wake up, work out, hit a twelve-step meeting, and have brunch with a subset of the crew from the meeting — and thinking, *Wow, I'd kill to have her life.*

"I didn't know that."

I thoroughly understood envy. It was one of my biggest character defects. Onto each friend I drew near, I projected my distorted ideas about miracles, and in each projection, I reified the hierarchy that dictated my thinking. And the distortions didn't end when I got into recovery; I brought it all with me, just like I brought my sense of humor, my combination oily-dry skin, and my tendency to see the world in black and white.

How often had I sat in recovery meetings listening to some friend or acquaintance report a victory in a battle I was still waging — when Jolie got engaged, when Emily and her husband jetted off to France, when Callie booked the honeymoon suite in Oahu — and a thick envy would consume me? My envy was spiny, sticky, nearly ever present. I tolerated it, like white noise.

I'd never been envious of guys. A mild envy over my brother's charisma, lifelong friendships, and ease of conviction irritated me now and then, but I could easily convert it to admiration. There was nothing sharp that could draw blood. I understood by middle school that the world valued boys more than girls, that those preferences were systemic and historical, and that I would have to negotiate our culture's view of our relative values for the rest of my life. It never felt personal. He simply drew the winning lottery card according to the logic of our culture: straight, white, male, clever, charismatic, tall, good teeth, great hair. And anyway, he was there during the drinking years, too, so no one raised him up as a "miracle" either.

"Envy and jealousy are the worst. They've stolen more joy than menstrual cramps," I said.

"So what would it look like?" Meredith asked.

"What?"

"What would it look like to get better?" She tapped on the table. "We should write a vision for ourselves in friendship. When we are healed, who will we be? What will it look like? How will we change? Let's write it and share it. It'll become a map for where we're going."

15

Meredith suggested writing a vision, but I couldn't do it. Was it unrealistic to wish for intimate friendships without complications? Were ease and intimacy incompatible? I picked up my pen and drew the shape of a triangle over and over again. A clue?

"Come meet us," my friends Emily and Marnie beckoned into the phone one Wednesday afternoon in 2004, when I was still mired in chronic dissatisfaction with my romantic life, and John was three years in the future. This was the same Emily who shimmied at my bachelorette party, toasted my announcement that John and I were trying to have a baby, and fielded my calls from bathroom stalls across Chicago. Before we settled into a solid friendship dyad, we were part of a triangle known as Marnie, Christie, and Emily.

"We're at Marshall Field's. Second floor

by the bras." I heard Emily in the background as Marnie gave me directions.

At my law office four blocks away, I toiled as a second-year associate, reviewing the financial documents of a giant grocery store chain. I could slip out and join them for an hour or so. Why not? I grabbed my coat and race-walked under the el tracks toward the seven-story Marshall Field's feeling two things: grateful that they called me to join them and envious that neither Emily nor Marnie had anywhere else to be on a Wednesday afternoon. Oh, and a third thing: jealousy that they were already together.

At the time, they were my closest friends, but the triangle we formed was uneasy. My leg was the wobbly one, the one mostly likely to splinter and crack. I had a long list of reasons why they were closer to each other than either was to me, among them: they both had husbands who supported them financially so they could write (Marnie) and paint (Emily) all day. Thus, neither had a boss, a billable hours' requirement, a work schedule, or lonely nights at home reheating leftovers from a firm luncheon. They'd never had to endure being single in their thirties or create an online dating profile. Plus, their husbands enjoyed each other's company so they double-dated to the cozy French bistro in Lincoln Square that Emily loved and the southern Italian trattoria in Oak Park that Marnie favored. They lived lives I could only dream of: married artists with sufficient means, mortgages, and plenty of free time to spend with each other.

Meanwhile, I had a boyfriend whose rent I covered, hoping once in a while he'd choose to hang out with me over playing video games.

I was desperately jealous of Marnie and Emily's common ground, and my insecurity hovered between them and me almost all the time. On more than one occasion, I'd called Emily, who answered the phone and asked if she could call me back in a few minutes because she was on the other line with Marnie. Each time I hung up on Emily with a curt "sure," and then did not pick up when she called back. I felt ashamed of being the friend who could wait her turn. I wanted to be the friend Emily dropped everything for. I wanted to be Marnie. On one unfortunate occasion, I called Marnie's home phone from law school, and Emily picked up, which so flustered me I could hardly speak. "I'm painting Marnie's vanity," Emily explained, which earned her vintage Christie curtness and a quick click of the phone line. Emily and Marnie answered each other's phones? It felt like the equivalent of a friendship ring. At twenty-nine years old, I hid in the law school bathroom, blinking back hot tears, convinced they preferred each other over me. My feelings, however immature, were extremely real and hard to control. I was the cusp friend — or so I believed — the dispensable one who would fall away easily if anything shook our little threesome. And when I disappeared, I wasn't sure either of them would miss me.

As I pushed myself through the revolving door of Marshall Field's, I thought: *If the building catches on fire, Emily and Marnie will save each other, and I'll be on my own, dying of smoke inhalation under a rack of coats.* As I wove through the warren of cosmetics counters, allowing the woman at the Clinique counter to thrust a piece of cardstock spritzed with perfume into my hand, I took note of a fire extinguisher posted on the wall by a rack of earrings. *Okay, Christie, you can save yourself.* I rode the escalators to the second floor and spotted Marnie's orange purse a few feet ahead.

She waved me over, and we hugged hello. "Where's Emily?" I asked.

174

We both turned toward the circular racks of bras and panties across the aisle and about ten yards away, where Emily, bent low, checked for a size on the bottom row.

"Look at her," Marnie said, her voice full of love and adoration. She sounded partly like a doting mom and partly like a lover. "Isn't she just the cutest?" Marnie stood and gazed at Emily with her hand over her heart for what felt like a full minute. Then she looked at me like she was waiting for my verdict. *Was Emily the cutest?*

Honestly, the rack of thongs obscured Emily's face, so I couldn't really say if she was as adorable as Marnie seemed to think. I mean, I loved Emily — sometimes on the way home from her studio she would stop by my law office to give me a hug and have a ten-minute chat on the sidewalk, offering me a humanity break during a stretch of working twelve to fifteen hours a day reviewing EBITDA (earnings before interest, taxes, depreciation, and amortization) documents. But I'd never talked about her like Marnie did. Actually, I'd never gushed about any friend like that. And I was positive Marnie never spoke about me in that hushed, reverent tone.

I felt like I'd crashed their date, even though they both seemed happy to see me.

175

After Emily bought a pair of shoes that Marnie already owned in two colors, I said goodbye to them out on the sidewalk and walked back to my office, thinking that sometimes it felt better just to be alone.

"I have a dark history with triangles," I told Meredith one Saturday after I'd written an inventory of my relationship with Marnie and Emily. I knew that struggling in a friendship triangle did not make me unique. I felt certain that every woman who passed through middle school understood the intensity and dangers of a friendship triangle. Until Meredith came along, though, I thought that the ubiquity of the triangle configuration and its inherent imbalances meant I didn't have to do any work around them, other than to avoid them in the future.

"What was your part in that one?"

"My insecurity. Jesus, I never let up. Never, ever." It's entirely possible that Marnie and Emily liked each other more than they liked me. But my focus on their common ground, affection for each other, and wealth blocked me from receiving their love for me and enjoying our time together.

Meredith laughed. "Yup. When I go out with my friends Samantha and Kelly, it feels like they are the whole planet — they live in

176

the suburbs, and they have children in college — and I'm just a little satellite." Meredith hunched her shoulders to make herself look small and pathetic.

So I really wasn't the only one addicted to apartness in friendships.

"The triangle with Marnie and Emily mimicked the one with my mother and sister. It played into my whole *I'm different than them, blah blah blah.*"

"Right! And Samantha and Kelly are the sisters my mother would adore, and I'm just lame old Meredith with the bad posture and drab clothes."

I laughed loudly and pointed to her deep purple shirt with a matching scarf. She seemed not to appreciate how absurd the criticism about her clothes sounded.

"Yeah, but —" Meredith's voice broke off, and she looked at the ground. We'd never really discussed her wardrobe, but now I realized it was the source of some distress. I waited for her to continue. "You know where I shop, right?"

I shook my head.

"I don't buy new stuff." Her eyes flitted over her shoulder. "I can't buy nice things — new things — for myself. I can only shop at Salvation Army. It's not a money thing. I just can't . . ." Her voice trailed off.

I suddenly understood that Meredith shopped at a charitable organization, not out of economic necessity or some principled middle finger to capitalism but as part of self-deprivation. And she was deeply ashamed of it.

"Maybe someday we could shop together," I said. I could teach her the fine art of trolling through the designer castoffs at Nordstrom Rack.

"Samantha and Kelly sometimes invite me shopping, and I can't make myself say yes. It's one more way to keep myself apart."

"How can we stop doing this to ourselves?"

"I think we can catch ourselves when we slide into these old beliefs about not belonging. You call me if you feel it, and I'll call you."

"I swear to God, I will never willingly enter another friendship triangle."

"Let's cross that bridge when we get to it."

I thought of the times when I called Emily crying, saying in not so many words, "You love Marnie more than you love me." Emily always listened and assured me that she loved me and would always have my back. "You're like family to me," she said every single time. And I believed her until my neurosis flared, usually the next time she opted to finish her conversation with Marnie before calling me back or when I heard the report of their latest double date.

Marnie was less tolerant of my bullshit. Once, she heard my voice fall when I realized she'd told Emily she'd made an offer on a new house before she told me. Marnie put her foot down. "Don't do this. I told Emily first because she called right after we made the offer. Had you called two seconds earlier, I would have told you first." Marnie offered tough love — *Stop acting like no one loves you* — and Emily offered endless reassurance. Both of them loved me well, but the insecurity I brought into the triangle meant it wasn't enough to keep me steady.

I could see all of this clearly now, and I was positive I wasn't that person anymore. I might feel a twinge if I heard about two mutual friends getting together without me, but I no longer slammed down the phone or demanded constant reassurance from my friends.

But by sharing the particulars of that triangle with Meredith, I felt the pangs of that old insecurity. The way my stomach clenched when I knew Emily and Marnie were together or the way a cold panic would seize me when Emily said, "Let me call you right back when I get off with Marnie." My body remembered those cramped days, and how impossible it felt to breathe and relax because I was always poised for the abandonment I was positive was coming.

I wish I could say this unstable configuration transformed into a healthy, stable triangle because I eventually mustered up some self-esteem and stopped demanding that my friends prop me up. But that's not what happened.

First, Marnie and Emily had a disagreement about a ski trip to Canada they were planning. The tension between them grew, and they eventually stopped speaking to each other.

"I think we are done," Marnie reported to me.

"I don't know how we get back together," Emily confirmed.

I'd like to think I was a compassionate, even-keeled friend to each as they faced this crisis that started as a travel squabble and eventually led to a total breach. Of course, part of me was relieved they were on the outs — it meant both of them would turn to me. I became the primary friend I always wanted to be; I was no longer the weak link. For a few weeks, I reveled in my status as the only friend on speaking terms with all parties, but then I realized how stressful this fractured triangle was. Could I mention Emily to Marnie? Would Marnie be angry if she knew I was having dinner with Emily? I had to choose my words carefully with each, because what if they reconciled and later compared notes? I felt like a kid caught in a contentious divorce.

As the months went on, Emily and I forged a way ahead in the new, cozy non-triangle reality, but Marnie and I lost our bearings.

Our last conversation started out normally. It was an early-summer Saturday afternoon. Marnie called and invited me to her house in the suburbs to hang out. "We're going to grill, maybe swim."

"I wish I could, but I have to work. Big filing on Monday." I'd answered Marnie's call from my office, where I sat surrounded by piles of my client's financial papers. Out the window, boats carrying tourists up and down the shimmering Chicago River sailed by, taunting me with visions of an alternative summer day.

A few hours later, Marnie called while I was still in the office but away from my desk. "I don't appreciate your lying to me about having to work. If you didn't want to come over, then you should have just said so," her voice mail said.

Her message went on and on, full of accusations that I'd lied about my availability. I stood in my office, my heart thumping with panic as it always did when someone expressed anger at me. What in the world had gotten into Marnie? Who voluntarily stays at the office on a summer Saturday until late in the evening, waiting for the partner on the case to release her? The four other attorneys on the team and I would return to the office the next morning at ten a.m. to do it all over again. None of it was optional. Marnie knew that my law firm expected me to be on call twenty-four/seven.

I didn't call her back that afternoon. Or the next day. A week passed. My anger softened to confusion. I waited for her to call me back.

She didn't. I didn't reach out either.

And that was the end.

Even though I'd spent most of our relationship obsessed with my status relative to Emily, I'd called Marnie my best friend for several years. We'd met in recovery meetings and bonded immediately. I adored her wit and her tough-love style. I'd traveled to Georgia with her when she researched her hometown for her memoir. For several Christmases, she invited Emily and me to her house for homemade pasta and gravy, which remains one of the best Italian dishes I've ever eaten. When I graduated from law school, she and Emily threw me a party in the park down the block from her house in Oak Park.

And yet one angry voice mail and I never called back?

It was easy to place the blame on her. After all, just a few months earlier, she'd scorched her relationship with Emily. I considered my decision not to call her back healthy and laudable. I have no memory of discussing my decision to ghost in therapy or at any meetings. I did not lay out all the complications of the friendship for a neutral third party to help me. I, alone, managed the broken-apart triangle and the subsequent strain of having a relationship with two friends who no longer spoke to each other.

I did not ask for help. At most I reported to others that we'd grown apart.

But the bright side of breaking up with mean ol' Marnie was that now Emily and I could share an uncomplicated friendship. No more triangle. No more strain. Problem solved.

■ ■ ■ ■

At some point, when Meredith and I were out for coffee, we discussed my friendship triangle with Marnie and Emily again. My fear was that my bad habits — the insecurity, the obsessing, the conviction I was the weak link — still lived inside me but simply went dormant when Marnie disappeared.

"It's all still in me," I said. "I can almost feel that particular insecurity inside me, like a faint pulse. Now, I feel like Callie, my baby, and I form a version of this triangle." In a recent conversation, Callie had said she was afraid that once my daughter was born, Callie would be squeezed out of my life. No matter how much I reassured her that I would continue to love and need her — maybe more than ever — she didn't believe me. To Callie, my daughter was the golden miracle baby about to yank my love and affection away from her.

"Of course. It's not a coincidence that you're in this situation, because now you can see how far you've come. And you'll get a chance to do it differently."

I sighed. I'd been willing to do so much emotional work to get healthy enough for a relationship with John, but this friendship stuff felt more deeply rooted and more intractable. I had so many bad habits. Insecurity. Jealousy. Codependence. Conflict avoidance. Fear. Anger. Meredith was certain that her God would heal her and all this work — the writing, talking, sharing — would take her where she wanted to go. I didn't share her faith.

"Do we ever really change? I mean, appreciably. Is that really possible?" I asked.

"This from the woman who used to cry through every meeting because she was going to die alone?"

"Faith is not my strong suit." I'd probably be better off if I had an unwavering belief in God, but I wasn't there yet. In my head, God was mixed up with religion, repression, homophobia, genocide, extremism, and rigidity. I couldn't extricate God from all of that.

Meredith nodded. "Could you do the trick that some recovery people do? The one where GOD is an acronym for Good Orderly Direction. You could pray *for* Good Orderly Direction instead of *to* God." I'd heard this before, but I was ambivalent about the acronyms of recovery. On one hand, they reeked of hokey homespun wisdom and turned me off. And there were so many of them. KISS (keep it simple, sweetie). ODAT (one day at a time). FEAR (false evidence appearing real). SHAME (should have already mastered everything). On the other hand, they helped lots of people manage their runaway emotions so maybe there was something to them after all.

"I guess it's hard to argue the downside of Good Orderly Direction. I could certainly use some of it."

"And you must believe in progress, right?"

"Sure." As doubt-filled as I was, I'd watched people get well around their eating disorders and dating patterns, family relationships and finances; I'd seen it in myself and in countless others. Progress definitely existed.

"When we feel pain around friendship or notice anything that brings up shame, anger, or loneliness, then we're making progress."

"Sounds fun."

"The alternative is denial."

"I'm such a slow learner. Please don't give up on me."

"Never."

16

John and I welcomed our daughter Zara into the world on a July morning two days after my thirty-fifth birthday. I kissed her tiny nose and the faint raspberry mark on her forehead she earned trying to scoot through my birth canal, and whispered all kinds of promises to her.

I'll always love you.

I support all of your feelings, including anger — you never have to stuff your feelings.

You will always be safe with Daddy and me.

Our last night in the hospital, the nurse on duty urged John and me to sleep. "I'll take the baby to the nursery," she said. "When she wakes up, we'll bring her right in."

I didn't want to let my Zara go, but I was reeling physically and emotionally from the C-section, and sleep seemed like a wise choice. The nurse rolled our daughter out in her bassinet, and John and I settled into the dark room. I closed my eyes and took some deep breaths. Tomorrow we would be sent home with this little baby, and there would be no one to wheel her away so we could sleep. We had to do it now.

From down the hall, I heard a baby crying. Was that Zara?

"Do you hear that?" John whispered.

"Do you think it's —"

"No way. Couldn't be."

I closed my eyes again, and the baby cried on. I sat up. "It's her. I know it's her. Go get her."

Before John could stand up, the nurse reappeared in the doorway. "She won't settle. We can't have her waking up the other babies." She wheeled Zara next to my bed and left the room. I picked her up and offered her my left breast. She settled instantly.

John and I looked at each other across the room and burst out laughing. "Holy shit, this kid knows what she wants and won't stop until she gets it."

I held her tight and felt proud. Two days old and expressing her feelings like a champ. I thought of all the ways our culture projects onto little girls and shuddered to think of all the ways I, too, would project onto her throughout her life, no matter how much therapy and recovery I had.

"Oh, sweet girl, here we go," I whispered.

After our daughter was born, I leaned on my friends like I never had before. I needed them: my family and John's lived several states away, so our village was composed of people who didn't share our bloodline. Like all new parents, I'd never been so fucking tired in my life, and I was deeply freaked out by the C-section — how I'd been carved open and stitched back together. I couldn't bear to look at the scar and whenever I thought of it, I felt nauseated. When I closed my eyes to rest, I pictured my OB dragging a sharp blade across my abdomen and my vital organs quivering on a metal table.

A few days after we got home, Emily and her husband, Rob, visited. They held the baby and delivered news of the outside world. They also brought Thai food, and a wave of joy and adoration that buoyed my weary spirit.

After dinner, while the baby dozed in Rob's arms, I burst into tears. I wanted my baby desperately and loved every inch of her, but I also felt a thick darkness hovering — the fear that I'd never see my body as whole again, never cross another 5K finish line, never dash off to coffee with Meredith,

Callie, or Emily. A sense of profound loneliness threatened to devour me. I said the words before I fully understood.

"I think I'm depressed, y'all." I laid my head on the table and let myself cry harder. How awful to have a beautiful baby and feel smothered in unexpected despair. I hated this feeling. It made no sense! I had a beautiful baby; a present partner; a safe, clean home; and a savings account. I also had great friends in Emily and Rob. Jolie had offered to bring food the next day, and two other friends were scheduled to drop off lasagna and soup over the weekend. What was wrong with me?

Emily placed her palm on my back and rubbed a soothing circle. "It's okay," she said. "This is a lot. And you just had major surgery."

Three days earlier, I'd cried in the hospital room because every time Zara latched on, it felt like a tiny knife grinding into my breast. Beside my bed, a sixty-something nurse with a Slavic accent gave me a talking-to. "Some mothers have a hard time. They are used to controlling their lives. You a lawyer?" I nodded. How did she know? "Yes, of course. You are not used to this little baby who won't do what you want. You are not used to physical pain. And women today have babies without their family around. You are more alone than you should be. You are going to have a hard time. A very hard time."

Her harsh words offered a strange comfort.

"I have friends to help. And my parents are coming in two weeks."

"I hope it's enough for you. I hope they are good friends."

Now with Emily's hand on my back, it felt like enough. I would be okay. Tired and sore, but that was how most mothers felt five days after giving birth.

"You should tell Dr. Rosen how you feel. You don't have to suffer," Emily said. "Send him a message right now."

John handed me my phone, and Emily sat with me as I typed a message to Dr. Rosen. *I love my baby so much, and I feel depressed. It's really dark in my head and getting darker. Please help me. Meds?*

A few days later, I had a prescription for antidepressants and my therapist's affirmation that I deserved to enjoy my baby. I thanked Emily for the support in asking for help.

Meredith came over in those first early weeks and brought a picture book called *I*

Will Love You Forever. I held my daughter as Meredith read the words to us both. Zara slept, and I cried my eyes out. Hormones and exhaustion whipped me to and fro, and our ragtag village of friends held me together. It was so beautiful and uncomfortable — all I could do was nurse my baby and cry.

Jolie brought homemade bean soup, braised greens, corn bread, and brownies. Astrid, a woman I'd known for years from twelve-step meetings, came over once a week with her four-year-old daughter, and they took turns holding Zara so I could lie on the couch and close my eyes. Another woman from my therapy group named Rebekah brought over a kugel, one of John's favorite dishes from childhood.

The meals, the presents, the texts, the outpouring of support — I absorbed all of it and let it soak through me. These women knew to bring big enough meals so that we'd have leftovers. They recommended remedies for my sore nipples. Each one held my hand and led me toward joy.

One month after Zara was born, we packed up the baby and drove to Callie's house to celebrate her birthday and her new pregnancy. She was eight weeks along, and her little one's heartbeat was strong and solid. She opened the door and held me tight.

We did it, we whispered to each other.

Out on her back deck, I rocked Zara. When she got fussy, Callie led me to her bedroom so I could change Zara's diaper and catch my breath.

"How are you?" she asked. "I mean, really?"

"I'm okay. I think we're turning a corner." The darkest edges of the depression had lifted, and we were getting a few more winks of sleep each night. I could almost imagine a day when I would get in the car alone and linger in Target all by myself for a whole blessed hour.

"And you? How does it feel?" I asked, nodding toward her belly. From the deck, we could hear her husband, Grant, laughing and telling stories.

"Honestly?" she said, looking over her shoulder to be sure that no one could hear her. "I'm scared. Really scared. Will I still be able to go to swim practice? Will Grant and I still have sex? I've been really nauseated, and I'm worried I'll never recognize my body again. And I can never tell anyone I feel like this because we've worked so hard for this baby — all the money, time, tears, shots, and all the fucking appointments."

I nodded. I'd been scared to admit my depression because I was afraid it would sound like I didn't want my baby. It helped to think back to all the women who'd come to meetings through the years telling the truth about their experience of motherhood. They taught me that we could want our babies and also feel terror, shame, dread, and pain. The insistence that new mothers feel nothing but joy is a form of violence. I would not participate in that lie.

"I know you want your baby. It's okay to have all kinds of feelings. I'm here for it."

"Thank God," Callie said. "I can't do the self-sacrificing smiling routine for the next twenty years of my life."

"Fuck that. Let's be real. Because this is hard. I'm still bleeding every day. My left nipple has a blister on it. I'm waking up drenched in sweat and breast milk. I cannot imagine ever having sex with anyone again. I mean, anyone — not John, not Mark Ruffalo, not Ralph Fiennes, not L.L. Cool J — I mean, no one."

"This is serious."

"I'm telling you, my libido left the building with my placenta."

Right then, Zara started wailing. I lifted her to my shoulder and patted her back. Callie and I couldn't really talk over the cries, but we'd had a moment. In her bedroom with my daughter's fouled diaper, we had our first moment together as young mothers, and I felt the joy of connection. I also felt the shift of our roles. Now with my newborn, I felt like a big sister to Callie and her eight-week-old fetus. I vowed to be generous and always tell the truth about my experience.

17

"I've been having vivid dreams," I told Meredith one morning over breakfast when Zara was about six months old. Or she was a year . . . Or a year and a half. Time and memory tumbled this way and that during my early motherhood. I missed my mental acuity; I still do.

Meredith raised her eyebrows. "Please tell me every single detail."

We laughed because we had a running joke about how boring it was to listen to someone recite the details of their dream. This guy Gus who came to our Saturday-morning meeting consistently took up a solid five minutes of sharing time to tell us about the strange vistas and surreal scenes he visited during his REM cycles. Meredith and I rolled our eyes every time.

I pulled a piece of paper out of my wallet with seventeen tick marks on it and passed it across the table to her. "This is how many times I've dreamed about Lia, my best friend from high school, in the past few months. When I wake up, I make a mark on this paper that I keep in my wallet. Seventeen times."

"Always the same dream?"

"No. Sometimes we're in high school, sometimes college. In a few we're adults, and I'm visiting her in a big city with skyscrapers and huge apartment buildings. But after every single one, I wake up heartbroken. Twice, I woke up crying. I've never done that before. In each dream, I'm running late or have just missed her, and I'm devastated. For many of them, I can remember every detail — the drapes in her parents' living room, the china pattern on the plates, the wood grain on her front door. It's hyper-vivid." I diagnosed the dreams as unresolved grief and guilt for that lost relationship.

"Maybe you should reach out to her," Meredith said. "You could reconnect."

"I'm too ashamed. And I don't know where she is."

I hadn't stayed in touch with anyone from my high school, and Lia wasn't on social media. But that was a lame excuse because my parents saw her parents at Mass every Sunday. In two phone calls, I could get to Lia. She'd invited me to her wedding the summer before I started law school, and I'd felt such joy to see her — so beautiful, so radiant, so in love — but my shame tripped me up the whole weekend. In our conversations, I awkwardly made fun of my haircut and my status as a single woman, and then I skittered away so she could talk to the friends who deserved her attention. Most of her half dozen bridesmaids were strangers to me — I didn't know their names or how they knew Lia — which was proof of how far I'd drifted away from her. She'd been my best friend in high school, but I didn't meet her husband until the rehearsal dinner. I had no idea how they met, what she loved about him, where they were honeymooning. The wall I put up when I started dating Kal still stood between us, cemented now by my shame and regret. At the reception, I kept close to my parents, watching Lia and her friends from afar.

I had so many choices that weekend — jump into the dancing fray and party like we were high school sophomores again; call myself out for ghosting and express an interest in reconnecting; tell her that I loved her, missed her, and wished her and her husband every blessing. I did none of that. I hid, cowered, and then slinked away.

"I'm scared it's too late," I said.

When I thought of reaching out to Lia, I shut down. I couldn't bear to face the guilt, shame, and sadness; I feared they would consume me.

"What are you afraid of?"

I looked out the window blinking back tears I hadn't expected. Meredith touched my hand. I stopped blinking and let the tears slide.

"It's grief. All that I missed. It hurts the way death hurts."

"I know that feeling. I have a friend from medical school who I turned my back on when I dropped out. I couldn't face her because I was so ashamed. Still can't — it's been almost thirty years. I want to reach out, though. I also have that with my old boss and the team I worked with. I left abruptly, and I really loved those people. They were like family." Meredith had tears in her eyes, too.

"Is this where we reassure each other that the opportunity to connect will arise if we are patient and watch for it?"

"Yep," she said, wiping under her eyes. "After we cry, we reassure."

I shook my head. "It's not enough to just reminisce about lost friendships. We have to do more."

"We will." I raised my eyebrows. I wanted

timelines, dates, something to put in my calendar. *Call Lia and make amends for dropping out of her life.* "When the time is right. We aren't just 'reminiscing' " — here she made air quotes. "This is the work of recovery."

Meredith had a point. In twelve-step world, step four suggested taking a "searching and fearless moral inventory," of situations and relationships that troubled us. Step five suggested sharing that inventory with someone else. That was exactly what we were doing. Reaching out to someone we'd harmed was part of step nine, which came only after getting clarity about our character defects (step six), asking God to remove them (step seven), and making a list of everyone we'd harmed (step eight). But I wanted a slightly quicker fix for my discomfort, not a long, arduous slog through the steps.

"I want it to go faster."

She leaned forward and held my gaze. "When the time is right, I guarantee you that you will find yourself in the position to make amends to Lia and yourself for your friendship failings. Just like I'll get to see my friend and my old boss and colleagues. Our lives are made of patterns that always repeat. I think they repeat until we learn how to be different inside them."

I felt agitated, anxious to be better already.

"How? Let me guess. More work," I said.

Meredith nodded and took a sip of her coffee. "If you're like me, and I think you are, then 'more work' usually means 'more pain.' "

I slapped my forehead with my open palm. "More pain? Is that always the answer?" She didn't mean I would have to stick my hand over an open flame, but I would have to face the pain I'd caused others.

"How did you recover from bingeing and purging?"

I pursed my lips and looked out the window. My recovery from bulimia had been slow going. And now two decades had passed since I started going to meetings and letting go of my eating secrets. I no longer binged and purged, but I still struggled at times with the attendant parts of my eating disorder: obsession with body image, days of restriction, periodic episodes of overeating, self-loathing about my appetites. Some days I swam in guilt about what I'd eaten the night before. Some days I felt uncomfortable in my body, despairing that it was "too big" and fretting about every calorie consumed. Sometimes I ran miles on the lake on an empty stomach. I sometimes lost minutes of my life envying women who seemed at ease in their bodies, or I lost hours scheming about how I could make my body smaller. To me, all of those behaviors fit squarely in my "eating disorder" box. These episodes didn't last as long as they used to, and I always talked them over with my friends in recovery. Recovery didn't mean no more hard days; it meant no more facing hard days all alone.

"It takes a long time to get well," I said.

Meredith smiled and lifted her coffee cup. "I'll toast to that." She'd left me a message earlier that week about skipping dinner more than once in the past few days. She knew a thing or two about disordered eating.

I tapped my cup of hot tea to hers.

"Did you make any friendship amends related to your eating disorder?" Meredith asked after telling me a story about writing a one-hundred-dollar check to a former roommate from whom she stole food and money.

"Sure." I had practice coming clean about food I stole, but not for the ways I let down the people I loved by drifting away.

18

In 1992, I was a sophomore in college, zooming toward an emotional and physical collapse from bulimia. Rock bottom looked like fainting in the shower after bingeing and purging on a pizza I'd rescued from the trash can in the dorm's common area. The silver lining of almost dying from literal garbage pizza was that I became willing to do anything to get better. A friend who'd gotten sober in AA our senior year of high school recommended a similar recovery program for people with eating disorders, so I looked up the meetings in a giant phone book on the shelf in my dorm room. In my first meeting, I realized that if I wanted to keep my head out of the toilet, I would have to work the steps of the program. I set my sights on a sponsor — Teresa, a soft-spoken woman with rosy cheeks and clear brown eyes who had graduated from my high school a few years ahead of me. At some point, she told me to make a list of all the people I'd harmed when I was bingeing and purging. Top of the list was Kate.

Kate was my roommate and closest friend and in the time we'd lived together, I'd helped myself to her food, never asking in advance, instead swiping pieces of this and bites of that. She wouldn't have cared that I ate one of her Hot Pockets or sneaked a handful of pretzels, but acting in secret and stewing in shame were the centerpieces of my eating disorder.

Two months before I found recovery meetings, Kate and I sat in our usual spot in the library studying for a political science test.

"I'll be right back," I said. I walked out of the library and then sprinted to our dorm room three blocks away. There, Kate had stashed two bags of Halloween candy in her closet, part of a care package for her boyfriend. I tore open one of the bags and ate five or six Reese's peanut butter cups standing inside her closet. Jamming the candy into my mouth so quickly made the chocolate and peanut butter glob together and stick in my throat. I ran to the sink and stuck my mouth to the faucet, drinking enough water to clear my airway. Ten seconds later, my hand reached back into the bag. This time, Hershey's milk chocolate. In less than five minutes, I'd eaten a third of the bag. Then, panic. How could I hide what I'd done? My brilliant idea: run across the parking lot to the campus market, buy a bag of replacement candy, and switch it out for the one I'd demolished. Did I polish off the half-eaten bag right then? Probably. I know I purged in our bathroom before running back to the library where Kate sat hunched over her textbook with a highlighter.

"That took a while," Kate said, looking up. "Who'd you run into?"

"Someone from my women's lit class. I don't know her name." My cheeks flushed from the sugar, the purging, and the sprints across campus. Lying to Kate made me feel hot and dirty — my clothes were suddenly too small, the library now boiling hot.

When I got into recovery, I told Teresa all about this incident — and others like it — and she advised me to tell Kate the truth about my eating.

"Kate," I said solemnly, on a Sunday night as we sat on our beds deciding whether to watch an episode of *Northern Exposure* or catch up on reading for our classes. I tried to act naturally, but my voice sounded lower than normal, and my hands were shaking.

"So. Well. Um. I've gotten into recovery for my eating disorder, and in order to stay clean, it's necessary for me to make amends to people I've harmed. I've stolen food from you the whole time we've lived together. I've lied about how much I was eating and hidden my bulimia from you. I'm getting help now, and I need to come clean to the people I've harmed. I'm sorry for all the ways my eating disorder has harmed you and our friendship." As soon as I got all the words out, I waited for relief to wash over me, but all I felt was embarrassed. This was the hardest conversation I'd ever initiated.

Kate, ever loving and supportive, knew I'd been suffering, even if she didn't know the details. "I'm so glad you're getting the help you need. I'm here for you. And I'm proud of you for getting help."

We hugged and decided it was a TV night. The relief of coming clean arrived by bedtime.

From that day forward, Kate supported my recovery. She knew that drinking too much triggered my desire to binge, so she'd put her hand over my cup when she could tell I'd had enough spiked punch or keg beer. When I was late to sorority chapter meetings because I was at a twelve-step meeting, she covered for me. She wanted me to be safe and happy; I wanted the same for her.

Kate's friendship was an incredible gift for someone in her first year of recovery. Once I came clean, I never had to hide who I was or what I needed. When we graduated from college, we backpacked through Europe where, in Italy, she waited patiently at our hostel while I attended a twelve-step meeting; in France, Switzerland, and Spain, she let me pick the restaurants because the foreign foods were freaking me out, and she wanted me to be comfortable with the menu.

After our European summer, I decamped to Chicago, and she began her business career in Texas. I should have been able to hold on to the friendship. I had all the tools of recovery plus an email account and a cost-effective long-distance plan, but I drifted away. In the same ways I longed for Lia, I now longed for Kate, yet took zero steps to reconnect. Sometimes, I'd hear a Hootie and the Blowfish song that Kate loved or think of one of our many inside jokes, and I'd miss her. In those moments, I had perfectly rational thoughts, like *I should call her* or *I'll invite her to Chicago!* But I'd quickly convince myself it was too late — one phone conversation or visit couldn't dent the distance between her life as a businesswoman in Houston and my graduate school existence in Chicago. Then, I'd picture her big life — filling out expense reports, bar-hopping with a lively new roommate, hobnobbing with consultants and junior oil execs — and feel certain she wasn't missing me.

So much second-guessing. So much projection. So much of my imagination devoted to imagining her glorious postgraduate life. So many missed opportunities.

19

Adult life happens so fast. One minute you have a baby girl, two twelve-step recovery programs, therapy sessions, a full-time job, a stable marriage, and then you blink, and you are back in the labor and delivery department breathing through contractions, hours away from your son's birth.

John and I found out we were pregnant with a second child on the morning of Meredith's wedding to Gage at the Briggs Mansion in her hometown of Rockford, Illinois. That May morning, I'd turned on the shower, laid out my pink dress and silver sandals, and then, on a whim, peed on a pregnancy test stick. We'd only been trying for two months. I was skeptical that pregnancy would happen while I was still nursing Zara, but I knew it was possible. As the bathroom filled with steam, I busied myself with finding the right necklace and plugging in the straight iron. When I glanced back at the stick, two bright red lines glowed in the little window.

Meredith had asked John to be the official photographer of the wedding, so I watched Zara while he zipped all around the room capturing moments from Meredith's special day. She wore a cream-colored silk dress, which I'm proud to report she bought brand new at that most sacred of temples, Nordstrom Rack; her face radiated the light and joy of a Catholic saint depicted in a stained-glass window. Her bridesmaids, Emily and another woman I knew from meetings, Anna, wore cornflower blue dresses, and John snapped dozens of pictures of them holding hydrangeas and flanking Meredith on a grand wooden staircase. I wasn't hurt that I hadn't been chosen as a bridesmaid; I knew how much Meredith loved Anna and Emily. During the reception, I introduced myself to Meredith's sisters — perfectly pleasant gray-haired women in their late fifties and early sixties who shook my hand and smiled warmly — so I could report that they were "nothing special" compared to her. When I met her eighty-something-year-old mother, I went on and on about how talented and beloved Meredith is to all of us, and stopped just short of telling her that I'd cut a bitch who made Meredith feel small and unworthy.

"I'm so happy," Meredith whispered to me when I hugged her after the ceremony.

"It shows."

She was a few weeks away from her sixtieth birthday.

When the party wound down, Meredith pulled me into a little alcove by the front entrance. Half the guests had already hugged her goodbye and started the drive back to Chicago. The stragglers lingered in the main room where Anna's daughters twirled their skirts to the music. Meredith's face held an expression I couldn't recognize.

"What's up?" I asked.

"It's a lot to take in — all this love." She gestured around the room. "All these lovely people, and Gage is so wonderful. Even my mother was pleasant." She grabbed my arm. "But I'm obsessing."

I laughed and hugged her. "You're not the first bride to obsess. About what?"

She pointed at a round wooden table a few feet away, where party favors had been fanned out for guests to grab on their way out. Meredith individually wrapped shiny new pennies as a parting gift because she loved the *In God We Trust* emblazoned above Lincoln's head. It was the most Meredith thing ever. Next to the pennies, someone had splayed dozens of small plastic baggies — I couldn't tell what was in them.

"See those baggies? Those are pieces of fudge!" I nodded. Somewhere John held Zara, who was probably gumming one of them. "They're hideous! I didn't want them here. I'm so angry. What the fuck?"

"Bebe?" I knew that Meredith's friend Bebe had offered to help with the party favors and that their negotiations had broken down. Bebe offered to make fudge — regular and sugar-free! — but Meredith didn't want little baggies of fudge handed out like goodies at a grade school bake sale. Apparently, Bebe wouldn't take no for an answer. Meredith had practiced what language she could use to let Bebe know it was a no-go on the fudge. *Thank you so much for the generous offer, but fudge in a plastic bag is not the direction I want to go.* Yet, here they were.

"How'd they get there?" I asked.

"Bebe brought them and arranged them like they're goddamn Godiva samples, but look at them? They look like literal shit."

"You want me to move them?"

She waved her hand. "It's not worth it. Most people are gone. I'm furious at Bebe. She asked me what I wanted, and then she didn't listen."

"Mere, honestly, I'm not surprised by this. Bebe's a little" — I searched for the right word to describe Bebe, whom I'd seen swanning around the reception draped in what looked like multiple black shawls — "undersocialized."

"She made it all about her!"

"Anyone who trespasses on a bride's big day like this lacks what my country grandma would call 'home training.' "

"It's my wedding. She shouldn't have offered to help if she wasn't going to abide by my wishes."

"Totally agree. What a whore." I winked for the first time in my life and tried to hold my face still.

Meredith was about to say something and stopped herself. She smiled. I smiled back, happy to witness her very human moment of fury, to be audience to her rant. To see her struggling in real time with a friendship issue.

"I'm being crazy right now," she said.

I shook my head. "Not as crazy as someone foisting off weird fudge packets against a bride's explicit wishes. How about this? You let it go for now. Focus on Gage. Later, you and Bebe can hash it all out. Right now, though, maybe go enjoy the final moments of your wedding reception?"

Meredith nodded. "You're right. Screw the fudge. I'm going to find my husband."

She wiggled her hips and kissed me on the cheek.

"Tomorrow, after you catch your breath," I said, "maybe you can make a list of all the things you love about Bebe."

She narrowed her eyes. "Very sneaky. Turning my suggestions back on me."

"Oh, also thank your God for this opportunity to work on this friendship."

"You're cruel."

I didn't tell her about the pregnancy test because I didn't want to make her wedding day about my womb. I texted her a few days later with the news.

Hurray for you and your family! Sweet Zara is getting a sibling!

We found out on the morning of your wedding. This kid will always remind me of you and Gage and your special day.

Mystical connection.

Eighteen months after we welcomed Zara, our son Elias arrived via C-section forty-eight hours before an epic snowstorm, which every news outlet predicted would dump more than twelve feet on Chicago. The hospital, worried we wouldn't be able to make it home safely, sent us home a day early. Gobs of snow fell and fell and fell, and the drifts grew from eight feet, to ten, to twelve. Zara still wore diapers and expressed deep feelings of curiosity that quickly turned to dissatisfaction when we brought home her brother. On our sixth day home, we ventured out of the house for a late breakfast because we were all losing our grip on reality. The whole city was like an igloo, hushed and cold. Parking was challenging given half the spaces were filled with snowdrifts. We found a spot at Jane's in Bucktown, but had to wait thirty minutes for a table and another thirty for our food. None of us had slept more than three hours at a time for almost a week, and everything looked, felt, and tasted as surreal and unfamiliar as the cold, white world.

When we pulled into the garage after brunch, Elias started to cry, and I gathered him from his car seat to take him upstairs to nurse.

"Up, Mama," Zara said, raising her hands so I could pick her up, too. And I wanted to; my arms had plenty of room. But the doctor told me not to lift more than twelve pounds or I would risk tearing the stitches from my C-section.

"Sweet girl, I can't lift you, but let's go upstairs together."

Zara stomped from the garage to the living room and then collapsed to the floor, crying and wailing. "MAMA!" was the only word I recognized among her pained shrieks. I held the baby and looked on helplessly. My scar ached, and I was afraid my body wouldn't be able to manage holding my newborn son and crouching on the floor with my daughter. She scrambled to her knees and began to bang her little forehead on the hardwood floor. Her curls bobbed wildly up and down. She cried. I cried. The baby cried. John got on the floor with her and held her so she couldn't hurt herself. She lacked the language to tell us how put out and disappointed she felt about this new baby in my arms. How enraged. How devastated. My rational brain knew she would be okay — John would hold her physically; we would both hold her emotionally; and she would move through her blaze of rage and frustration. We would all make it to the other side. But watching her suffer also reminded me of how I felt about my little sister, she with the perfect name who was a perfect upgrade for faulty, depreciated me.

When we got Zara settled on the couch next to me, she looked wrung out and exhausted, her little cheeks red and hot to the touch. "You did some good feeling work," I said, affirming her emotions the way Dr. Rosen always praised me when I ranted or tantrummed during sessions. I told her all the things I imagined she might want to hear: *You're safe and beloved always. I will never leave you behind. I know you feel scared and angry. He's not here to replace you. One day you'll be so glad to have a sibling to commiserate with you about what it's like to have me as a mom.* I held her and said her name over and over. It felt like a prayer.

By week two of mothering two children, I felt a dull sense of panic about my ability to properly care for these two little beings and give them what they needed. My bar was perfection and my default setting was despair. Bad combination. When it was time to rest, my brain immediately leaped to self-accusation. *I'm a shitty mom. I was so selfish to have children. They would be better off with someone else.* I left a voice mail for Dr. Rosen describing my dark thoughts. I didn't have a plan nor did I want to die, but the fatigue and stress had tripped a trigger of anxiety and hopelessness deeper and wider than I'd known before. At my postpartum checkup, my OB was emphatic: "You do not have to suffer." She insisted I take an anti-depressant. Dr. Rosen agreed. We'd already been down this road after Zara's birth, when I'd taken Zoloft for six months and then tapered off once we were sleeping more than four hours a night.

"I'm going to take it, but I'm nervous, even though I've done it before," I confessed to Callie on the phone. Really, I felt ashamed that I couldn't control my emotions. I believed I should be managing with greater ease after my second child — I'd done all this before! — but I wasn't, and it felt like a personal failure.

I stood under the el tracks outside of Dr. Rosen's office, my breasts heavy with milk, and my skin still hot and swollen along my C-section scar. Getting to therapy so soon after Elias's birth required a great deal of effort, but I was desperate for the support and comfort of my group.

"Hello?" I said. I pulled my phone away from my ear to see if Callie was still there. "Callie? Are you there?" Callie's son was now ten months old, and I trusted her to understand my anguish because she'd struggled in her early motherhood, too.

"I'm here," she said, but I heard something distant in her voice. I assumed the worst, as I always did inside her silences.

"Why are you acting weird? You think I shouldn't take meds?" In that moment, I couldn't admit my own fears about taking medication again or own my disappointment that I needed it. I wanted so badly to be the blissed-out mother I thought I was supposed to be, but I was actually a mother who needed a prescription for Zoloft to get through the hard, early days of Elias's life. It took half a second to project all of my own ambivalence about meds onto Callie. "Wait, maybe you think I should take it? Which is it? What is happening right now?" The panic raised my voice a few octaves. I started walking toward the Blue Line train that would carry me back home. I had thirty minutes to get home before my breasts began to leak. I'd synched my therapy session and my nursing just right, and I didn't have much extra time to spare on a post-session meltdown on the street.

I heard Callie sigh elaborately.

"What?" I said, shrill as ever. "What is it? You're judging me!"

"I feel like you just set me up. There's something you want to hear from me, but I don't know what it is. This feels," Callie paused, and I stomped down Washington past the Disney Store, furious and hurt. "I feel like you set a trap. Almost like you want me to judge you."

"What the fuck, Callie? I don't want you

to judge me. I'm struggling here. I don't know what I'm doing. I want to take care of my babies and stop hating myself for five minutes. It's not good for anyone if I drown in darkness and despair."

"Your medication is between you and your therapist."

"That's it? That's all you have to say?"

"I don't know what else —"

"I have to go. My train's coming. I'll talk to you later." I hung up on Callie and rode the train home to my babies, seething inside.

20

"Can you fucking believe her?" I said to Meredith over the phone, trying and failing to speak quietly as Elias slept on my chest. "I wanted her to weigh in, to big-sister me by affirming the positive steps I'm taking to care for myself during these intense postpartum weeks. When her son was born, I didn't judge her for feeling like she 'lost her spark.' Once, when we were on a run a few months after she'd given birth, she spent two miles railing against the pressures we put on mothers to be self-sacrificing and to smile through their suffering. I thought Callie, of all people, would support my mental health."

"People have all kinds of strong opinions about meds. Maybe in that moment she couldn't sort through her own stuff and support you."

"I'm telling you, she was judging me. She wants me to grit my teeth and not take the help the doctors are offering me? Why am I friends with her?"

Meredith laughed. "She's one of your closest friends."

"She's a traitor to me and all of woman-kind."

"You love her."

"I'm so angry right now."

"It sounds like you're hurt, too. And both of those are part of love."

"Fuck this kind of love."

"Okay, maybe when you calm down, you can think of all the things you love about her. Text your list to me."

I sighed and let my head fall back on the pillow. I didn't feel grateful for this newest conflict with Callie. I was so tired it felt like my temples would explode, and every time Elias latched on to my left breast, it felt like daggers shooting through my nipple. "Will it help?"

Meredith clucked. "Will gratitude help? Of course it will. I recently wrote everything I loved about Gage, and now I no longer want to divorce him. I did it with Bebe too but I'm still pissed about the fudge."

"So it doesn't work for friendship?"

"All the tools for romantic relationships work for friendships."

I knew, even then, that one day I would

owe Callie an amends for how I behaved in this conversation and for projecting onto her all of my shame about being depressed and unable to hack motherhood without pharmaceutical intervention. And I still felt angry at her for judging me.

I texted the list in bits and pieces to Meredith over the next few days:

Callie is my only friend who's ever been into running.

Callie was a bridesmaid in my wedding.

Callie joined me for the last six miles of the Chicago Marathon in 2006 and helped me finish the race.

Callie took dozens (hundreds?) of phone calls from me when I was upset about guys and dating and shitty relationships.

Callie always reminded me, when I was fried at work, that I could stop, go home, go to bed, and get up early the next morning to complete the task.

Callie works hard, tells the truth, and invests emotionally in all of her relationships.

Meredith sent a smiley face emoji after I texted my gratitude list to her. *Good girl,* she wrote.

I'm sure I rolled my eyes.

Callie and I got past the medication conversation because neither one of us ever mentioned it again. I quietly filled my prescription at the Costco pharmacy and hoped the little green pills would cut the darkness as it had after Zara was born.

Very quickly, however, we fell into other conflicts that I never saw coming until I heard her deafening silence on the other end of the phone. The first happened after I told her about a playgroup I joined on Thursday afternoons. I'd invited her to join, but she couldn't because of her work schedule.

"I feel so isolated," Callie said.

"I know what you mean," I said. I felt that loneliness and isolation, too, which was why I had taken steps to connect with other new mothers.

"Yes, but you have a playgroup and I don't."

Was I supposed to apologize? I hated the feeling of not knowing how to make it better, even though she wasn't asking me to fix her. This was a much smaller version of the guilt I felt when I got pregnant before she did.

A second tiff was slightly murkier.

One day, Jolie, a friend from the Saturday breakfast crew who had a son six months younger than Zara, invited me to go thrifting with her in Lincoln Park. We buckled our babies into strollers and looked through the secondhand play mats and cashmere blankets that affluent families in Lincoln Park had discarded. I found a wool cardigan for Zara and a snowsuit for Elias.

The next day, I mentioned this outing to Callie in passing, and she abruptly got off the phone. What was wrong now? Our excursion took place on a day that she worked. I would be happy to go again with her if she wanted, though she wasn't really the thrifting type. I felt angry that we couldn't find an easy rhythm and annoyed that she was mad at me. Again.

Callie left me a voice mail a few days later.

"Christie, I felt so hurt —" I can't remember now if I deleted the message right then or if I listened and have since forgotten, but I remember sitting in my minivan with my kids in their car seats, waiting for me to turn on the ignition and drive us home from the pediatrician's office. Earlier that day, I'd gone to a recovery meeting and heard people sharing on the topic of "toxic relationships." Allyson, one of my favorite women there, shared about a friendship that had fallen apart recently. "I just let go. We'd been fighting all the time, and I needed some space. It was a gift I gave to myself." Her words reached inside and grabbed hold of me, like a lifeline.

I wanted that space. I was tired of being tense around Callie. Maybe I should do what Allyson did and let go. Give myself some space.

"How do you do that, 'get space' in a friendship?" Meredith asked a few days later over tea when I told her about it. "If you're in a romantic relationship, you say, 'I need space,' and you stop sleeping together or you start sleeping with other people and slowly drift apart. What does this space look like in friendship?"

"I have no idea," I said. "I guess it means, Don't call me, I'll call you."

Callie didn't like anything I did these days. And the tension between us twisted inside me, making me feel monstrous. If I didn't get space soon, I was going to make a big mess of this friendship. I was ready to run.

Meredith leaned across the table. "You sound clear about your anger, but I'm wondering about fear. What's scary about your relationship with Callie?"

What did she mean?

"I smell fear. Your dynamic with Callie reminds me of my relationship with Lily, a friend I was afraid would devour me — her personality was so big. I felt totally dominated and lost around her loud clothes, bright jewelry, grand hand gestures, booming voice. So much bigness. When I realized how afraid I felt that I might disappear around her, I learned to set boundaries. A lot of them. But before I was able to do that, I had to know what I was afraid of."

I stared at the wet tea bag in my almost-empty cup. I was definitely afraid of Callie being mad at me. I was afraid of having to walk on eggshells every time I had a plan with another friend that didn't include her. I was afraid of that sigh of disappointment I sensed on the other end of the line every time I did something she didn't like. I felt responsible for her unhappiness, even though I understood intellectually that she was struggling in several areas of her life. But Meredith was right about fear: now I was really frightened of what I would do or say if I didn't get some space soon. I was afraid that it was time to break up, but I didn't have the courage or skill to extricate myself.

"I'm afraid we will never get out of this bad pattern. I'll go on hurting her, and she'll be disappointed. But if I pull back, she'll notice and feel hurt, which will make me want to fix it. She'll think I'm deserting her, and I promised I wouldn't."

There was no way out. I didn't want to

wait until the accumulated bitterness and hurt feelings extinguished all the joy between us. I couldn't remember the last time I'd laughed with Callie. Maybe on a run when I told her I wasn't sure how much maternity leave to take, and she cracked a joke about the glass ceiling. Maybe. The levity between us had hardened into something sharp and ugly. We'd just had three tense conversations in as many weeks.

But you don't just walk out of a friendship. She'd been a bridesmaid in my wedding. She had that prized spot on my speed dial. She was my big sister. Who would I run a 10K with next summer?

I hung on because I didn't want to be an almost-forty-year-old woman who couldn't figure out friendship. Broken bonds and irreparable rifts belonged in middle school, not motherhood. In my most hopeful moments, I imagined we were one tearful heart-to-heart conversation away from a deeper intimacy, and one day we'd look back and laugh on these dark days when we were both figuring out how to juggle motherhood, marriage, careers, and friendship. In those shiny fantasies, the solution was simple: I had to stop feeling responsible for her happiness, and she had to stop shutting down every time she feared abandonment.

The catch, of course, was that I was ready for Callie to change, but unprepared for the emotional work — boundary setting and tolerating her moods without making them all about me — I had yet to do myself.

21

John dressed the kids, while I finished pumping so Elias wouldn't starve while we were at the church.

"Do you have the directions?" he asked.

"On the counter."

The baptism ceremony for Callie's son started at ten, and it was our first dress-up event as a family of four. Zara wore a flowered dress with a sash, and Elias wore his best blue-and-white-striped romper. I wore a dress with a lot of stretch to accommodate my distended belly and swollen breasts. Though I'd slept little the night before, the blue-sky morning perked me up as we cruised down the highway to the church in the suburbs where Callie's husband, Grant, grew up. After the thrift shop tiff, Callie and I reached a détente, and now my family and I were showing up for her son's baptism. I felt like my best self, not the prickly, small-hearted version that got me into trouble with her.

In the lobby of the church, we mingled with Callie and Grant's family members. I snapped a picture of John holding Elias right next to a simple wood carving of Jesus Christ, and the way the light fell across their faces suggested they were especially sanctified. I spotted Callie talking to the minister and waved when she caught my eye. I chatted with her brother and his wife, whose little girl immediately bonded with Zara.

The ceremony started on time, but the service went a little longer than we anticipated. We watched from a row near the back as Callie and Grant, along with their son's godparents, held up their son and promised to raise him in the faith. My heart swelled watching Callie with the son she'd wanted so badly and worked so hard to have. Her beautiful baby boy.

During the closing prayer, the minister blessed all of us present, especially Callie and her family. I bowed my head in prayer. Then, two things happened at once: Elias started wailing and Zara started whining that she wanted to go outside. When I pressed my finger to my lips to remind her to whisper, she raised her voice even louder. John and I exchanged panicked glances, and he nodded his head toward the door. "We have to go," he whispered. The service had been lovely — a celebration of the life of a family and little baby boy I loved — but my children were on the verge of ruining the moment. John led Zara out through the back doors, and I bounced the baby for a few seconds to see if he would settle. He'd already downed the bottle and now he wanted the breast. While I'd whipped it out in the mall, restaurants, the park, and an arboretum, I'd never nursed during a suburban church service, and wasn't sure it would be appreciated. I pushed open the wooden doors in the back of the church. Before I exited, I tried to catch Callie's eye, but she was facing the minister; there was no graceful way to get her attention.

We'd made it almost to the end. I felt proud that I'd gotten out of the house and through most of a religious service. It was good; we were good; I was good.

So when we talked the next day, and I heard that singular Callie silence I knew so well, I lit up with indignation. My insides went nuclear with rage when I heard the sigh and the disappointment that we left "so early."

"So early? We made it to the closing blessing. Five minutes after we got into the car, Elias blew out of his diaper, and Zara melted down, screaming so loudly we had to roll the windows down in the car. Believe me, it was good we left when we did."

She disagreed. I'd expected her to be grateful that we'd celebrated her son's religious milestone. But it wasn't enough. Why couldn't anything I did ever be enough?

Inside me, a door slammed shut. I was done. Whatever friendship or chemistry we had in the years before we became mothers had been charred by resentment and disappointment.

I would take my space. I would punch through the wall closing in on me in our friendship and leave a Christie-shaped hole in it. I would raise my arms up over my head and run far away.

Not even Meredith could convince me I should stay.

Callie called twice, and I didn't listen to either message. Delete. I didn't call back. I wanted to be free, for us both to be free.

I ghosted.

22

Weeks passed before I told Meredith about the ghosting. She favored hard conversations, vulnerability, and showing up, and what I had done with Callie was the opposite of that. And I didn't have the courage to disclose how exactly I'd handled the situation. In therapy, I described the dynamic between Callie and me in broad strokes. *We make each other miserable, and one of us is always upset. I'm stepping back.* That was all I said: *I'm stepping back.* But Meredith would want to know the details. She wasn't going to let me off the hook so easily.

"Callie and I broke up," I told her one morning as we rode the Red Line train after having breakfast together.

Meredith raised her eyebrows and grabbed the pole as the train lurched to a halt. It was the tail end of rush hour but still too crowded for us to find seats.

"How'd that go?"

"She's not happy."

"Did you literally say those words? 'We need to break up.' " Meredith's eyes were wide, her mouth shaped in a perfect "O" of surprise.

I shook my head and looked away. "She's called twice, and I'm not calling her back. I've had enough."

Meredith nodded.

"You're disappointed in me."

"Oh, honey, stop. I'm just listening. How do you feel?"

"Honestly?" I looked at Meredith's glacier-blue eyes and told her the truth. "Fat. I feel fat."

She guffawed so loudly that two teenagers turned around to stare at us. It was true, though. For the past few days — since I'd become a ghost — I felt like my clothes didn't fit, and I imagined extra rolls of fat lining my stomach. When I exercised, my body felt leaden and too big to move. I didn't think it was funny.

"Fat isn't a feeling." Now that she was training to be a spiritual counselor, Meredith had a host of new sayings that she rolled out with startling authority.

"You have an eating disorder; you know what I'm talking about."

"Of course I do. I feel fat all the time."

I shook my head at the insanity of eating disorders, both hers and mine. Meredith was one of the thinnest women I knew — her clavicle bones jutted out from her chest and her ankles were the size of my wrists. Sometimes we emailed each other what we'd eaten during the day, and many of those days she ate less than my toddler. *Breakfast: cup of yogurt, grapes; Lunch: hard-boiled egg and chocolate milk; Dinner: bagel with cream cheese.* But eating disorders don't give a shit how much you weigh or how old you are or how "clean" your food is. Meredith had taught me that when she called me sobbing about drinking too much chocolate milk or eating too much yogurt. "I hate myself," she cried into the phone one week, and the next week it was me saying the exact same thing.

"If you weren't hiding behind body dysmorphia, what would you feel?" Meredith gripped the pole and stood slightly closer than I wanted her to. When I was deep in shame, I hated being close to other people. Too much vulnerability.

I swallowed hard, and my eyes stung. "Sad and angry. I'm not sure I'm friend material."

Meredith batted her hand as if to erase

my words. "Nonsense. You've got lots of friends. Emily and Jolie and all the breakfast crew ladies. And what about me?"

I gripped the train pole. "Yes, I've got you, Emily, and Jolie. But I'm stacking up friendship casualties. It feels gross. I'm almost forty and just lost another friend."

Meredith nodded and pulled her bag to her chest as someone squeezed by her at the Grand stop. She told me how she'd seen her mother over the weekend. "I'd like to break up with my mother."

"You could stop answering her calls and going to see her."

Meredith laughed. "That's not how it works with mothers and daughters."

"Or with friends, and yet . . ."

She pursed her lips and squinted at me for a few seconds, thinking. "Both you and Callie are in twelve-step recovery; you both go to therapy. You're both working out your roles. Mother, sister, daughter, friend. Your story with Callie isn't over. It's on pause."

The train pulled into the station at Chicago Avenue, and we filed up the grimy stairs into the sunlight. At the corner where we normally parted, we lingered.

"What if I'm doing the wrong thing? What if I'm supposed to stay in this friendship?" I asked, but before she could answer, I said what felt most true. "In my body it feels like the right thing to do. Right here." I made a fist and pushed it into the soft spot under my ribs. "I had to go."

"So that's your answer. Bodies don't lie."

23

The law of conservation of energy holds that energy cannot be created or destroyed, only converted from one form to another. A few weeks after my breakup with Callie, I struck up a new friendship with Anna, one of Meredith's blue-clad bridesmaids and closest friends. I'd seen her around in meetings for years. Whenever she spoke, her words were humorous, wise, and humble. Once, when our mutual friend Jill landed in the ER with a leg injury after a bike accident, Anna and I worked together to get her discharged, home, and fed for the night. I admired how Anna showed up for the friends we had in common.

I also envied her. Anna had dewy skin, a willowy figure, and thick blond hair that fell in soft waves. I was envious of her slim-fitting jeans, her tiny running shorts. And I struggled not only with a superficial envy of her conventional beauty but also of her inner grace and sparkling wit. Everyone laughed when she spoke and flocked to her after meetings to thank her for her insightful comments. I also coveted her free time. Once she had twin daughters, she quit her corporate marketing job, and I imagined that when the girls were at preschool, she had long, languorous mornings to read *The New Yorker* and weekday afternoons to linger over coffee with friends.

"I have a proposition for you," she said to me one morning after a recovery meeting in a drafty basement of a Unitarian church. "We should get together and write some children's books. Let's write stories for our kids about how big feelings are okay and that life is messy. Let's invent characters who know how to express their anger and sadness. Especially girls."

"Yes," I said, flattered by her attention and excited by her enthusiasm. "I'm in!"

I'd never written a children's book, but I'd read plenty of them to Zara and Elias, and I instantly felt drawn to the prospect of a writing project that could feed my creative side, which had been neglected during my years as a corporate litigator.

"Maybe it could be a series. We could create a main character, like Fancy Nancy, but with our own flair." Anna waved her hands and spoke fast, and her passion swept me up.

Anna's proposal arrived like a magic carpet. I'd just asked the head of my law firm whether I could work an 80 percent schedule that would also allow me time to parent my two children, and his response had been disheartening. "We can't let you work part-time," he said. "We're swamped; we have twice as much work for you to do than before you left on maternity leave." When I asked if he was going to pay me double my salary for twice the work, he laughed and laughed. We agreed to part ways.

"I'm now a children's book writer," I announced to an amused John over dinner.

Anna and I began to meet up once a week, alternating between our houses. Sometimes we hired a sitter and sometimes we let the kids loose in the basement, where her four-year-old girls would play with Zara and Elias, now two and almost one. We created a character we loved — a little girl named Katherine Rose who had a big mouth and bigger feelings she wasn't shy about expressing. Katherine Rose wanted the world to be fair, and when she brushed up against injustice, she wanted answers. Her parents celebrated her anger, told her it was beautiful, and taught her how to channel it constructively.

During our writing sessions, we'd eat lunch — salads with grilled chicken or turkey wraps with avocado and feta — before we got to work. After a few weeks, our pre-writing conversations meandered to our marriages, parenting, aging, friendships, childhood. And we enjoyed talking about therapy because, like me, she had joined a therapy group with Dr. Rosen. I liked Anna more after each session.

One afternoon, Callie's name came up.

"We had a falling-out," Anna said. I leaned forward in surprise. Anna and Callie had met in the same recovery meetings I attended, but I hadn't realized they'd had a rift.

"We did, too," I said, nervous to bring it up because I felt uneasy about my ghosting.

"I don't really understand what happened, but we stopped talking," Anna said.

"Same here." The tight knot of shame about my friendship with Callie loosened after I learned Anna had struggled with her, too.

I was grateful that Anna didn't offer more details. If she had, I would have gobbled them up as further rationalization for why I bailed on Callie. Anna's kitchen table, a site of creativity and new friendship, would have become a table of gossip and grievance. I didn't want that, and it seemed Anna didn't either. We both agreed that we loved Callie — and that still felt true, that I loved her — but we didn't know how to be in a relationship with her right now.

The next time we got together for a drafting session, Anna asked me for advice on how to spend her upcoming anniversary with her husband. "I want to go big, like New York City or someplace that's a plane ride away, but maybe we should do a bed-and-breakfast in Wisconsin or Michigan."

I voted for New York City and then confessed to Anna that I'd spent a reckless amount of money at Nordstrom Rack and didn't want to tell John.

"What'd you buy?"

"Stupid shit. Vanity purchases. A pair of Citizens of Humanity jeans because they made my ass look amazing. A patent leather navy Kate Spade purse. A lace cocktail dress I have no occasion to wear. Smartwool socks."

"It's June."

"Impulse buy." I put my head in my hands. "I can't tell John. 'So, dear, I quit my job at my law firm and then spent three hundred bucks on crap at a discount store.' "

Anna laughed. "You know you have to tell him. The secret will cost way more than three hundred dollars. And isn't the point of our recovery to have relationships — marriages — where we don't have to hide?"

See? She was wise, warm, and compassionate. Not remotely judgmental. I trusted her. Together, we ate our bougie lunches and wrote children's picture books; we built a friendship. She debuted on my speed dial at number four, only three slots after my husband.

My envy of all things Anna waxed and waned. Sometimes, I could hardly sit still because I was so busy wishing I had a body the same shape as hers. At her high-top kitchen table, I sometimes regressed to little Christie back at the dinner table in Texas, pining to switch places with Virginia. Like Virginia, Anna seemed to glow with beauty and grace. I noticed, and I compared myself to her before, during, or after each session. How did she get her hair so shiny? Why were her baseboards always spotless? How come after our meetings she had twice as many texts and missed calls from friends as I did? My envy, a secret stash I managed by ignoring it or sometimes hinting at it with John, didn't threaten the relationship. It sat next to me while we wrote, like a gun on safety.

Around this time, John had to travel more for work, and I found myself managing dinner and bedtime with both kids by myself for two or three nights every other week, a schedule that looked manageable on paper, but not always in practice. One night when John was away I found myself standing in the hallway between my children's rooms, each of whom was wailing in distress. It was almost nine thirty p.m., and I'd been trying to get them to sleep for more than two hours. All three of us were sobbing. I'd already sung, rocked, nursed, begged, and prayed for Good Orderly Direction; I ran out of ideas. The surround sound of my children's howling destroyed my thoughts before they could form. I dialed Anna's number, desperate for a lifeline. "Help," I said as soon as she picked up the phone. "What do I do?" She could hardly hear me for all the crying on my end of the line.

"Oh, I've been there. Take a few deep breaths. It's so hard. You're doing just fine. I'll stay on the phone with you while you come up with a plan." Her gentle voice calmed my frayed nerves. I loved her for every single word delivered in that soothing tone she was famous for. She suggested that just this once I let both kids come to bed with me. "You all need sleep. It will be so much better in the morning."

"But the books say you shouldn't do that. If they sleep in the bed with me, then they'll never have healthy relationships, they'll fail out of school, and my marriage will fall apart." That was what all the baby books said. Except for the radical attachment parenting one that said I'd already ruined my children by not stapling them to my body after their first breath, especially because I, likely a sociopath, had insisted on having my babies at a hospital and not at home. "I'm fucking them up."

"It's just one night. I promise. One night. Get some sleep."

Of course, when I brought them into my bed, my babies nestled into my body and relaxed within minutes. We all slept just fine once I surrendered to Anna's suggestion. I texted her the next day. *Thank you! You saved my night.*

Anna was my new friend. A good friend. I could do friendship even as a mother.

We wrote one book, then two, three, and four. I was part of a working, functional, female "we." After each session with Anna, I felt stronger as a collaborator, a parent, and a friend. That June, we flew to New York City for a weekend away. Anna and I saw two Broadway plays, ate brunch at a famous spot in the East Village, and spent an afternoon at the Strand. Before we caught our late-Sunday flight home, we walked to the Barnes & Noble and camped out in the children's book section.

"Let's research agents and publishers who might want our books," Anna said, her green eyes bright with ambition and energy.

We rolled our suitcases out of the way and pulled out volume after volume, checking the imprint names and writing a list in a notebook. I'd already gotten so much out of writing these books — I believed I was better at supporting my kids' feelings and communicating boundaries to them because our stories insisted on that for Katherine Rose. And my friendship with Anna buoyed me each week. Our time together left me feeling energized and refreshed, which was how I thought a therapy session should feel, though mine very often just stirred up intense feelings and then flung me back into the world, frazzled and teary. Flipping through a book about crayons coming to life, Anna declared that we could go the distance with our stories; we could be published.

"This is going to be great," she said. I felt so lucky.

24

Blogs written by mothers were having a moment — Dooce (Heather Armstrong) and *The Bloggess* (Jenny Lawson) and *The Momastery* (Glennon Doyle). Every morning, my in-box filled with links to blog posts written by witty mother-writers sharing stories about leaving their high-powered jobs, extracting pistachios from their kids' noses, and dividing labor with their partners. Every mother I knew read blogs to be entertained, to escape, and to curb the loneliness and isolation of mothering young children. A woman from my former law firm started a blog, and when I ran into her on the street, she told me how easy it was. She texted me a link to the website where I could set one up, and the next morning when John took the kids to Costco, I did it. I put roughly twelve minutes of thought into the name of my blog (*Outlaw Mama*) and started typing about my life as a former big-firm lawyer and mother of two who had no idea what she was doing with her life. I had zero followers, had never heard the word *monetize,* and had no end goal in mind.

I told Anna about my blog and sent her the link so she could follow me. She commented on my first few posts I wrote about Elias learning swear words and Zara eating dinner in her birthday suit. None of my posts contributed to urgent national conversations, but I was learning how to write and how to use my voice. And most of all: I enjoyed it. I could write when my kids were asleep at night or during their nap time. Since walking away from law firm life, I missed the rhythms of a busy office and the pressure of deadlines and intellectual tasks. A blog offered a taste of everything I'd put on hold. It was mid-2011, when the internet was a place for genuine connection, and the comments section was a place to find helpful advice and support from other mother-writers. Rest in peace, gentle era of the internet. My followers swelled from 4 to 123.

A few days before the month anniversary of my blog, Anna and I stood across from each other at her island, keys in hand. We had finished a writing session, and now we both had children to pick up.

"One more thing," she said, her voice a little formal. She cleared her throat. "I wanted you to know" — she looked down at her keys — "I started a blog."

"Great!" Lots of writers had blogs; she was a writer. Why the strange tone?

"I mean, I didn't know if you would care."

"What? Why would I care?" The World Wide Web, the giant cyber highway, surely had room for all of us. At least for Anna and me.

"You started first."

I waved my hands. "Girl, that doesn't matter. Send me the link so I can follow you."

Anna's shoulders released.

On the ride home, I found myself smiling at the thought of Anna's blog. I knew her meticulous attention to detail meant that her masthead and layout would look professionally designed, and she'd never ever publish a post with a typo. I laughed, thinking of the post I'd written about deodorant, in which I'd misspelled *deodorant* five times — and I knew about the misspellings only because a reader in Columbus pointed them out in the nicest possible way. That would never happen to Anna. She would write soulful pieces about the teachable moments of parenting, gently self-deprecating and always illuminating the lesson in each episode of discomfort. Her blog would shine, no doubt. She'd probably become a household name and get a book deal; the *Today* show would invite her to be on a panel to discuss swimming pool safety next summer. Yes, perhaps I did feel threatened, just a smidge, but I'd survive.

A few days later, I sat at John's desk and clicked on the link to Anna's blog. I instantly took note of the masthead — stylish font, engaging graphics, pithy name. At the bottom of the post, I saw the number 147 — the number of people following her blog. I sucked in my breath. She'd had a blog for twenty minutes and already had more followers than I did? My humiliation seemed a foregone conclusion. I ran downstairs and found John in the bedroom folding towels. I threw myself next to the unfolded pile and buried my head into my pillow.

"What happened?" John asked.

After a few long moments, I lifted my head. "Anna. She has a blog."

John held a towel midair and waited for more information. Her superiority was so real to me that I couldn't believe he needed more explanation.

"She has almost 150 followers after less than two hours."

John nodded slowly, understanding. He

pushed the towels aside and lay next to me on the bed.

"You can both have a blog," he said quietly.

"But hers will be better."

"Maybe. What if it is?" I lifted my head and considered John's point. Anna's blog had nothing to do with mine. No one was going to shut my blog down simply because hers had more fans. What was this really about?

She was already more beautiful, more beloved in the recovery world, and better at cleaning, skin care, cooking, crafting, and editing. I didn't want to compete with her; I could never win. I closed my eyes and projected three months into the future — Anna's blog spreading like a brush fire, my followers whittled down to my second cousins and an unemployed alcoholic guy I knew from college.

"This makes no sense, I know, but it feels like everyone will leave me for her. And she'll be too busy with her fame to work on our books. I'm going to lose everything."

"Everything?" John, ever rational, would not let my hyperbolic projections stand without question. "What about me and the kids? What about your joy in telling stories on your blog? No one can take that away."

I nodded. Of course he was right. On some level I understood I was overreacting, but on another, I truly believed that Anna's arrival on the scene would snuff me out completely.

I typed out a three-line email to Emily outlining my distress and pressed Send. Emily excelled at offering the perfect blend of comfort (*that sounds hard*), reality (*she's only got twenty-four more fans than you do*), and practical advice (*stop monitoring Anna's blog and get busy with your own life*). An hour later, still no soothing email from Emily, but I did have one from Anna.

Oh, I get it completely. I would feel the same way. Sending hugs.

Holy Mother of Viral Blog Posts! I'd accidentally sent the email meant for Emily to Anna!

"Anna, I'm so embarrassed. I don't know what to say. That email was for Emily." I'd picked up the phone as soon as I composed myself.

Anna laughed. "It's okay. Really. Someday soon, I'll be the one jealous of you. We're only human."

The call with Anna went well, but I still spent my next therapy session in tears, freaked out about her success and that I'd outed myself as a woman with the competitive heart of a middle school girl who had some serious growing up to do.

"This is not about blog posts," Dr. Rosen said, without a hint of a smile.

Ah yes . . . I'd heard someone in a recovery meeting recently say, *If you're hysterical, then it's historical.* This blog business wasn't really about Anna at all; it was about all the ways she reminded me of Virginia: her more diminutive body; her arrival on the scene after me; her instant and unwavering acclaim.

"I know, I know. Anna reminds me of my sister."

Revelations are fine and good, but it was small consolation to be nearing four decades of life and still be crying about my baby sister's ability to siphon off love and attention I wanted for myself.

"How long am I going to cry about this? I'm a grown-ass woman with children of her own. I can't do this forever."

Very helpfully, Dr. Rosen shrugged and encouraged me to keep crying.

I knew Anna and Meredith were close friends, so it was uncomfortable for me to disclose the depth of my anguish to her. When I did, Meredith nodded, like she knew exactly what I was talking about.

"You know," she said. "I have this dynamic with Olivia. I've known her for years, but a few months ago, we both landed jobs at Hazelden. She has more flexibility in her schedule, which means she gets more shifts. Everyone there likes her more than me — she's younger and flirts with all the male staff. She giggles more than I do —"

"You're no giggler."

"When she walks through the door, I hear her greeting everyone in this fake voice. 'Hi, Marcus! Good afternoon, Regina!' She says everyone's name and remembers personal things about them."

"What a savage!"

"Stop. You know how it is. When someone triggers my insecurity, then everything they do feels directed at me, even though it's not. I want to throw a stapler at her."

"Believe me, I know."

As always, Meredith showed me I wasn't the only one whose sister issues seeped into her relationships with other women and ignited a sense of inferiority. I was not alone. I felt my neck muscles relax. What a relief to know the great and spiritual Meredith wanted to hurl office supplies at Olivia.

When my Anna envy flared, I would think about Virginia and remind myself that it was no longer 1978, and I wasn't a four-year-old girl without language or tools to get my needs met. In therapy, Dr. Rosen signed off on the theory that Anna reminded me of my golden little sister, but he also pushed me to go deeper.

"What part of her life do you covet the most?" he asked.

"Her commitment to her writing." It wasn't the skinny jeans or the great curls that grabbed me by the throat. It was her freedom from a stifling day job that filled me with fury. I had never admitted that before. I'm not sure I even knew I felt that way. Years before, she'd set up a life with ample space for creativity. How could I possibly do that? I was still paying off thousands of dollars in student loans for my law degree. I believed that I'd eventually have to return to work as a lawyer because of my debt, but also because I had a warped idea of feminism as an obligation to make the same amount of money as my husband, plus I had years of Catholic indoctrination that life should be an arduous vale of tears. Never mind that I'd settled on law back when I was a lost young woman convinced she'd die alone and that the practice of law had never touched my heart's deepest longings to have a creative professional life. I had to stick with the law, period. Right now,

I was teaching part-time at my law school, but as soon as my kids were in school, I'd be back at a desk job, writing briefs and prepping for client meetings. Not Anna. She'd made it clear she was going to parent and write. Period. And I burned with envy that she could simply declare herself a writer and keep her days free for her creative work. Her schedule had nothing to do with me, but . . . how dare she allow herself the thing I couldn't help but deny myself?

"So, she has freedom and space that you'd like in your own life. What do you think would happen if you let yourself get closer to her?"

Intellectually, I understood Dr. Rosen's point. If I drew nearer to Anna, I would be closer to the creative, law-free life I wanted for myself. It would be good for me. When I looked at Anna's life, however, I didn't feel inspired; I couldn't see through the smudged lens of my envy. I wasn't ready. I loved her, but sometimes I also wanted to get really far away from her.

25

Obsession: an idea or thought that continually preoccupies or intrudes on a person's mind.

Was I obsessed with Anna?

I was definitely preoccupied, despite my sincere intention to evolve. When she published a blog post, I analyzed it line by line, and more than once, I convinced myself she'd "stolen" her ideas from me. One week, I wrote about my bulimic past, and when she alluded to her own eating struggles a few weeks later, I called her post a "smoking gun." I submitted an essay to a semi-famous website, and the very next week she submitted her work there, too. All of it was evidence in my case against her. Of course, I "borrowed" ideas from other writers *all the time.* But when I piggybacked on my friend Carinn's idea to submit an essay for an anthology, I was networking and being collegial. Not Anna — she was a thief, a backstabber. My heart slammed shut against her and any sense of generosity, expansiveness, and cooperation evaporated.

And as for the wise suggestion — from John, Dr. Rosen, Meredith, and Emily — that I stop reading Anna's blog, I didn't take it. I was too deep into building a case to prove Anna's betrayal. My writing sessions with Anna lost a sense of flow, and a tense stiltedness replaced the laughter and ease. Without any direct communication about what was going on, we skated on the surface of safe topics, like our kids and the weather.

We limped along for a few months, tinkering with the stories we'd written over the previous year, but we didn't move forward. I wanted out of the stale place we'd slipped into, but couldn't bear to face my part in the ruin of our friendship. I suspected that if we stopped getting together to write books, we would stop talking altogether. I hung on, hoping that something would transform the heaviness and bitterness I couldn't seem to shake.

When a former colleague from my Big Law days gave me a lead on a position at the federal courts that would suck up all my free time, I applied for the job. My kids were nearing preschool age, and it felt like the right job and the right time to get back to wage earning because working for the courts would give me a gentler schedule than returning to private practice. The position also came with a significant bonus: it solved my Anna problem because I would no longer have the time to write children's books with her.

Meredith coached me over breakfast one morning on how to tell Anna that I was returning to work and wouldn't be available to write each week.

"Be clear about your availability. Would you be willing to get together on the weekends?" Meredith asked.

"Maybe, though the weekends are family time." Beyond my competitiveness and envy — or maybe because of them — I no longer felt the pulse of life in the children's books I'd once loved so much. I wanted a break.

"Just tell the truth. And keep it simple."

Before I could resign as a children's book author, Anna surprised me with her own announcement.

"I'm working on a novel," she said. "So I'm not sure I'll have time —"

"Perfect timing because I'm starting a job at the federal court in two weeks."

We laughed at the serendipity of our mutual decision to move on to other projects. The tension coiled inside me eased a bit, though I couldn't help but notice she was following a creative path, and I was veering back to law. We hugged. We spent that last session at her kitchen table, rereading all of our Katherine Rose stories, laughing and saying goodbye to the character we'd created with our best intentions as mothers.

"Good luck at the new job."

"Good luck on your novel."

We clinked our La Croix cans, toasting ourselves and our new chapters. We were kind and mature. Our collaboration came to its natural end. A sense of warm goodwill and compassion for both of us surged through me.

I rarely saw Anna once I went back to work. John and I moved our family across town to be closer to the school we'd chosen for the kids. I rode the train to work and drafted legal opinions on habeas corpus and the Fair Debt Collection Practices Act. At night, I blogged and wrote a few chapters of a novel about a modern-day Jane Eyre who worked at a law firm and had a therapist I named Dr. Rochester. My novel was messy and ill-conceived, but it kept me in touch with my creative side while I dove back into my legal career. The internet slowly — and then quickly — became a place where reading the comments section of an article or a blog post felt like a crash course in human cruelty. The writers I knew left the blogging world and retreated back into their careers, marathon training, writing books.

I thought of Anna often, wondering about her novel. Sometimes I found that my curiosity was warm and benevolent, supported by a genuine wish for her to find satisfaction and success in her project. Slightly more often, I'd find myself bracing for the announcement that she'd sold her novel for $1 million dollars and had a film deal — *Julia Roberts and Viola Davis are attached!* I would look at my computer screen, open to a twenty-page Supreme Court case about sentencing or contract law, something so dry I had to read it four times to understand the legal points, and I would ball my hands into fists. My mind would drift to Anna and how lucky she was to write full-time.

I'd tell Meredith about using Anna to torture myself, and she'd nod. She'd heard it all before.

"No one's life is as good as you think Anna's is. You know that."

I knew all the quippy sayings that warned against comparing yourself to other people. "Compare and despair," Meredith sometimes said to me. I taped an Iyanla Vanzant quote on my desk: "Comparing yourself to others is an act of violence against your authentic self." In a daily meditation book that I cracked open occasionally, I'd dog-eared the passage that opened with Theodore Roosevelt's famous quote: "Comparison is the thief of joy."

In my texts to Meredith, I exaggerated my thoughts about Anna so much that even I had to laugh.

Do you think Anna is soaking at a spa right now while I'm preparing a cup of coffee for my boss who thinks I'm a secretary?

I'm obsessing that Anna is going to win a National Book Award while I'm still dicking around as a government lawyer.

Guess what? The babysitter just called to tell me my kid bit someone during a playdate. My first thought: this would never happen with Anna's kids.

Meredith would respond by telling me what she was obsessing about — the fudge from her wedding, which *still* irked her, or the latest with Olivia at work. In our texts we toggled between my obsessions and hers, wiping each other's brows and offering pep talks, and then we got on with our lives.

With Meredith as my witness-partner-friend-guide, I believed I was taking all the right actions. Slowly, my fantasies about Anna's perfect life receded, and I had every reason to believe that my work on friendship was paying off and that the hardest parts were behind me.

■ ■ ■ ■

PART II
WHAT HAPPENED

■ ■ ■ ■

26

It was the size and shape of a pea, big enough to see below Meredith's clavicle. She wore a blush-colored V-neck T-shirt and gray pants. The air outside was a chilly 66 degrees, but she wore flip-flops. She pointed at the pea and said she had to get it checked out. I felt no fear about the pea, because I had no idea that serious illness could be so obvious, so detectable with the naked eye, but also so harmless looking. I mean, it literally looked like she'd swallowed a pebble and right after it passed her epiglottis, it hooked left instead of proceeding down her esophagus to her stomach.

I knew she was a survivor of breast cancer.

I knew her mother and one of her sisters had survived several bouts each.

She didn't seem afraid, and so I wasn't either. She mentioned it halfway through our time together and shrugged it off. She loved her doctor and was looking forward to "catching up" with her. I pictured a seasoned physician with slightly scuffed black flats and a low ponytail, someone slightly older than Meredith who looked like Jane Goodall and asked her what books she'd been reading. My fantasy conveniently omitted that the doctor was an *oncologist,* and I didn't register that it was a little strange how giddy Meredith seemed about seeing her.

I didn't say, "What do you think it is?" I also didn't offer to go with her; I think I assumed that Gage would be there. When she talked about her appointment, her voice was easy, low-key. No alarm, no fear.

We spent less than ten minutes discussing her pea that morning. She gushed about her new semester of classes and how she'd gotten a promotion at Hazelden.

"No more overnight shifts! Now I have an office with a door I can shut, and I'll have more contact with patients." We celebrated her advancement over herbal tea.

She talked about the future. "Only two more semesters of classes until graduation," she said. She'd put off her statistics requirement again, saving it for last, but had a seminar in addictions for which she couldn't wait to do the readings.

"Gage is mad about my heavy school

load," she said, wrinkling her brow. "He likes it when I'm home."

"He also fell in love with someone with a dream of finishing her master's degree and working at a treatment center. You've never been a stay-at-home type."

"As long as I save time for sex each week —"

"He'll be fine."

Out in the street, we hugged, as we always did, when we said goodbye. I didn't say good luck at your appointment because I didn't think she needed it. I texted her later that day, something vague, like *Thinking of you* with a flower emoji. Maybe some part of me was afraid, but not ready to put it into language.

Meredith had become one of my closest friends, but almost all of our relationship took place on the phone, in snatches of conversation after meetings, or at our breakfasts downtown before heading in separate directions for school and work. John and I never double-dated with Meredith and Gage. I felt like I knew Gage as well as I knew any of my friends' spouses, but I'd hung out with him and Meredith only three or four times. She'd been to our house several times — I hosted her wedding shower, and she dropped off gifts when my kids were born — but I'd never been inside her house. Ours was a somewhat typical friendship among people who meet in twelve-step meetings. Fierce bonds are formed through private interactions that often don't involve spouses or other friends. Meredith and I shared common friends from recovery meetings, but we were part of distinct social groups. Her crew was older than mine — they had grown kids or full-fledged businesses and often attended seven a.m. meetings on Sunday mornings. Mine skewed younger — women in their child-bearing years who liked to brunch after a midmorning Saturday meeting. Beyond meetings, she didn't know my law school friends or any of my colleagues; I didn't know any of her friends from Rockford or her classmates. The insularity of our friendship made it safe. She became the home base I could return to no matter what kind of shenanigans were going down in my other friendships — even with Anna, one of the close friends we had in common. Whenever I brought a friendship snag to Meredith — regardless of who the players were — she always came down on the side of my spiritual growth, whether I liked it or not.

The rain fell in sheets from a steel-gray sky, and a giant puddle filled the entire intersection at State and Van Buren. Meredith's text said she'd call in five minutes. I gripped my umbrella and leaped to the curb in my green rain boots. I'd been sitting in the Harold Washington Library downtown, but my cell reception was spotty in the giant, ten-story building. I thought I'd have better luck at the Barnes & Noble café. It was a few days after an appointment at which they'd ended up scanning her whole body.

I hung my dripping umbrella on the back of a tall chair and scooted myself close to the table. I plugged in my laptop cord and slipped a notebook and pen out of my backpack. DePaul students sat with books cracked open on the tables around me, and a man I'd seen asking for change outside now loitered by the magazine rack.

The phone buzzed, and Meredith's name glowed on the screen. When I picked up, her voice sounded far away. She was not sixty-something Meredith; she was a frightened little girl when she spoke.

"It's my liver."

What the fuck. The pea was nowhere near

271

her liver. How was this possible? My hands shook as I slid my computer out of my way and placed both elbows on the table to brace myself. The liver was the worst. Except maybe the brain. The brain was definitely worse.

"And my brain."

Fuck.

"The doctor says it's the liver that will kill me. It's in my lungs, too, which is why I've had a cough for months." Why hadn't I noticed the cough?

"Is Gage with you?"

"He's here."

"What do you need? Do you want me to come over? I can bring you dinner. Have you called your therapist? What are the next steps?" I had so many questions. "Sorry, I need to shut up. I know. I'm sorry."

She breathed. I breathed.

"This is really bad," she said.

"Okay. Yes." Why lie?

"There are so many things I want to do."

Lines of dialogue ran through my head, but each one seemed wrong in so many ways, not the least of which was that they didn't fit me or my heart or our relationship. I pictured a TV mom telling her stricken son, "We'll fight this!" Or a woman in a movie who tells her friend she knows people at Sloan Kettering. In real life, I knew a couple of shrinks, a cardiologist, and an ER doctor — no one who could save the day.

All of my genuine, unscripted questions sounded lame, upsetting, or intrusive. How much time do you have? What are the treatment options and when do they start? What stage is this thing? Will the chemo make you bitchy and even skinnier? Will you leave me?

Thank God I said none of them.

"I love you. I'm right here."

"I'm calling all of my friends," she said. "Setting up times to talk to them. I'm not leaving it on voice mail."

"God no, of course no voice mail. Do you want any help with that? Are you sick of talking about it?"

"Not yet."

"I'll do whatever you want." Please don't get off the phone and leave me with this terrible feeling.

"I know. We'll talk soon."

When I hung up, I shut my computer and gathered up my things. I needed a moment alone in a bathroom stall. If I'd blown up friendships over alcoholic love interests, jealousy/envy, and an inability to set boundaries to get the space I needed, how was I going to do this with Meredith? I wasn't entirely sure what "this" was, but I imagined I was about to adopt some new vocabulary words: *chemo, wig, hospice, goodbye.*

I pressed my shoulder into the bathroom door, and it didn't budge. Fuck. BATHROOM KEY AVAILABLE AT CIRCULATION DESK read the laminated sign on the door. I walked over to the circulation desk and waited behind a guy asking about graphic novels. The graphic novel guy had lots of questions. I wrapped the black nylon strap hanging from my backpack around my index finger until I could feel my pulse, then I released the strap and wrapped again. And again. I sighed heavily — my best passive-aggressive customer service sigh. Now I needed to be alone *and* to pee. Why couldn't they hang the key from a hook that I could reach myself without having to ask?

"ID please," the staff member said when I asked for the key.

"I just need the bathroom key," I said. My fingers, still wrapped in the backpack strap, pulsed with my heartbeat, but I kept my voice steady.

"We'll need your ID to give you the key."

"I don't have my ID." I'd taken the bus, so I didn't have my driver's license. "I have a library card and a debit card. Which do you want?"

He shrugged and glanced past me to another patron. I heaved my backpack onto his desk. "Look, you can keep this." I shoved it toward him. "I swear I'll come back. I really need to go to the bathroom. Please. Please." Panic-sweat formed between my breasts. I could feel it. I begged, and now I was crying. "Please."

Without looking at me, he handed me the key and took my Visa debit card as collateral. In the stall, I leaned against the door and wrung my hands. I scrolled through my phone thinking of who I should call. I didn't want to call any mutual friends because it was Meredith's news to tell. John was driving the kids home from a camping trip and not able to talk. I reached Jolie and said all the scary words Meredith had said to me. "Liver." "Brain." "Lungs." I wanted to punch the stall door but worried there were cameras and I'd have to forfeit my debit card.

Outside the rain pounded the streets so hard that each drop bounced back up and fell again. My umbrella turned inside out, but I let the buses pass me by. I walked and walked. When I got home, I peeled off my wet clothes and turned on the hot shower. If I felt nauseated at the news, how on earth did Meredith feel?

Three days later, we sat across from each other at our favorite spot on Michigan Avenue that was nothing special, just a chain café, but it had become ours over the hours we spent in the booth in the back. Neither of us ordered, and no one seemed to care. The tables around us sat empty, almost like there was a force field surrounding us, keeping strangers at bay.

Meredith talked dispassionately about the treatment plan and the next series of appointments. But then she softened and seemed to return to her body and her feelings. She sighed deeply and tears appeared. Finally.

"I hate hearing everyone's pity," she said, sipping the thermos of coffee she'd brought from home.

"Are you sure it's pity? It might be sadness, grief, fear —" I had lots of feelings about Meredith's news, but pity wasn't the word I would use for any of them.

"It feels like pity."

What the hell did I know? I didn't want to push her — bully her into feeling what I thought she should — but I hated watching her turn other people's well-intended if feeble gestures of love into something unpleasant. Could I help her see it another way?

"What's the worst thing someone's said?"

She rolled her eyes and sat up. "It's hard to pick. My friend Julia insisted I get some crystals and go to this shrine in New Mexico. Sherri talked to me about my diet and forwarded me articles about all the foods that could shrink the tumors."

"Did you read them?"

She grimaced. "I don't have time for that."

"People can be so terrible."

"No one is talking to me in their real voice. Everyone sounds so hushed and sad. Makes me feel like I'm already dead. It's very lonely."

She asked me about my weekend with the kids. I didn't know this was day one of a new pattern: we'd talk about her illness — updates, appointments, symptoms — and then she'd insist on dispatches from the world of the well. Details about the potluck at school, my coffee-making duties at work, my ongoing obsession with Anna. I punched up my anecdotes, trying to get her to laugh, happy to serve as the butt of a joke.

"John and I have been too tired at night for sex. I'm pretty sure he's going to leave me for Anna."

"My boss returned my latest draft brief with tons of edits and markups. Pretty sure she's going to fire me and hire Anna."

I played it up, and our laughter seemed to drain some of the dread creeping ever closer.

One morning, in the early days of her illness, she got up to order a fruit cup at the counter. I watched as she handed the barista dollar bills from a raggedy, overstuffed wallet that looked like a relic from the previous century. I shook my head when a penny fell on the floor and rolled under the counter. She looked exactly the same as always. Same bird arms, same blue eyes, same hunch of her shoulders. She had the same knob on her wrist where she broke it when she got tangled in her dog's leash and fell. How could this woman be dying?

When she sat back down, she had a serious look on her face.

"Gage is a mess."

"Of course. Do you want me to send you guys a meal?" Offering to send her and Gage a meal was about to become my nervous tic.

"It's a little soon for that, isn't it?"

"Is it?" Please God, I hope so.

"Yes."

"Okay, but say the word and I'll send you spider rolls and miso soup."

We were quiet for a long moment. I considered a dozen topics to introduce, but knew my voice would sound hollow and frantic, and she'd just complained about no one using their real voice around her. I couldn't fix this for her with witty banter about the Bulls defense or Gwyneth Paltrow's advice that women "steam clean" their vaginas.

"I'm so jealous of everyone who doesn't have this. I hate everyone who isn't sick."

I nodded and felt a lump in my throat rise, bringing tears with it. I stared at a smudge on the booth above Meredith's shoulder; if I met her eyes, I was going to cry. Was I allowed to cry? I wasn't sure. I didn't want her to have to take care of me, but I didn't want to withhold my feelings. I imagined myself in her place, watching "healthy" people live their lives, making doctor's appointments only for annual checkups and flu shots. I could feel vicarious rage surging through me. If I lost my ever-living shit over Anna's superior blog posts, how would I feel if the stakes were life and death?

"Everything about this sucks." Hopefully, Meredith wasn't looking for anything insightful or wise from me. "Should I point out that, actually, you are *envious* of everyone not battling metastasized cancer?"

Meredith smiled.

Since her call on Saturday, my fears about supporting her as she faced her physical demise had grown more intense. In quiet moments, I thought about Lia, Kate, Marnie, Callie, and Anna. The drifting I'd let happen. The ghosting. The projecting. The thought of failing Meredith made me feel sick to my stomach, but I knew I would. Of course I would. Look at my track record. I dreaded my future failure so much, it made me want to pull away now so I wouldn't fuck it up later. I had to tell her.

"I'm going to fail you, you know. All the 'Good Orderly Direction' in the world won't be powerful enough to stop me."

She looked startled. "No, honey, you won't —"

"I will. I know I will. We both know I'll do something stupid. I'll get scared and back away. Or you'll want some space, and I'll take it personally. Or I'll be envious. Something bad is going to happen between us. I know it." I'd tried so hard not to cry, but there was no stopping the tears.

"You're going to do just fine."

"Meredith, you know I have blind spots. What if I'm jealous of all the attention you get? Oh my God, I can see it now. Our friends will call me to talk about you, and I'll be, like, 'Yeah, Meredith, sure, she's in ICU, but don't you want to know whether I got bangs or won my oral argument?' Or what about when you have less energy, and you choose to spend time with other friends and not me." I grabbed her hand and held her gaze. "Think of the day I hear a health update from Anna. You'll be fighting for your life and I'll be outside your hospital room obsessing over why you reached out to her first."

This worry was as real as the table between us, her giant black tote bag, my unmanicured cuticles. I looked into my future with Meredith and saw a series of obstacles, points in time when she would need me to step up or get out of my own way and friend her as she needed to be friended. She would need me to surmount my internal hurdles and show up as her faithful, stalwart friend. How could either of us have any confidence I could do that?

Meredith smiled and cocked her head.

"You can't even deny it," I said. "You know I'm going to fall on my face over here. The consequence will be that I let you down. This is a foregone conclusion. No one knows the holes in my friendship résumé more intimately than you."

"Okay, so what if you fuck up?" She was laughing. She didn't have time for friends who were only half-baked; she needed fully cooked companions who could serve her as her body broke down.

"It'll be unforgivable. What if I do something bad, like, at the end, and there isn't time to make amends or make it right."

"So fuck up early and get it out of your system. Or I guess I'll have to haunt you."

"Maybe we should part ways now; it might save so much pain."

She squeezed my hand hard enough that all of her stacked golden rings pressed against my fingers.

"You're not going anywhere. I need you, and we'll figure it out together."

"I want to go on record: I'm scared of failing you, and it makes me want to leave so I don't have to watch myself fail. And when I do, I'm going to probably say, 'I told you so.' "

"There is no record, Christie. There is only this moment. You're here now. Keep doing what you're doing."

A few days later I got a two-line email from Meredith. *I believe in you. Thought you should know.*

27

"I'm in your lobby," Meredith said when she called on my office phone. "Come downstairs and get me." I'd switched jobs from the part-time clerkship to a full-time position with a government agency. The adjustment to working every day hadn't been as grueling as I feared, and I was in a good rhythm at home and at work. Elias, now five, had the same school schedule as six-year-old Zara, and we had a loving, committed after-school babysitter who made it all possible.

A strange thing happened with me and Meredith when she got her diagnosis — I started leaning on her more, rather than less. Every time we talked, which was several times a week, she wanted to hear about my life, not discuss her chemo and radiation. She knew about my kids' social lives, their reading levels, their interest in *The Wizard of Oz*. I kept her informed on my sex life

283

with John and the quotidian struggles of working for the federal government. Sometimes we went whole weeks without talking in depth about her illness. The weekend before she stopped by my office, we'd had a lively conversation about our shopping habits, and I confessed that I was stuck in an annoying cycle of making impulse purchases at T.J. Maxx and Nordstrom Rack, and then feeling put out when I came to my senses and had to return the weird silk-shirt dress or silly plastic shower caddy.

I found Meredith in the lobby, holding her school tote and two large brown Trader Joe's shopping bags full of books. When she spotted me, she held out the bags.

"What's all this?" I asked.

"I brought you some books."

The titles involved shopping, commercialism, capitalism, and how buying things never cured the soul's aches.

"I Shop Therefore I Am," I read aloud. "Are all of these books about —"

"Shopping and spending."

She beamed at me as I took the shopping bags out of her hands. I thought of that box of scarves all those years ago.

"You act fast." I'd just told her about my latest shopping nonsense a few days before.

"Gage and I are cleaning things out. We

might put the house on the market. Maybe make a change."

I didn't like the sound of that.

The first round of treatment had shrunk her tumors, and most days Meredith expressed hope about her condition and her future. She might have five years. But still, I sensed this cleaning was inspired not by Marie Kondo but by impending mortality. I searched Meredith's expression for a signal she knew something she wasn't telling me, but saw only her joy at having curated a perfect collection of books for me.

"Come on up," I said, leading her to the elevators.

I'd never had a friend stop by this office before and felt shy about letting her see the shabby carpet, the cheap bookshelves, and my windowless room the size of a closet, where half the ceiling lights were burned out. Long gone were the days of my fancy private law firm office with the view of the Chicago River and the matching mahogany furniture.

"So this is where the magic happens," she said, laughing. From my two mismatched visitor's chairs, she chose the one with the less-frayed cushion.

"Don't laugh. I buy my own highlighters

and bring them to work. Budget cuts are real."

"I used to share my desk with the receptionist at Hazelden, I get it."

She pulled out a carved wooden box and a woven doll with a multicolored dress the size of my palm. She pushed it across the desk toward me.

"I think Zara would like these."

"A colorful doll and a box to hide treasures? She'll be thrilled."

"Tell her that I sent them to her."

I picked them both up and put them in my lap. There were intricate flowers carved into the domed top of the box. I opened the box and it smelled faintly of floral perfume and stale hairspray.

"Did you keep this in your bathroom?"

"For about twenty years."

Smiling, I thanked her and put the box and the doll next to my purse so I could take them home to Zara. The part of me that understood Meredith was in the process of letting go curled in on itself. *Nah, nah, nah, I can't hear you, I can't see you. This isn't happening.*

I was touched Meredith wanted these objects to go to Zara, since they hadn't spent much time together. When I'd hosted Meredith's wedding shower at my house,

286

Zara, then ten months old, charmed all of her guests. Like a doting auntie, Meredith always glowed over the stories about my kids.

"I've been so envious of all you mothers — all these years, so upset every time the subject turned to babies." As Meredith spoke, her face still held the bright joy from the lobby. "I don't want to push the pain away anymore. I want to lean into it." She slid a white envelope across the table with my daughter's name on it. "I wrote her a note. I wanted her to know I was thinking of her."

I nodded, the knowing part of me still chanting, *No, no, no.*

Meredith had lost most of her hair during the first round of treatment. With her thick brownish-gray hair mostly gone, her eyes glowed a more searing shade of sky blue that was so intense I wondered if the chemo literally enhanced the color.

"That's my favorite thing about you," I said, and she looked puzzled. "Your envy. It makes me feel so much less alone."

She took my hand in both of hers. "You're never alone, you know."

"You either."

When I walked her back to the lobby, I felt expansive, like my body held the whole horizon. I knew I would never abandon Meredith, no matter what happened. That truth made me feel strong, like all things were possible.

I could be a friend.

I *was* a friend.

28

"I heard a rumor," Brad said, as he sat down and pulled a cup of soup out of a white paper bag.

The group therapy session had begun moments before. Not everyone was settled in their seats yet. Max was hanging his overcoat on the back of his chair; Dr. Rosen was adjusting the shades to keep the glare of the bright April sunshine off Patrice's face. Regina was riffling through her purse for a check for Dr. Rosen. My mood was lighthearted as I took my usual chair — the air smelled like spring, and I had no pressing issues to bring to the group.

"Oh Jesus," Patrice said, exasperated by Brad's long-standing habit of dragging salacious tidbits about the lives of people we hardly knew into our sessions. "Let's not spend the whole session dissecting a stranger's sex life."

"It's not a stranger," Brad said. He pulled

a baguette out of the sack and dipped it into his soup. Now that he had everyone's attention, he paused for dramatic effect.

"Well?" Patrice said, throwing up her hands.

His eyes darted to me for a split second and then away.

"I heard Anna might join this group."

Patrice scoffed. "Where'd you hear that?"

Brad picked up his soup and held his spoon aloft. "On the Rosen-grapevine. I'm friends with Renée, who's in the Monday-afternoon group with Anna. Apparently, Anna wants to shake up her therapy routine, join a new group. Rosen gave her a few options." He dipped the spoon into his soup. "Including this one."

Everyone turned to Dr. Rosen, even though we were all intimately familiar with his resting shrink face and knew it would offer no clues. No sense in asking him directly either. We could blather all we wanted, but he would never disclose, confirm, or deny any information about patients in other groups.

Max asked Brad how definite Dr. Rosen's offer was. Brad admitted he didn't know.

"This is third-party information we can't verify," Patrice said. "Why don't we table this discussion until Dr. Rosen officially announces a new member, *and* we're sure it's Anna. Until then, it's nothing more than a rumor."

Max turned to Dr. Rosen. "Cute."

Dr. Rosen raised his eyebrows, like, *What do you mean?*

"Come on. This is provocative. Unnecessarily so." Max, who'd been with Dr. Rosen the longest, had become an expert in challenging Dr. Rosen's unorthodox ways. "We all know Christie is hung up on Anna. This is a bit much, even for you."

"I don't want a new member. I'm not in the mood," said Regina, our resident crank. Regina hated change generally and particularly despised the getting-to-know-you rituals involved in welcoming a new member.

Everyone laughed to hear her expressing the exact sentiments we expected from her.

"Anna's pretty hot," Brad said. "I met her years ago in a recovery meeting."

"Ew," Patrice said. "You're not supposed to creep on people in meetings."

"She's very attractive."

"I definitely don't want some pretty little thing coming in here," Regina said. "Do better, Rosen."

After a few minutes, the group tired of the subject and moved on. Brad finished his lunch and asked for help negotiating a commission at work. Patrice reported on her latest trip to visit her grandchildren in Dayton. Max's chair squeaked, and he chided Dr. Rosen for being a "cheapskate" who refused to invest in higher-quality furniture. Regina went to the bathroom at the halfway mark.

The minutes ticked by until there were five minutes remaining. It was almost time to stand up, gather our things, and launch back into our workdays.

"Christie," Dr. Rosen said, when there were four minutes to go. "Why is your arm bleeding?"

Patrice gasped. "Christie! Oh my God! What happened?"

Max, seated to my right, scooted toward me and placed two of his hands under my left arm. He drew my arm toward him so he could inspect the bloody track I'd secretly carved in my skin.

"Seriously, Christie, why?" Patrice sounded angry, and I couldn't blame her. What had I done?

Dr. Rosen leaned forward in his chair. "This is about Anna?"

I opened my right palm to him and shrugged.

He left the room and returned with an ancient first-aid kit, stiff from neglect. Max transferred my hurt arm to Dr. Rosen's open hands, as if it was a sickly newborn. Dr. Rosen daubed a cool, ochre-colored ointment on my wounds.

My group mates and Dr. Rosen asked me questions I couldn't answer. Did they really expect me to have a reasonable explanation? Wasn't it obvious from, you know, the blood, that I was somewhere beyond language and logic?

I didn't understand why I'd gouged my arm in secret for over an hour.

I didn't understand why I hadn't asked for help.

I didn't understand why I was so resistant — resistant enough to hurt myself — to the possibility of Anna showing up in my therapy group.

I didn't understand why I was so out of my mind when it came to Anna — so regressed, so envious, so sure I'd die if she arrived.

Dr. Rosen administered aid, while my group mates looked on in confusion. I kept shaking my head.

"I'm sorry," I said. And I was. Sorry to pull a dramatic stunt and sorry for not being able to articulate why I had done it.

"You cannot bring Anna into this group," Patrice said to Dr. Rosen. "You just can't."

29

A few days later, I rolled up my sleeve to show Meredith. We'd met outside our coffee shop and let the tourists and office workers stream by us.

"Oh, honey." She held my arm.

"You're fighting for your life, literally trying to save your body, and I'm ripping up my flesh. What the fuck, right?" I rolled my sleeve down. "Let's go inside."

The scratches on my arm had hardened to a scabby rust color. The skin still felt warm and tight. It reminded me of the flesh on either side of my C-section scar that was hot to the touch and swollen for months after I'd given birth, both times. At night, when I rolled onto my hurt arm, a throbbing pain woke me up. I'd been wearing long sleeves to hide my arms from my children, even though it was almost May and the buds were days from bursting all over Chicago. Worse than the stinging pain of my self-inflicted wound was the shame of what I'd done. I was a forty-two-year-old woman with years of therapy and recovery; I was a veteran of "working on myself." I'd addressed so many issues, including friendship, but now I'd torn my own flesh because a woman, someone I used to call a "close friend" but was deeply envious of, might join my therapy group?

Across the table, Meredith waited for me to speak.

"I don't know what happened. One second I was fine, and then someone said Anna's name, and I snapped."

"It can't really be about Anna."

"Yes and no. Of course, not totally. But she's fucking involved. I mean, at least in my mind."

I'd thought a great deal about why Dr. Rosen would bring Anna into my group. I could imagine he believed that amazing breakthroughs would come to pass for me if I was forced to face all my feelings about her *while sitting in a circle with her under psychiatric supervision.* Maybe he believed that the alchemy of a group that included Anna would transform me from a dissatisfied lawyer into a full-time artist who no longer saw her sister's shadow in every attractive, powerful, successful woman. Hell, he very well might have believed that bringing Anna into my group would, once and for all, put me in touch with my own luminescence so I could stop projecting it onto every other woman who crossed my path. I'd end up more empowered, centered, and free. But my body had revolted, and it was hard to reconcile my hurt arm with all the alleged advantages of sharing a group with her.

"I understand those scratches." Meredith held out her hands, and I placed my arm in them.

"You've done this?"

"Not scratching, but I've skipped meals *at* people I was angry with or jealous of. I talked to my mom over the weekend" — Meredith's sister Ginny had recently moved their mom to Washington State, which relieved Meredith of the torturous visits to Rockford every other weekend — "and of course she droned on and on about how wonderful and thoughtful my sister is. Mom's health is failing, but she's got just enough breath to remind me to be a good wife to Gage or else he'll leave me. After the call, I drank a quart of chocolate milk. I felt sick halfway through, but I didn't stop. And I drank that milk *at* my mom. My stomach ached, and I felt like I was going to burst. My mom was with my sister, eating her creamed corn and pudding, and I was seconds from running to the bathroom to puke."

"Damn."

"I'm in my sixties, putting my goddamn affairs in order, and I'm upset that my mom loves my sister more than me, which actually makes sense because my sister moved her across the country so she could die with family. She *should* love Ginny more than she loves me. My sister is better at loving."

"I can't believe that's true."

"Feels true.

"I've been beating myself up for being in my forties and hurting myself over Anna."

"Fuck age."

"I can't be in group with Anna, Meredith. I'd rather find another therapist. I can't do it. I know you love her, but I can't do it." Suddenly, I hated Meredith for loving Anna so much. Bridesmaid-level love. "I'm not ready to face all the work her presence would demand."

Meredith nodded. I thought of a picture John had snapped of Meredith and Anna at the foot of a wooden staircase right before Meredith's wedding: their heads tilted toward each other, and both smiling wide for the camera. You can feel the love and affection radiating off them. Friendship. Sisterhood. Obviously, Meredith didn't feel about Anna the way I did. Did she hate me for having this ugly, self-defeating envy, this fury that led me to tear at myself? Did she know I hated her a little bit for loving Anna so much?

"Do you hate me for this?" I nodded toward my arm, knowing she would say no but also needing to hear her say it.

"Oh, honey, no. I *am* you."

While it was comforting to hear that Meredith could relate to me, I wanted us both to be different. For all the work we did on ourselves, shouldn't we have achieved more emotional stability? Was it too much to ask that we not harm our bodies with our fingernails or chocolate milk when confronted with intense fear, anger, sadness, and grief? How much more work did we need to do? And was it even a matter of our working harder, or was this one of those spiritual paradoxes where we would find profound, unshakable serenity once we stopped working so damn hard to change ourselves?

I didn't hate myself for having blind spots or for tripping up, but it messed with my identity as someone who was mostly sane and functional — someone with the gritty emotional work of her life behind her. I would have sworn that I was done committing great harm to myself. But that simply wasn't true, and I didn't want to accept that a cornerstone of my identity had turned to dust.

The following week, I went to a recovery meeting downtown during my lunch hour, and I didn't recognize any of the faces around the circle. The anonymity made it easier to admit that I wanted to be further along, spiritually and emotionally, than I was. I alluded to "self-harming behavior," and a few women around the room nodded. God, I loved those nodding women. I didn't know their names, but I knew they'd schlepped from their offices to this church basement across from the Cook County Clerk's office to admit to everyone present: "I hurt; I want to feel better; I need help." Women had been nodding their heads at me since my very first meeting at age nineteen. More than half my life. Those nodding heads had done more to heal my shame and regret than anything else I'd ever experienced.

As I walked back to my office after the meeting, I felt less defensive and despondent; I felt softer toward myself. I visualized some future meeting when I'd nod at some hurting woman who was dismayed by something she'd done to herself.

Give me some of that Good Orderly Direction, I prayed under my breath as I rode the elevator up to my office.

30

Typically, Dr. Rosen would announce a new member's arrival one month before they showed up in person so the group could "emotionally prepare" for expanding the circle. Once I heard the rumor about Anna, I opened every session with the same question: "Are you bringing her in here?" Dr. Rosen would cock his head and furrow his brow, but say nothing.

"It was just a rumor," my group mates reminded me. "No official announcement yet."

I'd made my position clear. I sat with my scarred arm propped on the armrest, as if to warn: *Don't forget! Don't you dare bring a new baby home. Don't push me.* I pressed my injury into service to communicate to Dr. Rosen that I was as yet unavailable to be in a group with Anna.

But I wasn't the boss of therapy, and so part of me understood that I was being manipulative. Anyone who has to rip their flesh to get their needs met is not exactly perched in the seat of power.

"Am I allowed to ask you to not bring her in here?" I said in more than one session.

That couldn't be right. I was a patient. How could I tell him how to run his practice? I had no right to demand how he populated his groups. While I'd learned in therapy to ask for what I want, I knew the lesson didn't encompass my asking him to block Anna's entry. But I needed him to know I wasn't ready. "Please don't do this."

When I left therapy sessions, I longed to call Callie. I didn't know the status of her friendship with Anna, but I imagined they remained distant. A few years earlier, I'd bonded with Anna over Callie, and now, in true middle school fashion, I wanted to bond with Callie over Anna. Surely, Callie would understand. She, like Meredith, understood this side of me. Callie would never judge me; she'd struggled with jealousy, too. That was part of our poison — her jealousy of my other relationships. Callie, too, had a radiant, golden younger sister. I never knew her to self-harm, and we weren't in touch, but it helped to know she was somewhere in the world, making her way with a heart as tender and deformed as mine.

"My mom died." Meredith's voice on the phone was soft, sad.

"Oh, Meredith, I'm so sorry."

It was an early morning in mid-June. I'd been running on the lakefront path, but stopped and stepped off the path into the grass when Meredith's number flashed on my phone.

"I feel really weird. And sad. I want to skip breakfast."

"Keep talking. Tell me how it feels."

"I knew this was coming. She was ninety-three. But I also can't believe she's gone. I gave up on trying to get her to see me, really see me, a long time ago. And now that she's gone, I feel like I should have tried harder."

"Oof. You tried really hard. Think of all those trips to Rockford. All that chocolate milk you guzzled to coat your grief."

"And yet, somehow I also feel guilty I'm not sadder."

I stood a few feet off the running path underneath a row of crab apple trees in front of the Field Museum. Early-morning joggers shuffled past, and cyclists whizzed by in garish-colored jerseys. I searched for the exact right things to say. It was my turn to be wise and full of faith. I did my best to channel my inner Meredith.

"You will have days when you do feel sadder. Right now you're in shock. And honoring whatever feelings are coming up is a good way to walk through grief." Not bad. I think I stole those exact words from Meredith, who'd once said them to me.

"I really want to skip breakfast."

"Meredith. What would you tell me if my mother had just died and I wanted to skip breakfast?" Also not bad — direct her to tell me what I should say to console her!

She laughed. "I would say that skipping breakfast was a way to delay the grief. I'd probably offer to stay on the phone with you while you prepared and ate your breakfast."

"Great idea! So what are you going to make?"

I turned south and started walking back home. I pressed the phone to my ear and heard cabinets opening, glasses clinking, silverware shuffling. Meredith only committed to making her breakfast — a raisin bagel and a hard-boiled egg — not eating it, but in my memory I can hear her chewing and swallowing, bravely wading into the grief she feared would sweep her away.

31

In mid-fall, a break in Meredith's school schedule coincided with a break in her chemo schedule.

"Meet me for lunch," she said. "Somewhere that requires a reservation. And somewhere downtown on the Red Line."

We picked Atwood at the corner of Washington and State, across from the old Marshall Field's building and Anthropologie. I wore a dress and heels and ditched my giant nylon mom-purse for a small leather one. When I arrived, I spotted Meredith at a table, sipping water and watching tourists stream toward Millennium Park. Her signature stacks of rings decorated two fingers on each hand, and her pink cigarette pants matched her pink lipstick; other than being slightly thinner than normal, she looked as spry and alive as anyone else having lunch on this Friday afternoon. We both ordered the salmon entrée. We laughed when the distracted waiter spilled ice on our table. We shook our heads when we told stories about our husbands. We bemoaned our to-do lists. Neither of us said any scary words about cells or ports or chemo. When the waiter cleared our plates, we both ordered tea. I had a brief due in court by the end of the day, but the pleasure of peppermint tea with Meredith after lunch was enough to make me stay. The brief could wait.

After the first cup, we nodded when the waiter offered to refill our hot water. Time expanded beyond our table, beyond downtown Chicago. Time was the ocean; it would never run out.

"I think she would be good for you," Meredith said out of the blue — we'd been talking about how much Adele's music made her cry. But her energy shifted, and I knew she was referring to Anna by the way she leaned forward and lowered her voice. "If she came into your group, it would be good for you. She's a good person. She's doing the work —"

"I know she's a good person! That's precisely my point!" My voice came out louder than I intended. The couple seated next to us looked over. "That's the part I can't stand. She's better than me on all physical, moral, and spiritual scales —" I felt a tightness in my chest and heat in my cheeks. Our lunch had been lovely; why was she doing this?

"She's still thinking it over — joining your therapy group." Meredith met my eyes. "I hope she does. I wish that for you."

I sucked in my breath and twisted the napkin with both hands. The expansiveness I'd felt earlier retracted. Everything shrank to a tiny point between Meredith's eyes. I hated her for saying it, for going off script.

"I wish you were on my side."

"Oh, honey, I *am* on your side." She reached for my hand. "I'm for your growth, your healing. If she comes into your therapy group, you get to relive the experience of having a perfect baby sister come into the 'family.' " She did air quotes around *family*. "You're going see how okay you are. How beloved, no matter who else is in the room. This is going to transform everything. I want this for you. I really do."

I believed that she believed every word she was saying. I understood that my script — Meredith's love for me meant she had to hate Anna, too — was immature and toxic. Wisely, Meredith threw it out. Instead, she treated me like an adult who could handle complex, painful relationships, as well as the truth. She wanted my healing, and she was willing to tell me the truth. Part of me understood that. And part of me wanted to flip the table, send the teacups and salt-shaker sailing, and then storm out. But there was a third part. A sliver of me was a tiny bit willing to walk toward Anna to see what I might discover about myself. That part of me shared Meredith's faith in me.

I breathed, and Meredith breathed. And when she broke into a smile, I did, too.

"I'm this close to bringing up my arm because I'm afraid you forgot about —"

"I would never." A stricken look displaced Meredith's smile. "Never ever."

"I know. Really. I do. Maybe it's time for me to stop using my arm as a shield against every mention or reminder of Anna."

"I want you to hear that I think you deserve this. Some pain is good pain, right? When someone recovers from frostbite, it hurts like hell." Meredith wriggled her fingers, her rings softly clacking against one another. "Think about it. All that feeling and sensation returning to your fingertips or toes is screaming pain. That's what heal-ing is. It's not warm lights and lavender pil-lows. It's guts. It's blood. It's body parts shocked with new blood flow that feels like a too-bright searing agony pushing you to the brink of death. When they put people

308

suffering from frostbite in a bath to warm them up, they often give them narcotic pain medication."

"Where's my fentanyl?"

"Right here." Meredith gestured at the space between us, like our friendship was the only opiate I needed. Perhaps she was right, but it wasn't the same as a pill or a patch that could bring euphoria and take away my appetite.

On the walk back to my office, I felt jittery. Rattled. I hadn't expected Meredith to bring up Anna. Most of my other friends avoided the topic. Once Emily mentioned that she'd heard on the recovery grapevine that Anna's novel had attracted interest from a literary agent. I burst into tears and got off the phone faster than if she'd said, "I'm on the other line with Marnie." When I calmed down, I texted Emily to please not say her name around me. "I can't handle it." I'd never set a boundary like that. Anna had become part sister, part ex-boyfriend, and all Voldemort.

For months, I waited for Dr. Rosen to officially announce the arrival of a new member. Every time he cleared his throat, I'd think: *Here comes the news! Please kill me now!* I filed my nails short so I wouldn't be able to do any damage when the announcement arrived. But he kept not saying it. Just in case, I interviewed other therapists, my Plan Bs in case Anna joined the group. One of them, a middle-aged man named Ryan who wore dark denim jeans and feathered his blond hair, said he could "absolutely" help me, which felt comforting, but his salesy vibe ("I'm the best there is, Christie") soured me. He also asked me for a hug at the end of the session. Hard pass.

Over the phone, I described the scratch to a therapist named Rena, thinking she'd guarantee me a prime slot on her schedule, but at the end of our screening conversation she told me to stay put. "Sounds like it would be really good for you if this woman came into your group, and you could work some of this out." I hung up in tears. Bite me, Rena.

I kept a list of a few other therapists just in case.

Meredith, whose health was relatively stable as she faced the next round of treatment, was not a fan of my Plan B project. "You don't even know if Anna is coming. And if she does, maybe it's God's will. If and when God gives you this opportunity, maybe you should accept it," she said.

"When you don't like God's offer, you're

allowed to counter," I said.

I still longed to call Callie every time I thought about Anna sitting in "my" therapy circle, but I couldn't bring myself to reach out after the pain I'd caused.

So I breathed. The scars on my arm faded to a light dove-feather gray. I wrote briefs at work and went to potluck dinners at the kids' school. I bought crap I didn't need at the Rack, despite the stack of books from Meredith that counseled against it, and sent holiday gifts to my family in Texas.

At some point, Meredith came to one of our coffee sessions with a new suggestion. "Write an inventory of all the character defects you bring into your friendships."

I laughed. "I need a five-hundred-page notebook."

"Start with page one. I'm doing an inventory, too. It'll be fun."

When your friend in her second round of chemo invites you to do an inventory of all the character defects you bring into friendship, there's only one answer: "Sure, let me grab my pen."

I wrote several pages about my petty jealousies, starting with grammar school, and then a few more pages on the adult versions. At the end of that section, I scribbled: *If you could die of envy, I would not be alive*

311

today. Then, I filled in line after line about troublesome triangles, followed by my history of ghosting. The magic of this assignment was that I thought I'd write forever, that my shortcomings were never-ending rivers the spilled past the horizon. They weren't. Eventually, I ran out of examples. My list was complete.

The harder part was diving into the ways I failed my friends by not showing up for them.

"I'm a shitty friend," I told Meredith over the phone in the middle of the writing.

"This is supposed to be an inventory, not a weapon to hurt yourself. Think of it as taking stock. Don't draw conclusions. That's not the purpose."

"It feels terrible."

"Then write three pages about your strengths as a friend."

Gag. Flash to vapid self-affirmations, like a skit on *Saturday Night Live*. *I'm a wonderful person, worthy of love, and I deserve good things.*

"I'll help you get started. Write: I went to see the musical about Cher with Meredith."

I burst out laughing. It was true — I'd taken a half day off work to sit next to Meredith at the Oriental Theatre downtown, watching the story of Cher's life unfold on the stage. And while there was a time when I got a kick out of *I Got You Babe* back in high school, I had no desire to see this musical. I'd agreed to go because I loved Meredith, and she'd just been diagnosed. Even though I was laughing and writing this example, I thought the exercise felt forced, cheesy.

"Write: I drove Meredith to Rockford in the pouring rain to see Willie Nelson."

"Wait, that was my idea! I'm the one who loves Willie."

"But you did all the driving and paid for the tickets."

"Fine. I'll include it."

"Write: I took Meredith to see Lin-Manuel Miranda speak at the Lyric Opera House."

"Also my idea."

"You paid, and you took me with you."

I rolled my eyes. This was like a black-belt workout. "This might be harder than writing all my shortcomings."

While I generally followed directions like a good soldier, I felt completely resistant to the suggestion that I write my strengths. Yes, I went to the baptism for Clare's daughter and visited galleries to see Emily's art shows. I called or texted Kate every year on her birthday, and when her mother died,

I flew to Austin to pay my respects. But big whoop. You don't get a gold star for the basics, and showing up for major life events was basic. Wasn't it more important to list out the instances when I'd fallen short of minimum friendship requirements? That was what I wanted to change.

"Also, don't make this too hard," Meredith said.

"This?"

"Friendship. Your standard is perfection, so you're going to fail every time. It's a setup. If you expect yourself to be a perfect friend, one who's never jealous and who shows up for every single thing, you're going to fail. Can you just be a good enough friend? What about that?"

A good enough friend? The phrase felt like a deep exhale. It gave my lungs room to expand in my chest. It felt attainable. Good enough. I certainly appreciated that concept in my parenting — I didn't expect myself to be the "perfect" mother to my children. Sure, I wanted to meet all their needs and never falter, but I could easily see that it was impossible. The greatest gift someone gave me when I was a young mother, frantic about doing right by my innocent, beautiful babies, was introducing me to D. W. Winnicott's concept of "the good enough mother."

At a parenting class in a yoga studio years before, the instructor cited Dr. Winnicott and assured us that we didn't have to meet our babies' every single need for the rest of our lives. "It's okay if your baby experiences frustration while she waits for you to finish your shower." This class leader, the first person in authority to tell me that it was okay to put my own needs first every now and then, gave me a key to unlock the prison I'd made of motherhood. In those words, *good enough mother* — backed up by a famous British pediatrician — I heard permission to love my babies in the best way I could, even though I fell short of perfection every single day. It freed me up to enjoy my babies and skip the guilt — or at least not drown in it — when I left them with John or a sitter so I could wander the Target aisles by myself for an hour.

Was there a famous doctor I could cite for the proposition that one need only be a "good enough friend"? And if science couldn't back me up, could I decide to accept this standard for myself? Hearing Meredith say it helped me imagine forgiving myself for all the ways I'd struggled and failed in my friendships, and all the ways I would fail in the future. It also helped me

see my self-flagellation for what it was:
unproductive and boring as hell.

32

"She's not joining your group," Meredith said one morning after a meeting, and I didn't ask any further questions. I accepted the gift.

"Don't hate me for having a heart filled with joy and relief right now," I said, doing a little happy dance on the sidewalk. Meredith shook her head.

The news that Anna had decided on a different therapeutic path brought a relief that bordered on ecstasy. More than a dozen people had suggested her arrival would be a great benefit to me, spiritually and emotionally, and I'd understood their thinking. I didn't even disagree. Anna lived as an artist-mother who spent her days in ways I could only dream of. Sure, being closer to her might unlock my own inner artist-mother and free me as a sister and friend, but now that it was off the table, I felt like breaking into song: "Hallelujah" (Handel's famous chorus, not Leonard Cohen's dirge).

When Meredith and I parted, I glided down the sidewalk; I fist-pumped my shadow. *She's not coming!* Yes, this was a missed opportunity to do deep work I alleged I was willing to do, but who cared? She wasn't coming! Who wants to dance with me?

I relaxed back into my group sessions.

I rubbed shea butter over the scars on my arm, and I threw away my list of backup therapists.

And then, a few weeks later, I ran right into Anna.

Our mutual friend Katherine texted a group of us to see if anyone could stop by the hospital to visit her husband, B.J., who'd been admitted for some tests. I stepped into the cool lobby of Northwestern Memorial Hospital and beelined to the tiny bookstore next to the information desk to grab a thriller that B.J. had requested. As I scribbled my name on the credit card slip, I saw Anna walking toward the elevators. *Shit.* My stomach hitched. I clutched the copy of *Sharp Objects* to my chest and followed several yards behind her. When she turned to the elevator banks that led to B.J.'s room, I abandoned my thin hope that she had other reasons to be at Northwestern Hospital. I considered lingering in the lobby until Anna concluded her visit, but I had to pick my kids up at school by three and didn't have an hour to spare hiding behind a stone pillar waiting for her to leave.

I walked as slowly as I could, without drawing attention to myself, but when I turned the corner there she stood, tracking the elevator's progress to the first floor.

"Hi, Anna."

"Christie!" she said, her face lit up with a genuine smile. "You must be here to see B.J."

Other than at a Christmas party, I hadn't seen Anna in two years, and I hadn't spent one-on-one time with her in almost three. My skin had long since healed, but the shock of standing three feet from her made my arm tingle. I folded my arms across my chest and held the book so it covered the scars. Shield the arm, shield the heart. We stepped into the elevator together.

The elevator rose several floors and two other visitors stepped in; we shifted to the back right corner.

"Wait," Anna said, turning her whole body toward me. "Isn't today your birthday?"

I nodded. It was my forty-fifth birthday, and I was surprised and touched that my birthday lived in her memory. It was exactly the kind of complicating experience that made my head swim. *She was kind. She offered me kindness. Why can't I let her in?*

"Happy birthday! I hope you're doing something celebratory tonight."

We fell into step in the hallway, and once we made it to B.J.'s room, we sat shoulder to shoulder on the couch by the window. It was confusing to admit to myself that her presence comforted me. Her lively energy kept the conversation going. When B.J. expressed anxiety that his family trip would be canceled because of his illness, Anna reminded him that there was still plenty of summer left even if they had to reschedule. She was graceful and lighthearted. I handed B.J. the book, keeping my left forearm covered by my right.

When a nurse knocked and mentioned a test the doctor wanted to run, Anna and I stood up to take our leave. We retraced our steps and walked back through the lobby. We swirled through the revolving door and stood in the radiant, inescapable July sun on the corner of Ohio and McClurg Court. We paused and hugged, she again wished me a happy birthday, and we parted ways.

In the cab, I texted Meredith immediately. *Oh my God, I just saw Anna. Spent an hour with her in B.J.'s hospital room. HOLY SHIT. I think it was okay. It's really not about her. It's me. I know it's me.*

Seeing Anna brought her back to her right size. My imagination had blown up Anna and her perfection until she'd become a caricature, an untouchable beauty like Mila Kunis filled with the unwavering goodness of Mother Teresa and the global popularity of Beyoncé. But none of that was real. The phantasm in my head left no room for the actual flesh-and-blood Anna. From our short visit with B.J., I understood that. This was progress.

What a wonderful birthday present, Meredith wrote.

33

Have I made Meredith sound like a saint? A blue-eyed, uber-spiritual, tiny-boned angel with golden rings stacked on her fingers, sent to guide me? I'm afraid I have, and Meredith would hate that. I would hate that. I want to tell the truth about her, give you the whole complex picture. She wasn't a saint before she got sick, and she didn't become saintly when she got sick. Much like me, she could be a real pain in the ass.

Sometimes she would call me, tired from treatment, and go off about Bebe and the fudge debacle from her wedding years earlier. "Meredith, don't you have bigger fish to fry?"

Sometimes during our coffee dates, she would pull out Tupperware filled with quinoa and slices of boiled egg from her rundown grocery store, even before she got sick and chemo threw her appetite out of whack. Maybe it was delicious, but it looked like food you'd feed an arthritic lap dog, and it pained me to see her forgoing edible food to save money or cut calories.

Sometimes she refused to ask for help even when she desperately needed someone to drive her somewhere, hold her hand, or help decode the communications from her insurance provider. She wanted to do it all herself.

Though she owned two buildings in Chicago and had a full-time job with benefits, she still struggled to spend money on herself. She had plenty of problems, but financial security wasn't one of them. Early in her illness, she asked me to meet her at my place of worship, the Rack, to pick out a hat before her hair fell out. I found her in the accessories section holding a jaunty black leather baseball cap over her head. She smiled at herself in the mirror and turned her head in several directions, admiring her reflection.

"It's perfect," I said, and she nodded but put it back, mumbling that it was "too expensive." I returned to the store the next day during my lunch hour, and improbably, the hat was gone.

When I told her I'd tried to find the hat for her, she seemed annoyed.

"I don't need that hat!"

"I want you to have it. You looked so happy in it."

"The one I got is fine."

"Sure, denim bucket hats are a look. But —"

"Leather's too hot. I don't want it."

"Fine, but let me say this: it's hard to watch you be cheap at a time like this."

"Fuck you, Christie."

Her sharp response startled me, but I didn't back down.

"Fuck me? What the hell. The difference was twenty bucks. I think that when you lose your hair because of chemo, you should get whatever fucking hat you want —"

"Exactly. I got the hat I wanted."

"Okay."

"So stop judging me."

I apologized and our argument petered out, but it scared me, the anger that ignited between us. She was right that I'd judged her as depriving herself, but I couldn't help it. No friend in her situation was going to deprive herself on my watch.

Meredith had periodic full-body scans to see if her treatment was working. Whenever the scan days loomed, Meredith fretted, projected, and worried. Hope made her feel too vulnerable. The day before one of these scans, one she had a bad feeling about, she gifted me a pink quartz rock shaped like a heart. After the scans, her mood faltered as she imagined the worst. Fatigue and discouragement thinned her patience with herself and others. To me, her foul moods, which occasioned snarky remarks and tirades against customer service reps and blowhards at recovery meetings, made her seem more human. More like me.

Honestly, I loved it.

"I'm so fucking angry," Meredith screamed into the phone one afternoon. My habit was to pick up her calls on the first ring — everyone else's could go to voice mail. "I can't take it." I heard her fists pounding on the steering wheel.

"I'm here. Get it out. Rage on. Maybe pull over to be safe."

She screamed and cried for a few minutes. A few deep, jagged breaths later, she explained that she'd spent hours arranging for her doctor's office to transfer her files to a new clinician whose team had better outcomes than Meredith's current medical team.

"I drove to the first office downtown. Paid for parking. Had to wait for twenty minutes. The nurse was rude to me, even though I called ahead. Then I had to drive across town in terrible traffic to the new office and do it all over again." Meredith sobbed again. Deep sobs. Sobs I'd been expecting for months. I breathed and let her cry. One of my coworkers stuck his head in my office, and I waved him off. *Not now.*

She caught her breath and continued. "I did all that, and the second office just called. There're records missing. I have to do it all over again tomorrow! Mother-fucker!" Her voice dissolved into more sobs.

I could tell from the noises she was making that she was crying with her mouth open. Wailing. Animal sounds. I gripped the side of my desk and took deep breaths as I listened. The sound was raw and haunting. I'd never heard anything like it. I sat still and focused on my own breathing. *In and out. In and out.*

"I yelled, Christie. I yelled at the nurse. I was awful. I really was."

"It's okay. You can make amends to her. I'm sure she sees this all the time. She knows the errand you were on. She knows the stakes."

"God, she was such a bitch."

"Do you want me go with you tomorrow?"

I would have to move around an oral argument with a court in Indiana, but I would do it.

"No. I'll figure something out. You have to work. I'll feel worse making you miss work."

"I can come."

"I know."

"Can I send you dinner so you can relax tonight?"

"Sushi sounds good."

"Text me what you and Gage would like. I'll have it delivered around six."

We paused. I shook my head. Had I rushed us to sushi dinner when she really needed to stay with her grief and rage? I didn't want her to think I couldn't handle the depth of her emotion.

"Mere, it sounds really hard." I teared up. If I had to spend two days shuttling records between oncology practices, dealing with traffic, parking, and grumpy nurses while sick, I would absolutely lose my fucking marbles — and I'd scream until my voice box burst into flames.

"This isn't who I am. Yelling at nurses? I don't want to go out this way. What's happening?"

"You're tired and frustrated, and you're sick. It's understandable. You deserve to get these feelings out, and it's going to be messy. Kind of like you're always telling me that I'm probably always going to be messy."

"But for you, it's living and healing that's

messy. For me, it's dying."

I wanted to push that thought away. *You're not dying, stop that.* But how violent and disrespectful, how selfish and inaccurate. By pure grace, I kept my mouth shut.

Meredith sighed. "Maybe it's all messy. Living, dying, all of it. Mess, mess, mess."

"I'm here for your mess."

"I know."

A few days later, the new specialist recommended a regimen of treatment at the University of Chicago, one hundred blocks away from Meredith's house.

"When does it start?" I asked. We stood together on the sidewalk after a meeting.

She shook her head. "It's too far."

"Too far? What do you mean?"

"Too far to drive back and forth every day. It's disruptive. It doesn't feel right." She folded her hands, signaling the discussion was over.

"Meredith, this is life or death."

"They don't know if it'll work."

"What'd Gage say?"

"He said it's up to me. It's my body. I'm the one who has to drive there every day."

My shoulders tensed. Why wouldn't Gage insist she do the treatment?

"Have you made up your mind?"

"Yes. I'm staying at St. Francis."

I pressed my lips together. This defeatist discussion about mileage and inconvenience made me want to shake Meredith's shoulders. Her decision to continue with her treatment at a podunk regional hospital with zero cutting-edge ideas about how to keep her alive smelled like suicide. I could accept her decision to buy a cheaper hat or drive out of her way to save a few bucks on groceries, but I could not accept this. Why was she giving up? How could I call myself a friend and let her deprive herself of the best treatment possible?

"Isn't part of the reason we live in Chicago so that we can take advantage of the amenities like the University of Chicago hospital? There are options — like you could rent a place near the hospital during your treatments —"

"Then Gage can't get to work easily. It's not all about me."

"Um, yes, it is."

Meredith cocked her head and pursed her lips. There was a line between us, and I'd stepped over it. And refused to turn back.

"Your friends could drive you," I said. "We can set up one of those Google docs —" My voice rose over our heads and floated to the top of the school building behind us.

"I know you're trying to help —"

"What about Mayo? Or MD Anderson? Or Sloan Kettering? Now might be the time —"

"I'm already under a lot of pressure —"

"I'll call them up. We can road trip —"

"This is not what I need."

"Minneapolis is a day trip, and I have friends in Houston who could tell us where to stay —"

"Stop. Please."

I pressed my lips together hard. Yes, I was pushing, pressing, insisting. I knew people who'd been saved by finding the right specialist at a fancy institution. The University of Chicago cured the stage IV tongue cancer of famous Chicago chef Grant Achatz. My neighbor commuted from Chicago to MD Anderson for a liver condition, and his numbers were looking good. The solutions, I believed, were out there for the tenacious, the bold, the willing. I wanted to see that in Meredith. Where was her will to live?

But she'd shown me her *no* — arms crossed, head shaking, lips pressed together. She wanted to do this her way, and now it was time for me to let go.

I nodded my head but didn't speak because of the angry tears I knew would fall. I was angry at Meredith for not insisting on the best treatment. And I hated how I felt. Impotent. Out of ideas. Ashamed. I stood there, nodding my head up and down, up and down.

She pulled her arms around her chest as if giving herself a hug. "I have to go."

I stepped forward to hug her goodbye, but she turned and crossed the street without looking back.

As she disappeared into the rest of her weekend, I knew two things: that I fucked up this conversation and that I was right about the University of Chicago.

At my computer that afternoon, I looked up the world-famous institutions I believed could save her and jotted down some notes to text her later. Maybe there was no one else in her life saying these things to her. Her mom had passed away, and her relationship with her sisters was distant. I couldn't give up just because she was uncomfortable leaving her neighborhood for treatment. A good enough friend would keep trying.

34

A week went by, and Meredith and I didn't text or call each other. We had no coffee dates on the books. The distance yawned between us. I picked up the phone to text her several times a day, but stopped. When I thought of her, my body warmed from the hostility and hurt feelings that I wasn't ready to address. Each time I balked, I told myself, *Tomorrow's better; I'll text her then.* Or *I don't want to bother her.* Every day I hoped she would text, but she didn't.

"Can I ask you a question about cancer treatment?" I said to a woman at a water fountain on the lakefront path. I'd joined some neighbors for a run at dawn, and one of them was a physician at the University of Chicago.

"Sure."

We started running again, south on the path behind McCormick Place. A line of ducks walked toward the water that was a deep untroubled blue on this late fall morning.

"My friend has metastasized breast cancer, and she's getting treated at St. Francis on the North Side." I paused to scoff at the regional hospital that hadn't won any awards that I knew of and never appeared in the local news for saving a celebrity's life. "I want her to go to the University of Chicago so she can have the best treatment."

The doctor whose run I'd just hijacked listened carefully and asked a few questions, some of which I couldn't answer, since I didn't know the particulars of Meredith's condition. But all that mattered was getting treatment at the best hospital in the city, right? I asked this U of C physician's opinion because I was sure she'd confirm my theory: the best was the best, and Meredith deserved the best.

"You know," the doctor said, her blond ponytail swishing back and forth in the shadows we cast on the trail in front of us. "There are studies that show that patients who trust their caregivers and are comfortable in their surroundings have better outcomes."

"Better outcomes?"

She glanced at me, like I should know

what she meant. "They live longer, and the quality of their lives is better."

I swallowed hard and pinned my gaze to our shadows on the pavement.

"You think I shouldn't push her to the U of C?" I trusted this doctor with the authoritative tone and the impressive cardio output. Before I cornered her, I'd heard her say that she'd worked two overnights during the week — she was heartier and smarter than I was. I would do what she said, but I had to make her understand who Meredith was and why she needed top-notch treatment. This doctor didn't know Meredith or how she deprived herself out of habit — the Salvation Army, the never-realized trip to Italy, the insistence on tap water. "I can't tell if she truly trusts the team at St. Francis or if she's denying herself the premier treatment at the U of C because she doesn't believe she deserves it."

"If I had a friend with that diagnosis," the doctor said, "I would defer to her choices. It's hard to be on the sidelines, but you have to respect her decision. If she doesn't want to drive a hundred blocks every day for treatment that *might* extend her life, then that's a valid choice. You never know. At the U of C, she might feel like a test case or 'just a number,' and that experience might hasten her decline. Put it this way, do you want your friends telling you how to spend your last days?"

Last days? The doctor's words shook the walls of my denial.

Meredith's life was coming to an end, and I'd done this all wrong. Why did I think I knew what was best for Meredith? I was a lawyer, not a doctor. I shook my head and watched my shadow self on the pavement finally absorb the friendship lesson I'd ignored. Meredith didn't owe me the treatment I wanted her to have. I had no idea what honoring her own life meant to her. I needed to listen, to support, to get out of the way.

Dear Meredith,

I'm so sorry I pushed the treatment I wanted you to have on you. It's just that those places might have exactly the treatment that you need, and I really want you to have what you need. I want that more than anything. Please know that I'm not trying to control you.

Dear Meredith,

I respect your choices and support whatever you decide. I did a little research on the program at Vanderbilt, and thought it might be useful to check out. Would you be interested if I set up a call?

Dear Meredith,

I'm sorry for putting pressure on you. I really want to do this right. It feels like the right thing to tell you that I'm willing to fly anywhere on Earth to find you a doctor who understands what's happening to you and has a solution. You tell me all the time to pray to accept abundance and to trust the universe and my Higher Power. Is it possible that your Higher Power put me in your life to help you find treatment?

I tore up every handwritten apology letter I started as soon as I reread it. I couldn't stop myself from imposing my vision of her treatment. It was time to let go, but somehow, I couldn't get all the way there.

Two weeks after Meredith crossed the street to get away from me and my bullying, I flew to Austin with my family for Thanksgiving. Meredith was on my mind constantly. *Thinking of you! Happy Thanksgiving!* I texted Meredith on Thanksgiving Day. The next day I typed: *I love and miss you.* Meredith "liked" both of them but didn't type a response. I prayed to let her have all the space she needed. Every time I thought of her, I sent her love and blessings for good health and joy. At least once a day, I imagined her pouring her heart out to Anna or sending long, intimate texts to some other, closer friend — someone who loved her better than I did. I reminded myself that it was none of my business who Meredith turned to and that if I really loved her, which I did, then I had to let her lean on whomever she wanted.

My sole job, I told myself, was to keep my feet planted in the friendship no matter how painful, scared, or jealous I felt. I would not fuck this up further by withdrawing or finding an excuse to back away.

Emily, who always offered sage counsel, reminded me, "Meredith is in a place that none of us can imagine. She might need space from every single person. Her silence may have nothing to do with you at all."

The day after Thanksgiving, I ran a few miles along Lake Austin and through the hip South Congress area, where bearded men and women in platform shoes lined up for cold brew and breakfast tacos. I stopped to take a picture of a Willie Nelson mural with my phone. When I looked at the image later, I saw that I'd also captured a street sign in the background. The cross street: "Meredith Street." I sent her the picture with a smiley face emoji.

She wrote back right way. *I love and miss you, Sweetie. See you when you get home.*

I cried to see a typed message from her — right there on the sidewalk, bawling my eyes out, spinning in a circle as I covered my face with my hands. *She still loves me! She's okay! We're okay! She misses me!*

The next time we went to coffee together, I slid a note across the table.

Dear Meredith,
  I have your back. Always.

Love,
Christie

She held my hand across the table, and I did the holiest thing of all: I shut the fuck up.

35

A few months later, Meredith pulled a small black velvet bag out of her purse after a meeting. She tugged on the yellow cord that cinched the top and pulled something out.

"Here," she said, offering me a second pink quartz rock shaped like a heart.

"What's this for?"

"Big scan tomorrow." So this was now her thing: giving out these rocks on the eve of a scary scan. "I'm worried about my liver." She pressed on her abdomen with both hands and grimaced. "I can feel it." She pointed at the rock in my hand. "I'm giving these to all my friends. Carry it tomorrow and think good thoughts for me."

Hanging from Meredith's shoulder was her giant tote bag full of textbooks, school papers, notebooks, a daily meditation book. The tote bag of a woman with plans for the future. Graduation was months away, and she planned to be there, even though the trek to school on the train sapped more energy every day. I squeezed the rock.

"You'll never believe this," she said as we walked toward her car. "I got a call from Celia Rodin offering me a full-time job when I graduate. She wants me to be the spiritual counselor at the treatment center she runs."

"What?" I yelped and stopped on the sidewalk to face her. Dr. Rodin and her team specialized in treating eating disorders, addictions, mood disorders, and trauma. This job satisfied Meredith's deepest professional and spiritual goal — it was the point of all her overnight shifts, all the papers she wrote on addiction and codependence, all the schlepping to Loyola for night classes and group projects with students one-third her age. This was it. A dream realized.

"Your dream job waiting for when you graduate?" I raised my hand for her to high-five me, and she hit the bull's-eye of my palm pretty hard, considering her scrawny arms and the way the chemo forced her into daily, three-hour naps. She beamed, I beamed. No one deserved a dream job more than Meredith.

"It's exactly what I always wanted."

"How many people can say that?" I'd never said that; I couldn't even visualize a dream job unless it was sitting in a comfy chair reading books all day for six figures and full benefits, including dental. I felt like bursting into happy tears; I couldn't think of a time when I'd been so happy for a friend. "Goddamn, you did it. I fucking love this news!" I pumped my fist in the air; Meredith stood still.

"It's like actors who say it's enough to be nominated for an Oscar. I feel that. It was nice to be asked."

"You're not taking it?" A deep sadness clouded my elation.

Meredith shook her head, and I realized my mistake. "No, honey." She tapped my fist that held the rock she'd just given me.

Could she do it even for a few weeks? Could she work one day a week for as long as she could? What if the scan offered good news — great news, even? What if the liver issue was just indigestion from those Tupperwares of quinoa? What if the job brought her so much joy that it forestalled the cellular process that had gone so wrong in her body? What if she said yes and waited to see what happened?

We stood in silence, both of us watching the tears form in the other's eyes.

"I so wish you could take that job, Mere."

"Me, too."

"Do you hate me for holding on to hope?" I put the rock in my pocket and held up my hands to the sky, painting her my vision. "I can see you, walking in that treatment center touching the lives of those suffering people — the anorexics who are scared to eat, the bingers who can't stop. They all want to spend time with you — they form lines outside your office for the chance to talk to you — and beg to have your email when they get discharged. They'll send you Christmas cards for years to come, thanking you for helping them gather the broken pieces of themselves and reassemble them into a useful, sane life. They'll name their babies *Meredith,* after the counselor who helped them so much." I put my hands down. "That's the vision I had when you told me about the job. I hope it's not insensitive for me to say all that."

"I love you for sharing that with me." She put her arm around me and leaned in close. "Do you hate me for abandoning you?"

"Honestly, a little bit." She squeezed my shoulder.

"Do you hate me for being honest," I asked.

"Not one bit."

That day she gave me the rock wasn't the same day she slid a box across the table, one filled with a string of pearls. But in my memory she handed me the rock, told me about the job, and then gifted me the jewelry box all at once.

"I didn't realize it was time for this," I said, when she handed me the pearls. I let them hang from my fingers. "Thank you."

"I feel lucky. Most people don't know how they're going to die. I do."

I wrapped the strand around my fingers and my wrist the same way I used to hold my rosary as a little girl. A few months earlier, she'd given me a gold ring studded with pearls, and I'd gasped to see something I was so used to seeing on her slender fingers on mine. I'd worn it once to a coffee date, and she smiled when she noticed it.

"I feel a little nauseated," I blurted out. The queasy feeling in my stomach came on suddenly, and I hadn't connected it to the jewelry or the rock or the job.

"That's sadness, sweetie. You feel sad."

I nodded and swallowed hard.

"I definitely feel sad." And afraid. Afraid of what was about to happen to Meredith's body, and then her mind and her spirit. I was less afraid of how I would do as a friend — I hit my goal of being a good enough friend these days — but I wondered if I could keep it up.

343

As if reading my mind, she said, "You don't have to do it perfectly. Just show up."

"They're growing. The tumors," Meredith told me over the phone when she got her latest scan results.

"Oh, Mere. I wanted you to get better news."

"Deep down, I knew."

The last time I'd seen her, she kept laying her hand on her side, saying she was worried about her liver. I saw the terror in her eyes and the wince of pain when she pressed her hand into her flesh. I'd hoped she was wrong. But over the past few months, I'd also begun to hear something different in her voice — a thinning around the edges when she talked about the future.

Now I understood I was hearing her readiness to let go.

"What comes next?" I asked.

"Hospice."

The word made me grind my teeth. It seemed premature and caught me by surprise. I thought hospice meant you could no longer walk, make dinner, hold a conversation. Meredith could still do all of those most days. But she was done submitting her body to the dwindling hope offered by one more round of treatment. No more *maybe* or *slim chance* or *possibility*. Going forward, she'd get medical care only to ease her pain, not to prolong her life.

Neither of us cried, though we sat in the vast silence of this new stage. One last time, I offered to bring over a meal.

"No, honey. I can't —"

"I know."

"One good thing is that I never have to step foot in another hospital ever again. You have no idea how happy that makes me. I want to snuggle with the cats and the dog, and look at Lake Michigan and the blue sky from my window. I want to be home. I belong at home."

I hated that we'd arrived at the hospice stage, but I heard acceptance in her voice and couldn't help but celebrate her liberation from having to work so tirelessly to save her own life.

On Mother's Day, my kids woke me up with snuggles and homemade cards. Zara handed me a water bottle, and then she and Elias shooed me to the gym for my favorite class. Afterward, full of endorphins and still humming the Lady Gaga tune that played during cooldown, I drove home with the windows open. Chicago turns slowly to spring, but on this May morning the sun sat high and proud, saluting the city from a sea-blue sky. John sent a text saying that the kids were preparing something, *so take your time.*

I passed our street and did a loop around the block. I would have done a second loop in the other direction, but I had to pee.

"Surprise," the kids yelled when I walked in the door. They handed me a piece of cream-colored cardstock with the word *Menu* emblazoned across it. Their hand-made menu consisted not simply of food but also activities. I could pair a fruit smoothie with a bike ride or pick grilled cheese and a movie. Elias hopped from one foot to the other, excited to watch my reaction.

"A movie would be so fun," I said. The year before we'd seen the RBG documentary on Mother's Day, and this year I wanted to see *Amazing Grace,* the film about Aretha Franklin. "But I do love a bike ride."

I peeled off my coat and sat down at the living room table with the kids to map out the day. My phone buzzed in my pocket, but I silenced it without looking at it. It rang again right away. I slipped it out of my pocket and saw it was Meredith. I held the phone up so John could see it.

"Answer," he said with a serious face.

"The kids and I will look up movie times."

"Hey, Mere," I said, ducking up the stairs. "What's up?"

I heard sobbing. Deep wracking sobs.

"I'm here," I said. "Breathe and cry. Talk when you can."

"I'm sorry," she got the words out, but then her crying smothered what came next.

"I'm —

"ruining —"

"your —"

"Mother's Day."

"Don't worry about that. What do you need?"

"I'm at Northwestern Hospital. I fell and shattered my elbow last night. I had to revoke hospice to get the ambulance to pick me up and bring me to the hospital."

"You fell?"

"It was the middle of the night. I thought I could still walk from the bedroom to the bathroom." She broke down and sobbed. "But I didn't make it."

"Meredith!"

"Can you come?"

"Yes."

John had joined me on the edge of our bed. He nodded. Of course I would go to her. When I got off the phone, I worried about the kids. We were supposed to spend the whole day together. I didn't want to let them down. But Meredith's voice. It sounded like an emergency. I'd told her I would come.

"Tell the kids the truth," John said. "That Meredith is very sick, and she asked you to come. It's an emergency. It's also a privilege. We can redo Mother's Day next weekend."

When I found Meredith's room down a bright white but eerily quiet hallway, there was a huge poster board hung on the door with thick white masking tape. The message scrawled on it looked like a child's handwriting. *DO NOT ENTER without first checking into the nurse's station. NO EXCEPTIONS.* The language sounded ominous, but the fourth-grade level handwriting made it seem like a joke. I walked around the corner to the nurse's station.

"I'm here to see Meredith in room 3510," I said to the kind woman in blue scrubs, her blond hair piled on her head.

"Are you Christie?"

"Yes," I said slowly. How did she know?

"You're the only one we're allowed to let in. She doesn't want to see anyone else."

"Glad I made the cut."

I returned to Meredith's room and swung the door open. Meredith sat in her bed, a

348

white plaster cast encasing her elbow and a dazed look clouding her features.

"Come in," she said.

I gestured at the door. "Friendly sign."

"I'm sick of people. I only want to see you and Gage."

I smiled, happy for her orneriness, the pulse of her life. Also flattered as hell to be one of the people on her two-person list. She patted the side of the bed. I walked over and sat next to her. She looked exactly as frail and hollowed out as someone who would be gone in ten weeks, though we didn't know that then. Her body swam in her hospital gown, and the patches of hair on her head were sparse. She asked me about my kids and how I was spending my Mother's Day.

"We're going to the movies later."

"I'm sorry I interrupted —"

"Nope. Don't do that." I looked at the machine she was hooked up to. "Are you in pain?"

"I'm okay."

"I'll get you more morphine if you want it." I had no idea how to do that, but it seemed like the right offer to make.

She shook her head. "I'm comfortable enough."

I wanted to ask her, *Why me?* Of all her

friends, the dozens of women who sat next to her during thousands of twelve-step meetings, why did she save me this seat, the one by her bed? I had that feeling I had when she handed me the scarves, the feeling that one of us — me — had misjudged the intimacy level between us. Either I was mistaken to be surprised by my front-row seat, or she'd mistakenly offered it to me. Meredith had friends she'd known for decades, and of course Anna and Emily wore those blue bridesmaid's dresses at her wedding. But how was it me sitting here now?

"Last night after I got settled here, I had a long hard cry. I let myself really understand what's happening, like way down all the way through me. I'm really leaving this world. So much of this whole experience of sickness has seemed like a movie, like a terrible thing happening to someone else. But now I know it's me. It's happening to me. I felt so scared and so sad. I've never felt anything like it."

"I wish you would have called when you were crying," I whispered.

"There are some parts of dying that no one can do with me or for me. I had to do it alone. This deep knowing that I'm going away is something I had to arrive at on my own. I called when I needed you."

"Thank you for calling."

She talked some more about the long dark night — how she fell, how the hospital didn't want to send an ambulance because she was a hospice patient, how the doctors ultimately decided against surgery for her arm, how she fully faced her death — I thought she would tell me she was "totally at peace" and "ready to go," like they do in the movies, but she didn't. She was done fighting, but she didn't want to go.

At one point, she ran her hand through the imaginary hair on her head, just like she used to do. She paused, hand on her naked scalp. "Did you see that?" she asked. "I forgot I have no hair!"

"I was mesmerized by the gesture —"

"Isn't it amazing? All of this? It's amazing. Me and you, sitting here, on Mother's Day. You have two kids, and you're sitting here with me? We're what we told ourselves we could never be: friends. Even though it's hard, even through an unwelcome transition."

"I learn a lot from you."

She grabbed both my hands. "We learn from each other, remember."

She leaned forward and hugged me, and I held on. She would have to be the one to let go first. It wasn't going to be me. We were crying and laughing. I loved her and I felt so afraid, and part of me wanted to make this the end of the story. I didn't know this would be one of our last sweet, lucid moments.

A nurse knocked on the door, and we broke our embrace at the same time. It was the same nurse I met at the station when I first arrived. She had a smile like a fresh orange slice and the unalloyed beauty of someone in her twenties who takes care of herself.

"Are you comfortable? Do you need anything?" she asked Meredith after checking something on the monitor by the bed.

"I'm okay. But let me ask you a question." Meredith lowered her voice, like she was initiating a conspiracy. "What is your skincare routine? You're glowing."

The nurse blushed and laughed. "Noxzema."

"Ha!" Meredith said. "Enjoy your youth."

I walked over to the window and looked up at the now-cloudy sky. I spied a sliver of Lake Michigan through the Streeterville high-rises lining the Chicago River. A cluster of people swarmed around the entrance to a popular brunch spot, all dressed up for Mother's Day.

When the nurse was gone, Meredith asked for news of the outside world. I told her about the kids' menu for the day and the playlist at the gym. In my memory, as I sat on the edge of her bed with my coat still on, my legs dangling off the side, I told her I'd been writing about her, though sometimes I remember having the conversation over the phone as I walked under the train tracks at 59th Street. We likely had two conversations. Maybe more, if you count all the snippets, passing comments, and outloud wishes folded into the layers of the big conversations. By the time I sat on her hospital bed, I'd already published an essay about her illness and our friendship, but I had more to say.

"I keep writing about you. About our friendship and what it means to me."

Meredith's eyes grew wide, curious. A little "ah" escaped from her lips. "Are you making me sound smart? You promised."

I hadn't told her — or anyone — that over the fall, I'd handwritten a novel in a black marble-covered notebook about a sick woman whose friends rent a beach house on the coast of Oregon, pool all of their prescription drugs, and help her die on her own terms. I had a cursory understanding of Oregon's Death with Dignity Act, a law that allowed terminally ill Oregon residents to use prescriptions from their physicians for a self-administered lethal dose of medication. In this novel, none of the fictitious women — not a doctor among them — knew what they were doing, but they wanted to grant their friend's wish to die surrounded by loving witnesses and her three dogs. When fictional "Meredith" died after swallowing the hodgepodge of pills, her friends took her dogs and returned to their suburban lives transformed by the experience.

"Last fall, I wrote a novel about a sick woman and her friends."

Meredith's eyes lit up. "A whole novel?" Then her face fell. "Why didn't you tell me?"

I shrugged, suddenly feeling guilty about not telling her. "I wasn't sure you would approve of my using your health crisis as a writing prompt. I wrote it by hand in a notebook, so it's messy. No one has seen a single word. The main character's great loves are her three dogs."

"Good girl. What kind of dogs?"

"Rescue mutts."

"Relatable. That's good. Did I survive?"

"Of course," I lied, and when I saw Meredith's relief, I knew it was okay to tell this lie; you're allowed to tell your dying friend that in the terrible novel you wrote about her illness, she survived and went on to direct a counseling program for women with eating disorders and lived well into her nineties.

"You should keep writing," she said, and I wasn't sure if she meant writing in general or about her specifically.

"I will."

She gazed out the window, and I looked at the monitor with its inscrutable numbers and flashing line graphs. I could fill the silence with all kinds of chatter, inquiries, and banal observations of hospital life, but I kept it holy and let it be quiet between us.

"Sometimes," Meredith said in a quiet voice, "I feel like you're my daughter; sometimes you're my sister; and sometimes you're my friend."

I knew what she meant. There were times, before she got sick, when she felt like my golden sister with her tiny thighs and her luscious hair. Sometimes she felt like a mother — when she patted my head and squeezed my arm. Sometimes she was all twelve-step sponsor, reminding me to *feel* and to *take inventory* and *go to meetings*. When she got sicker and frailer, I felt like she was the kid and I was her mother, gently reminding her to ask for help and go easy on herself. All those roles jumbled up and shifted, sometimes within a single conversation. Sometimes it felt like whiplash, but most of the time it was comforting. I had that with John, too — sometimes he moved from husband to best friend to father to brother to co-parent to roommate to accountant — all in one conversation about who should handle dinner before Parent Night at school. I'd learned to accept that intimacy with other people meant letting them out of their boxes.

"Did I really survive in your novel?"

Damn. I couldn't look at her as I said, "Not exactly."

"I knew it. You're a bad liar." She laughed.

"I'm sorry I lied. I was just working through what this all means."

"It's okay as long as you keep writing. Always write about the mess."

"I think what you're telling me is to write what I know."

36

I texted her every day, and she answered every third or fourth text. I blathered on about a flock of birds I saw flying in the shape of an arrow over the lake; the new band I'd discovered, the Avett Brothers; and my son's progress as a Little League pitcher. I sent her YouTube clips of the song "For Good" from *Wicked,* about two friends who changed each other's lives "for good" and "for the better." Even through the morphine haze, surely she understood the message I was sending.

I wouldn't let go first.

She'd text heart emojis and *I love you,* which buoyed me; after reading her texts, I felt a little high, like it was cheating to be able to communicate with her still, even though she was fading quickly.

One morning, I woke up to an ominous email with the subject line "Meredith Update." It was from Anna to me and several others.

> Meredith is at home and her pain is controlled. Gage asked if Meredith's friends could come and visit her during the week when he is at work. Email him to set up a time if you are available.

In the email, Anna reported that she'd just returned from a visit with her. My typical rancor and jealousy at the thought of Anna having an inside track to Meredith's deathbed at home didn't arise when I read the email. Well, maybe I felt a tiny twinge — I noticed Anna's primary role — but didn't go up in flames over it. Mostly, I wanted Meredith to be comfortable and comforted, and I wanted to participate in any way I could.

Finally, I discovered something stronger than my jealousy: death. Meredith was leaving, and all I wanted was to be one of the women helping usher her to the other side.

I pictured myself, along with Anna and all of Meredith's other friends, as ancient women in a village, working to help one of our own face the end of her life. We were there to form a circle around her, and in a circle there is no hierarchy. There could be no jockeying for the top spot — we were shoulder to shoulder, laying hands on Meredith.

> Thank you for the update. I'll email Gage right away to schedule a visit.

In my last visit with Meredith, she recognized me, though she drifted in and out of consciousness. She ate a slice of peach and a tiny bite of bread with a daub of Irish butter. She started a story about someone who'd come to visit her, but trailed off. When she couldn't follow her thoughts, she grew frustrated, her face twisting into a scowl. It appeared that despite her heavy medication, she retained the ability to beat herself up for not telling a coherent story. I wanted to beg her not to attempt anything as taxing as storytelling, but that seemed crueler than her frustration. I'd come to witness, not to control.

Her beloved cat wove between my legs as I sat across from Meredith, who was propped up on a cushioned window seat. Behind her, cars zipped down Lake Shore Drive as it curved between Belmont and Diversey.

I took in her diminished body, her addled mind, and I felt afraid. The urge to flee pressed against my urge to show up for her. Side by side. But I stayed in my chair and kept my eyes on Meredith's face. I'd read stories about other people's "last visits," and assumed I would look into her eyes and understand that she was already gone. But she was still there. Yes, the narcotic medication significantly altered her consciousness, but in quick flashes, I caught glimpses of her, the friend I knew so well.

"Your son. The baseball. Did he win?" she asked in a voice barely above a whisper.

"They won eight to five. Big victory."

Days away from the biggest transition of her life, and she asked me about my eight-year-old's Little League game.

Then she lapsed into a garbled speech I couldn't understand. Something about the Cubs and her therapist. I tried to assemble the words she tossed out but couldn't make meaning. Then, as soon as I surrendered any hope of cogent communication, she raised her voice and said, "I heard from my sisters." She raised her eyebrows, like, *Can you believe them?*

"What did they say?"

Before she could answer, she seemed to forget the topic and drift away.

When it was time to go, I helped her into her bed and sat on the edge, as I had in the hospital. She pointed at a painting on her wall — an impressionist image of a sheep standing in a dark field with white clouds overhead.

"I love that painting," she said, and then something that sounded like "So beautiful. Haunting."

I'd never done any hard drugs, but I was positive I'd never come up with "beautiful" and "haunting" if I was blitzed on painkillers.

She was still here.

I stalled on the goodbye by studying the small painting. Later, at the memorial service, Gage would offer it to me, and I discovered that it was actually one of Emily's encaustic paintings, made from colored hot wax. It now sits on my desk next to my computer monitor, reminding me of both Emily and Meredith — proof that friendship confers gifts that double back and land in different hands, widening the circle in ways you can't expect.

"Mere-Mere, I gotta go," I said. I let my tears fall as I wrapped my arms around her. "I promise that I'll check up on Gage. We have his back."

Into my ear, as clear and stern as she'd ever sounded, Meredith said, "You better."

She whimpered a little, and I cried.

When I released her, I saw that she'd fallen asleep. I laid her head back on her pillow and slipped out of the room.

On my way home, as I steered the car onto Lake Shore Drive, my hands and legs trembled. I drummed my fingers on the steering wheel. I fidgeted with the radio station every few minutes. I hit the brake with my right foot at the last second before hitting the bumper of the car in front of me. The anxiety was a blockade. When I surrendered it, sadness would rush in. I wasn't ready. I stayed in my head.

Had I done enough?
Should I have stayed longer?
Should I go back tomorrow?
Should I send Gage some food?
Is it too soon for flowers?
Did I say the right things?
When is the sadness coming?
What will it feel like?
How long will it last?
Why can't I feel anything except anxiety?
Is she okay?
Is she scared?
Is she in pain?
Does she know how loved she is?
Did I tell her I love her?
Do I have the courage to grieve?
How can I honor her?

362

Was I a good enough friend to her all the way to the end?

John's work took him to D.C. the next day, so while I made dinner I let the kids watch a movie about a dolphin that lost its tail. The summer heat had drenched us all, and I was counting the minutes until I could jump in the shower and wash the grime off.

On the counter next to the pasta box my phone buzzed. Anna. I stared at the phone and watched it hum. *No, Anna, I'm not answering.* I gathered up the kitchen trash and walked outside and into our backyard, ostensibly to throw the bag into the bin by the garage, but I stood in the grass holding the bag as if I'd forgotten where to go. There was only one reason that Anna would call me.

I set the bag at my feet and texted Max, from my therapy group, who was well acquainted with my feelings about Anna and Meredith.

Anna just called me and didn't leave a message. I can't do it.

You can't what?

She's calling about Meredith. Didn't leave a voice mail.

If she wants to tell you that Meredith died, maybe you should let her. Put your craziness

363

about Anna aside for tonight, and call her back.

I'm scared.

Call her.

I will.

Now.

"Hey, Anna. I saw you called." Throat tight, the register of my voice sounded weirdly low. I'd come in from the backyard and sat on the bench in our darkened entryway. The last fragments of a late-July sunset flickered behind our neighbor's elm tree.

"I'm calling about Meredith."

"I know," I whispered.

"She died a few hours ago."

The thickness from my voice spread to my throat, chest, and stomach. Every part of me thick and heavy, ready to rain.

"Thank you for calling. Are you okay?" My chest released, and a sob escaped, quiet as a thief. I leaned over to see if my kids heard me, but the dolphin was learning to swim so they paid me no mind.

"I don't know."

"I feel so sad."

"Me, too."

"And weird, too. I suddenly feel exhausted, like I could lie down and fall instantly asleep."

"I know that feeling."

"And I'm glad it's over." I asked about Gage and what he needed, and whether she wanted help calling people.

"I think he's all set for now. I'm good, too. It helps to connect with other people who miss her."

"Will there be a memorial service?"

"Maybe in the fall."

The fall? It was July 31, and I wanted company in my new grief. I wanted to gather with Anna, Gage, and all the other people. We should hold each other up; we should grieve together. But it wasn't my decision. I slumped against the wall, dreading the loneliness of the next few hours, the upcoming days. The next time I fought with a friend or heard a Cher song.

"I've never done this before, lost a friend like this," I said, resting my head against the hard plaster wall.

"Me neither."

"Are we doing what we're supposed to do? I feel twitchy with anxiety, like I'm not doing this right."

"I think there is nothing to do now except to feel."

When I got off the phone, I ran upstairs to the bathroom to cry a little more before serving pasta to the kids. They knew Meredith was sick, but it felt unfair to tell them when I wasn't ready to support them. I'd tell them in the morning. Or when John returned. All I could offer right now was spaghetti and a bedtime story.

37

The next few days blurred by. The pink rock always in my palm. Her gold-and-pearl ring on my finger. Phone calls with Emily and Jolie. A longing to keep my body close to the bodies of my children and John. An email to Gage offering to bring dinner, to help in any way. Cliché moments of slippage when I thought about texting Meredith, and then remembered. I told my kids in a traffic jam after a dinner out, and Zara and I cried all the way home as John and Elias silently looked on.

The days rolled by. We took a family vacation to Yellowstone National Park. I did what grieving people do: carried on in my life with a gnawing, pervasive sense of something missing, of having a wound no one else could see.

By mid-August, Gage requested help organizing a memorial service, and we scheduled the first planning meeting for a couple of weeks later. The committee consisted of Meredith's close friend Daniel, Anna, me, and Bebe, of the infamous wedding fudge.

"We need three speakers. So far, it's just me. Who else should we ask?" Daniel began.

Silence.

I thought Anna might volunteer. She was a perfect choice for so many reasons: she'd known Meredith the longest, and she'd write a beautiful tribute to deliver in her soothing voice that would have everyone laughing and sobbing at once. But she, like me, remained silent.

I wanted to volunteer, but I felt afraid to hog the mic or presume I deserved it. I squeezed the pink rock in my hand and said nothing.

"Okay," Daniel said. "Let's ask around and see if anyone wants to do it. Email us if you get a taker."

Not until I got off the call did I realize my mistake. The truth was that I wanted to speak at Meredith's service, but held back because I wasn't sure I was worthy. Yet I could also hear Meredith's voice chiding me, lovingly, for not stepping up. *Is that your codependence or low self-esteem, honey? Either way, it's not a good look.* She was the one who taught me that unworthiness is a lie we tell ourselves.

Hi, everyone, I would like to volunteer to be one of the speakers, I wrote to the committee.

Great! Daniel, Anna, and Bebe wrote back. Hard to read any hostility or resentment in their responses. No hints that I didn't deserve the honor.

We divided the other tasks among us: Anna would search for a venue. Bebe and I would design the program. Daniel would line up music and keep Gage in the loop.

When Bebe and I met to discuss the programs, she confessed, "I'm not good at computer stuff. Could you handle that?"

"Sure." Bebe was in her seventies and could hardly be faulted for not knowing how to whip out a program of events on her outdated desktop computer. But as soon as she handed the whole task to me, I felt engulfed in anger. I hung up the phone and then sobbed into my hands.

"What happened?" John appeared in the doorway of my home office.

"I can't make a program! I don't know how! Bebe said she'd help, but she handed it all over to me."

John gathered me into a hug. "I'll help you. We'll do it together."

I kept crying. "And the fudge!" I said into

John's shirt.

"What fudge?"

"Bebe brought that awful fudge to Meredith's wedding."

"You're crying about that? Now?"

Yes, yes, I was. My grief wanted a narrative for the rage and sadness coursing through me. If I had to borrow Meredith's years' old resentment, I would. The sane part of me knew nothing I was feeling had anything to do with fudge or with Bebe.

I was sad.

I missed my friend.

The next day, I stood in the checkout line at Staples holding a box of cream-colored cardstock. My kids, dressed in their Halloween costumes even though it was only September, goofed off by the colored pens. I paid and then moved to the line for printing services so I could enlist Staples' professional help in making the programs John and I designed.

When it was my turn, I explained that I wanted eighty copies, and he showed me how he planned to cut them. When he handed me the completed programs a few minutes later, I let out a huge sigh of relief. Behind me, Elias called to Zara, "Check out this silver Sharpie!"

I have no idea why I burst again then. I thought my rage tears after the call with Bebe would have bought me a few days' reprieve from public crying.

Maybe it was the box of programs that reduced Meredith's life to a small picture and a list of songs and speakers.

Maybe it was the buildup from weeks of fighting the feelings that stalk you when you lose someone you love.

Maybe it was the reality that grief is messy and unpredictable and impossible to control.

"Ma'am, are you okay?" the Staples clerk asked when I started to cry at the counter as I looked at the programs stacked so neatly in the box.

I nodded but kept my head down. Kindly, he averted his eyes and led the next customer to the station farthest away from where I stood.

In the parish hall of a Lutheran church on the North Side of Chicago, a large framed picture of Meredith anchored smaller pictures of her as a kid, as a young woman in the fray at the Chicago Board of Trade, as a radiant bride leaning on her new husband's shoulder. Against the far wall, shards of rainbow light from a stained-glass window

371

bathed a smaller table, illuminating a tray of store-bought cookies, a coffee urn, and a teapot, giving the whole scene the feel of a twelve-step meeting. No accident, of course, since most of us knew Meredith from the recovery world. The hall slowly filled up with people who knew her as a steady, unwavering presence in their weekly meetings across Chicago.

I hugged and chatted with almost a dozen women — all recovery friends I'd known for nearly twenty years. Some of us hadn't seen each other all dressed up in our soft pashminas and shiny shoes since our weddings years before. We stood in a tight clump near the door, folding in new arrivals as they entered the room. *Good to see you! How's residency? I'm sorry to hear about your mother's illness.* In hushed tones we talked about who was watching our children so we could be here together and how Meredith would have enjoyed the soft lighting and robust turnout.

How strange to feel the buoyant joy of connection on such a sad occasion. I felt intense tenderness toward everyone, including myself, so tender it almost hurt.

"I feel vaguely fluish," I whispered to Jolie.

She wrapped her arm around my shoulders and nodded. "Grief involves the whole body." I laughed because Meredith would have said something similar.

When I shifted my weight from my left leg to my right, my aching muscles begged me to sit down. I longed for a couch, a blanket, and a dark, quiet room. I'd never experienced this combination of emotion before: grief for my lost friend, anxiety about public speaking, and overwhelming bursts of love for the women standing around me.

It's not that I wanted to be somewhere else; I was just scared.

"She probably wouldn't have wanted us to go to all this fuss for her, though," someone said, and we all laughed because it was true. I thought of all the clothes she never bought, those pale egg-and-quinoa breakfasts.

When the music started, I settled into a hard metal folding chair about eight rows from the front.

"Nervous?" John asked, pointing at the notes in my lap.

"Beyond."

A few rows ahead, Anna sat next to her husband. I studied her beachy waves and her slight shoulders. Damn, her buttery leather jacket was perfect funeral chic. As I inventoried her luminous hair and her tapered ankles, I also searched my body for the urge to scratch, tear, rend — but nothing surfaced. Anna was no longer a threat or an enemy. She was a fellow mother, a woman in recovery, someone grieving Meredith. If I let her, she could be a friend again. Her body housed a soul that loved Meredith as much as I did. Someday, I might want to sit next to her and share memories of our lost friend. Maybe someday we'd make more memories of our own. Her presence could no longer be reduced to a catalog of the ways she activated my envy: hair, physique, occupation, wealth. I still observed and coveted some of her attributes (those blasted beachy waves!), but I saw through all that to the woman with whom I cried when I heard the news that Meredith was gone.

I visualized one of those huddles that athletes make right before a game, where each player sticks a hand into the middle of the circle, and then they chant inspiring words, like "Go, team, go!" For so many years of my life, I'd had it wrong. The hand I offered friends often became a fist I used to fight with them, with myself, with bystanders I perceived as threats. I no longer wanted to walk through the world with clenched hands, scanning the horizon for conflict, envy, jealousy, scarcity, women with Halle Berry cheekbones and gifted children. I wanted to offer an open palm, ready to give and receive.

■ ■ ■ ■

PART III
WHAT IT'S LIKE
NOW

■ ■ ■ ■

Dear Meredith,

When the world shut down in March 2020, I kept thinking of you. What if you and Gage still lived in that high-rise building with all those vulnerable, aging people? What if you had to face the end all by yourself? I wouldn't have been able to stand outside your window to wave goodbye because you lived many floors up in a unit with no balcony. I cried every time I heard a story about people dying alone. I also cried because I missed you, and everything was surreal and quiet, lonely and terrifying. I had no idea what I was supposed to be doing at any point during the day. My kids had their laptops set up downstairs and attended school remotely from the basement. Zoom became a verb. Zara walked a mile in place in her bedroom during P.E. one afternoon, while on the other side of the wall I Zoomed into group therapy.

I'm telling you, it was batshit crazy all over the planet.

I worked in my office, John in the attic. We brought in a college student who was stranded when her study-abroad program was canceled. She lived with us, and literally overnight, all five of us spent every day in the house together. I struggled with boundaries every single hour of the day. For therapy and twelve-step meetings, I sat in the car with the windows up and the heat on full blast.

We weren't supposed to go outside other than for thirty minutes of exercise. Daily constitutionals. "You're not training for a marathon, just a brisk thirty minutes," Mayor Lightfoot advised. After two weeks in the house, I felt like I was suffocating, and Dr. Rosen told me to take a walk every day and to smile at every single person I saw.

In May, we rode our bikes to the lake-front — the temperatures felt closer to late February, which means we bundled ourselves in puffy coats and wool hats under our helmets. We didn't care; we had to get out of the house before one of us ended up in the psych ward or in jail.

"Sorry, no access," the police officer

stationed at the entrance to the bike path said.

"But we just want to ride. We all live together. We'll stay away from other people."

"Go home."

Once, the sitter took the kids to the park in front of their school to look for cool sticks — like the goddamn Flintstones. What else was there to do? No one else was in the park, except for a guy sitting on a bench many yards away. After a few minutes, a police officer drove his squad car onto the grass, parked several yards from the kids, and flashed his lights. "Go home! No congregating," he said through the bullhorn. Terrified, the kids ran home, afraid they were about to be arrested.

We were in lockdown for the foreseeable future, and people were dying. Gruesome graphs charted the losses every day in the paper. Morgues in cities like New York and Seattle filled up, and they resorted to using refrigerated trucks to house the bodies. So many bodies, Meredith.

Through my house and throughout the world, the prevailing mood was dread and terror. It was difficult to find any Good Orderly Direction amidst all the death.

It was the weirdest fucking thing. Schools closed. Trips canceled. Restaurants shuttered. I went days without leaving the house. Work went remote. The computer became the only portal out of the house. In July, we put on our fancy clothes and huddled around John's computer when his brother Justin married his fiancé at the Taco Bell Chapel in Las Vegas.

It was less than a year after you died, but you wouldn't have recognized the world.

From the first week of the lockdown, I heard people talking about gratitude. Mostly in twelve-step meetings. As in, "I'm grateful for the chance to let go of running all over the place." "I'm grateful that I have a job that allows me to work from home." "I'm grateful that I'm not stuck on a cruise ship docked in Yokohama for four weeks." Valid, sure. But the forced gratitude grated on me. It felt compulsory, and I wasn't ready. I wanted to go to my my office downtown; I wanted Zara's science fair to go forward as planned; I wanted to fly to San Antonio for spring break with my parents. We'd already picked out the restaurants with the best mahi-mahi tacos!

I fought the gratitude for weeks. You would *not* have approved. At one twelve-step meeting, I was asked to speak on any topic of my choosing. My topic: you people can't make me be grateful for this fucking pandemic. Some of the old-timers side-eyed me as I deconstructed gratitude as patriarchal and oppressive.

I didn't exactly make friends during this period.

At night under the cover of darkness about three months in, I thought of you and jotted a few things down. A gratitude list. My kids' and John's health, our parents' health, our house, the ability to work from home, the food we cooked each day even though we ate lentils three times a week. My heart made space for gratitude, but I refused to perform it in public. I was still so furious and afraid. Fucking COVID-19 had stolen lives, fucked up the whole world, and I wouldn't be grateful to it for anything. Weirdly, it felt like a way of honoring the one hundred thousand people who had lost their lives.

Then, I got a message over Facebook.

Hi! Can you join Lia, Jade, and me for a Zoom this Sunday at 5:30 p.m.?? It would be so fun to catch up. Let me know! — Bree

Meredith, I screamed. A chance to reunite with my high school friends? *Yes,*

yes, yes, I want to join. At this point, in May 2020, I hadn't had any significant contact with Lia, Bree, and Jade since senior year in high school, twenty-nine years earlier. Sure, I'd gone to Lia's wedding, but I'd acted more like a fugitive than a friend, evading questions about where I'd been and slinking out early without saying goodbye. Remember all those grief dreams I had about Lia? Remember how you told me to reach out? I wasn't ready then. But now I was.

Yes!!!!! Yes, I'd love to.

Can you believe it? For the next forty-eight hours until the call, I felt different in my body. I felt new life breathed into the old musty version of myself who ghosted her friends in high school for a boy who didn't love her. I dragged her out of the darkness, polished her, and let her join present-day Christie. Bree's invitation wouldn't alter history, but it was a second chance. A shiny orb of space filled with promise opened up inside me. A chance to forgive myself and rejoin the friendships where I'd lopped them off three decades earlier.

The night before the call, I couldn't sleep. How many people get to reach back and touch their most wounded adolescent self and bring her forward into the present day? The feeling was the jittery, night-before-Christmas jubilance from child-hood, like something magical was waiting for me on the other side of the night. I held the pink quartz rock in my hand and thought about what you'd say to me if you were here.

"You deserve this. Just show up and be yourself."

"Carry your recovery with you."

"This is how you make amends: by showing up. Accept the invitation as a gift. Participate in friendships today."

Real talk, Mere: a few stray thoughts about whether they were going to yell at me for the girl I was at seventeen tempered my excitement. How absurd, right? Why would they take their time to track me down and send me a Zoom link only to shun or shame me? My thoughts went to weird places, though. Mostly fear. Fear I would squander the chance to reconnect. Fear about how it would feel to revisit these lovely faces, now three decades later. Fear about facing all I'd missed. If I'd laid it all out for you over coffee, you would've set me straight: "You're afraid. That's it. You've longed for this reconnection and now that it's happening you can feel how much you wanted it and how deeply the rupture upset you."

All I could think was: *Don't fuck this up, Christie.*

An hour before the meeting, I took a shower, taking great care to wash my hair and blow it dry, even though I had barely brushed it in weeks. I picked out a colorful sweater and small silver earrings. I held your pink quartz rock in my palm. John and the kids sat in the living room talking to John's mother on speakerphone, and I paced back and forth.

The math of my emotions: job interview nerves plus first date jitters plus meeting a celebrity. When it was time to log on, I took a deep breath and found I couldn't stop swiveling in my chair. I guess it was gratitude, even though it felt bigger and more multidimensional than that. I was getting a chance to show these women and myself that I wasn't the same girl who would vaporize the minute a hot basketball player with an abiding affection for drugs showed interest in me. This opportunity to reconnect with Lia, Bree, and Jade was the whole point of recovery, therapy, and working on myself: the chance to step into a situation I once couldn't handle but now could manage with grace because I'd changed.

I clicked on the link Bree sent, sure they would hear my heart hammering when my audio connected. Then I saw their faces. Bree was smiling widely, cheeks sun-kissed as she ironed silk camisoles for the clothing company she ran. Jade sat in her all-white kitchen, smiling and waving. Lia joined from her bedroom, where her three dogs lounged on the bed behind her.

"Christie! It's been forever. How are you?" Bree said, all smiles.

"Christie!" Lia beamed at me through the screen.

In their adult faces on the screen, I could see their younger selves, the ones I passed in the hallway or watched cheer-leading at Friday-night football games.

"Almost thirty years! Can you believe it?"

Thirty fucking years. My God.

We covered the biographical basics: where we lived, how many kids, how our parents were doing, who we still talked to from high school. As the minutes ticked by, atrophied parts of my former self circulated with new blood.

"Remember Ms. Palowicz's alegebra class?" Lia said. She ran across her bedroom and pulled out an oversized white book. Our high school yearbook.

She called out teachers' names, and I laughed remembering our strange college counselor, who had advised me to apply to the University of Transylvania, and our theology teacher, who told us about a couple who once got stuck having intercourse and went to the emergency room for medical treatment.

We zigzagged between past and present, and my stomach muscles ached in the good way from laughing so hard as we unearthed memories about our quirky Catholic corner of Dallas in the late eighties. The joy surging through me was real, though right next to it ran a parallel current of sadness. I felt the pang of grief when Lia mentioned seeing Bree on the weekend she got engaged in New York, and when Jade and Bree talked about meeting up for burgers when they both worked in Manhattan after graduate school. The joy of reconnecting at age forty-six meant I had to feel the years I lost, those years when I could have watched Lia run the Chicago Marathon or visited Bree and Jade on the East Coast. The shadow of all I'd missed hovered over me, both memory and warning: don't lose any more time.

Lia, the only one of us who settled in

Texas, lives fourteen miles from my parents' house. In the past thirty years, I could have seen her every time I visited my parents. It's hard not to regret all of the lunches, concerts, and dinners we could have shared. If I'd been in touch, maybe I would know her children well enough to give them funny nicknames. Maybe I could have met her husband's parents.

The three of them had visited one another in college and graduate school and then in their adult homes across the country. They'd stayed together; they'd done what I could not do. It hurt to see it up close, but I understood it was important not to run away from all that regret and longing.

"What happened to you?" Bree asked as the conversation wound down. "I mean, where'd you go after high school?"

That question had been swirling through the whole conversation for me, and it was a relief to address it directly.

"Senior year, when I started dating Kal, I lost myself. I let the turmoil in the relationship consume me. I lived in fear that he would leave or dump me, and it took all my energy to be his girlfriend. Everything else faded away, including y'all, my future, my family. Kal and his drinking swallowed my whole life. I let that happen. It was the beginning of a bad pattern in my life that I had to learn how to break. I feel sad for all I missed in your lives. I'm sorry for being someone who dropped her friends when the boyfriend came along."

All three of them nodded, as if they understood.

"I remember that guy. I had to learn so much in my twenties about relationships, too," Lia said.

"We won't talk about my first marriage," Bree said.

Jade nodded. "Glad you're here now, Christie."

You would have been so proud of me, Mere. Showing up and telling the truth. I didn't have to prostrate myself before them, begging for forgiveness for being a giant flake. I kept my explanation honest and tied to the facts. *I fell into an alcoholic relationship and lost my friendships.*

And get this: we still meet. Every Sunday. It's been more than seventeen months. The pandemic surges and wanes, and sometimes we have scheduling conflicts — Elias has a baseball game or Jade is at the mall buying underwear for her son. As life resumes its former, prepandemic contours, it's more challenging for all of us to carve out the hour on Sunday night. But for me it's a priority. I've missed only a few sessions, either because I was out of town or out with the kids somewhere I couldn't log on. I always text the group in advance to tell them I can't make it.

Each Sunday during the call, there is a moment when I look at their faces and remember how many years they were lost to me and how I'd had no idea how to get them back. I remember sitting with you at Panera by Millennium Park saying they were lost forever, that the best I could hope for was to work on the relationships in my life in Chicago. When I have that moment of grace? Gratitude? Wonder? Awe? I'm not sure of the word, but the feeling wells up inside me. Sometimes I think I might burst into tears and tell them, *Thank you for giving me this chance. Thank you for not forgetting me. I will never ever take you for granted again.* I can't imagine letting go.

A year after the pandemic started, John and I were fully vaccinated, so we masked up and pointed the minivan south to visit my parents. I texted Lia a few weeks in advance and offered to meet her for breakfast, lunch, dinner, a run, a walk, a coffee, a visit to the circus. Anything. She texted back right away.

Double date. Banditos in Snider Plaza. You have to have Tex-Mex while you're here.

John and I arrived early at the restaurant. My hands shook, and he squeezed them. He knew what this meant to me, even if he couldn't relate. He regularly talks to his high school friends — they're all on our Christmas card list, and every few years we meet up with his college friends and their families in Sedona or Lake Tahoe. Any time one of his friends comes through Chicago, John invites them to join us for a meal or to stay at our house. No thirty-year breaches in John's life!

Lia jumped out of her Uber and spotted me right away. In the parking lot, I hugged her tightly, half laughing and half crying. Her husband Matt wrapped me in a hug, even though we were strangers.

"Christie Tate!" he said, and then extended his hand to John, as if they were old friends.

I had the Christmas-morning feeling again — the feeling that I would be different on the other side of this dinner. Lia and Matt told stories about the night they met on a blind date and their early days of living in L.A. We laughed over queso and guacamole, and when I looked at Lia laughing at something Matt said, I recognized how it felt to love her and want her to be happy. *This is friendship.* I remembered being a fifteen-year-old and squealing on the phone when the senior boy she liked asked her on a date. I remembered driving to school with her at seven in the morning so we could eat breakfast with the elderly nuns before classes started. I remembered the joy and expansiveness of our friendship and how it felt to be inside the love we had for each other.

At the end of the night, she held on to me and said, "We are never drifting apart again," like it was a fact. I nodded.

I smiled all the way home, thinking of Lia — as she is today, as she was when we were young. She still closes her eyes and pauses for a half second before laughing. Her hands still move in the same pattern when she tells a story. She can still imitate anyone with such keen precision I want to march her to Lorne Michaels's office for a *Saturday Night Live* audition.

And even better, the next day she came by my parents' house with her daughter,

Sarah, who is now a sophomore at our high school. They'd come straight from school, so Sarah wore the same red-plaid skirt and saddle shoes we wore thirty years ago. Her blue eyes shine like Lia's, and her bronzed skin reminded me of sunbathing with Lia on the flat roof of my grandma's farmhouse. The feeling of warmth and affection I felt when I saw Sarah reminded me of how I feel when I see my niece or my friends' daughters. An urge to join arms with their mothers and chant an ancient song overtakes me. Go full *Red Tent.* I want each girl to know in her bones that we will always, always have her back and that she belongs first to herself, but then to us, and we will never let her slip away.

Lately, I've even felt it when I pass by teenage girls in the park or see young girls jumping rope during school recess, now that the schools have reopened. A few months ago, John, the kids, and I went to dinner in Chinatown in Chicago, and in the square next to the Chinese Zodiac statues, a group of seven girls — probably thirteen or fourteen years old — performed a hip-hop dance routine to a song blasting out of a boom box they propped up by the statue of the ox. We paused to watch their fluid bodies rolling, twisting, and jerking to the music. They weren't playing to the crowd by making eye contact or flirting or self-consciously averting their gazes. They danced for each other. At least that's how it looked to me. My heart swelled for them and their youth and their connection to music and to one another. I wanted to scream out, "I love you! Stay close to each other!" but instead I watched and savored the joy they brought me.

Sitting in my parents' living room with Lia, Sarah, and Zara, I imagined that the crooked line of my life has curved into a circle. I've traveled far enough to find myself facing Lia again. Lucky me. You once promised me I would have the opportunity to make things right and change the ending of the story. You, of course, were right.

Can you believe it?

Of course you can.

Miss you and love you,
Christie

Dear Meredith,

Here's what I want you to picture: it's January 2021, the pandemic continues its rampage across the globe, and I race around my bedroom on a Tuesday afternoon, changing my shirt three times (blue hoodie, then white blouse with a different blue hoodie, and finally a jacquard blue and purple top) and wiping off two shades of lipstick (spiced cider and blaze) to finally settle on sheer lip gloss. In the bathroom, I parted my hair on the right and then the left. I laughed at myself for acting like this was prelude to a first date with a crush I never thought would notice me. Annoyed by my own fussing about, I made myself pull my hair into a low ponytail and get into my home office. Once there, I rifled through the drawer for a pack of matches so I could light my candle, but I couldn't find any. Downstairs, I grabbed the flame starter from the kitchen (which bit me in the ass three days later when I needed it to light the fireplace and couldn't remember where it was). Back in my office, I grabbed one of your pink quartz heart rocks and slipped your gold-and-pearl ring on my finger. I knew I should meditate, but I couldn't quiet my whizzing brain.

At two, the moment of truth. I didn't have a date with Mark Ruffalo; I didn't have a job interview with a white-shoe law firm. Nearly ten years from the day that I vaporized our friendship, I logged on to Zoom for a therapy session with Callie and her therapist.

I guess I should backtrack: a few months earlier, in the fall of 2020, I reconnected superficially with Callie when I hosted a going-away party in my backyard for Emily, who'd just closed on a house in Catskill, New York. Callie, one of Emily's close friends, was on the guest list. Callie texted, offering to help with the hosting duties.

I wrote back right away, surprised by the rush of love I felt for Callie, the friend I'd ghosted for so many years.

Yay! Yes. I'm in early planning stages. Would love help. I'll be in touch with details. Hope you're doing great too!

We texted back and forth for a few

weeks, nailing down the time and date for Emily's party. Callie volunteered to bring sparkling water, and we brainstormed how we might commemorate Emily's goodbye. Callie suggested we buy a wooden box and ask Emily's friends to bring a note, memento, or a written wish for Emily to place in the box and take with her.

Callie and I moved through the party-planning tasks efficiently and easily, but then, the day before the big event, she sent me a text saying she felt anxious about seeing me again after so many years. She shared her intention for the party.

I will be grateful to be there, to see you, your yard, and any children who may make an appearance.

She assured me that even if she seemed distant or uncomfortable, that was simply her nerves overriding her gratitude and openheartedness.

As I read her text in my living room, I marveled at her grace and courage.

I replied:

This is a lovely text. I'm with you totally. I'm grateful for your thoughtfulness and adulting and putting this out there . . . I have no idea how I'll be tomorrow. I have some anxiety along with the joy that we will be together tomorrow after a very long time not together. My intention is to be present and open and undefended and to show love and take it in . . . I'm glad you're coming. And that we've connected. And that this is possible. Perhaps new chapters for everyone.

The day of the party, it was an unseasonable mid-sixties even though it was early November. The olive tree from my neighbor's yard that hung over our fence rustled like faraway applause. I'd bought blue hydrangeas and placed them in short vases around the table. The warm temperature meant we didn't have to swaddle ourselves in puffy coats and wool scarves, which felt like a gift. As I greeted everyone, I felt buoyed by the festive energy of seeing my friends all together, after so many months of lockdown. I was also nervous and found myself futzing with the flowers on the table, pushing a vase one inch to the right, then to the left, and back again. When Callie swung open the wooden gate to the yard, I felt a rush of emotions, including joy. I also felt safe — not afraid of the awkwardness.

More than once, I imagined you sitting in the backyard with us. You would have geeked out at the box we gave Emily, a beautiful blond bamboo. During the party, we each held a candle and read our notes to Emily and cried. So much heart and feeling — all very Meredith.

When it was my turn to share my good-bye message, I told Emily the truth: "I'm angry you're leaving and feel like you're abandoning me, and I support you totally. I'm privileged to witness your joy at starting a new chapter of your life in a place that is beautiful and meets all of your needs. I want that for you even though I'm sad for myself."

After the party, Callie texted:

I'm very interested in looking back at what happened between us so I can learn about myself and friendships. I had a vision that you could join me for a session with my therapist. Would you consider that?

I let out a long breath. Then another. Couple's therapy for me and Callie? It was a weird idea, but I didn't hate it. Hadn't you and I been doing some of this work all those years? Now, I had a chance to do explicit friendship forensics with Callie, who was as interested in looking at her part in our demise as I was with mine. I felt afraid but curious.

Callie's suggestion made me realize what I value most in friendship: someone who wants to own her own part and do the work of understanding herself. That's what I always loved most about you, Meredith. No one worked harder at understanding, excavating, and healing than you did. Honestly, Callie's idea of bringing in a professional sounded a little drastic, but so was a ten-year hiatus. Anyway, when have I ever turned down therapy? The idea grew on me. Callie had been with the same therapist for years; I remembered stories about her from our days of running on the lake together. It felt a little risky to see Callie's trusted therapist with whom she already had a yearslong relationship, but I didn't have the bandwidth to find someone else for us to see.

I wrote Callie back with perhaps slightly more enthusiasm about the idea than I felt: *Great idea! Let's do it.*

On the screen, I saw her therapist first, an older woman with blondish-gray hair, a kind smile, and a lilting, almost singsong voice. Callie hadn't logged on yet, and I was hyper-cognizant that this woman had likely heard plenty about me. I came this close to saying, "I'm the monster you've heard about all these years."

Thankfully, Callie joined us before I could open my mouth.

"Thank you so much for agreeing to this," Callie said, and even though we were images on one another's computer screens, I saw her tearing up, which made me tear up.

"I'm afraid this session will prove I was the bad guy," I said. "I'm pretty sure I was."

The therapist stopped me and explained that there were no "bad guys," and that the session was about understanding each person's experience of the relationship. I took a deep breath. I didn't believe her, this soft-spoken woman who'd been Callie's therapist for fifteen years. Surely, she hated me on Callie's behalf. I stared at the screen but couldn't detect judgment or harshness in any of the faces, except the square holding my own.

"I wanted to ask you about the end," Callie said. "I had Grant and my son, and you were next, the third-most important person in my life. And when you disappeared, it felt like you ghosted, I mean, that was my experience, that you ghosted. I don't know if that's the right word —"

I heard Callie tiptoeing around language, using I-statements, and sidestepping any accusations of wrongdoing on my part. I wanted to own what I'd done. As soon as I heard the word *ghost,* I understood it as a path to liberation for both of us. If nothing else, I would tell Callie the truth.

"You're right. I ghosted. I disappeared, Callie, and I gave you no warning or explanation." The relief of saying it out loud. I had ghosted. I could own it and set us free.

"Can you say something about why you disappeared, or ghosted? Why it felt like a better option than telling me what you needed."

Meredith, I squeezed the hell out of your rock. Stories swirled in my head, strands of narrative — some true, some aspirational, some flat-out false. I'd always been scared to tell Callie the truth. The truth about the space I needed or the responsibility I felt for her happiness. How I tied her apparent disapproval around my neck like a noose. If there was any future for us beyond this therapy session, I'd have to do more than simply admit I'd ghosted.

"I hated how I constantly disappointed you. I tiptoed around your anger in every conversation. If I mentioned another friend's name, you'd be so upset. And you'd withdraw, and I would go berserk wondering how to make it better. That happened all the time. It seemed like all I ever did was upset you."

Callie nodded. "I had such a hard time with early motherhood. I felt so lost and alone. I didn't have my feet underneath me. Maybe I wanted you to save me. I was so scared you would leave that I'm sure my misery pushed you away."

This was news to me. I knew Callie had struggled in early motherhood — who didn't? — but I hadn't connected it to the disintegration of our friendship.

"I didn't realize that your misery was about motherhood. I thought it was all about me — that I made you miserable, and I couldn't imagine why you would want to stay in the friendship when I was such a glaring, constant disappointment."

We went back and forth, explaining how those last months of our friendship felt to each of us. Callie drowning in new motherhood, me drowning in impotence to fix her or make her happy. The therapist interjected every so often, to be sure we were hearing each other, but mostly she let us go.

"I felt trapped in the resin of your disappointment."

"I felt trapped in motherhood and wanted

you to see me, hear me, rescue me."

"I'm sorry I couldn't see you or hear you."

"I'm sorry I put so much pressure on you."

Halfway through the session, I felt the weight I'd been carrying begin to lift, the blame dissolving. It was more than I expected from an hour-long therapy session.

"I really want to understand more about how I pushed you away," Callie said. "Do you remember any other incidents?"

I shifted in my seat and switched your rock from my right hand to my left. Outside, a light snow dusted my office window. How much could I say?

"Yes, remember when I struggled with postpartum depression after Elias was born? I remember standing under the el train right after Dr. Rosen suggested medication, and you went silent when I mentioned it. Not for very long — but long enough for me to project all over you — that you were judging me, that you —"

"I was. You're right. I was judging you about the medication. You didn't imagine that."

Right then, I felt the deepest part of the wound between Callie and me stitch itself back together. I'd come to the session with the intention of owning my ghosting and telling the truth. I hadn't realized that she would meet me there, in that space of truth telling, to own her own character flaws and the shadows that she brought into our relationship. She *had* judged me.

Her offering up that admission was one of the most generous acts of friendship I'd ever received. I felt like cartwheeling around my office.

In law school we studied speech acts in evidence class. A speech act, in a legal context, is when an utterance has legal significance. Certain words, if spoken in particular contexts, have the power to change a person's legal status. For example, if you and your spouse-to-be signed a marriage license and now the two of you stand before a member of the clergy who's just prompted you to say "I do," and you speak those words, those two syllables have the legal power to shift your status from single person to married person. Such speech is a kind of action. If your boss says, "You're fired," those two words transform you from gainfully employed person to someone who needs to sit down with a human resources rep to review your COBRA coverage.

Callie's words were a speech act — they

transformed me from the sole bad actor in the relationship to one of two people in a friendship that got messy. I'd carried so much shame about the part of me that ghosted Callie. In a dank, decrepit corner of my being, Christie the Ghost stalked me with guilt over what I'd done and kept me in constant fear that I might do it again.

Meredith, all those years with you — our coffee conversations, our phone calls, our check-ins after recovery meetings, the inventories you suggested I write — I had no idea if any of that would change me. Sometimes, I wondered if we were wasting our time and would be better off learning to bird or trade stocks. But the moment Callie owned her judgment of me, I was able to hear it and forgive her, thanks to everything I learned with you.

"All this time," I said to Callie, "I thought I made up that feeling of judgment, or just projected my own shame onto you, which maybe I did, but to hear you say that you were judging me is a huge gift."

"I had a lot of rigid ideas about motherhood and how help should look, and the truth is, I was scared. But I didn't say that. I didn't know how."

As with Lia, I felt incredible tenderness for Callie and for me — for the women we are today and the women we were ten years earlier in our newish marriages and the confusing, exhausting days of new motherhood, when we both had mothers who were gone or far away, and sisters who were busy with their own families.

At the hour's end, we agreed to meet again for another session in two weeks. Callie had more questions. The therapist asked me if I wanted to have any contact between this first session and our next one in two weeks.

"What do you want it to look like, Christie?"

I answered quickly.

"What if we send each other texts with our favorite memories of each other?" I said. The hour had been heavy with the weight of our rupture, but there was lightness in our history, too. I wanted those memories to be part of the conversation.

Callie loved the idea.

A few days later, I texted her my favorite memory: I hit mile twenty of the Chicago Marathon in 2006. The streets of Chinatown were lined with people ringing cowbells and cheering us on. More than six miles lay ahead of me. Callie, a veteran marathon runner who'd planned to take the year off and didn't sign up for the race, darted through the crowd and joined me at exactly the moment when my screaming hamstrings tempted me to leave the course and to find somewhere to sit down for a plate of dumplings. We'd planned for her to join me, but I didn't know how much I needed her until I saw her bright smile and laced-up running shoes. "Let's go," she said.

Once we'd covered six miles and the finish line lay two blocks ahead, she urged me to savor the moment. "Listen to the crowd. You just covered twenty-six miles on your own two feet. Remember this feeling! There's nothing like it." My whole body erupted in chills as I took in the sights and sounds: people lined up six deep behind the barriers yelling out names and ringing cowbells; the muffled sounds of the announcer calling out names as they crossed the finish line; the smell of bodies all around me sweating the last two-tenths of a mile; my arm brushing against Callie's as we headed to the giant sign emblazoned with sweetest word I could think of: *FINISH.*

For the final block, she tried to veer off so I could cross the finish line by myself, but I grabbed her arm. "No, stay! I need you all the way to the end." Right as I cleared the final yard of the race, I burst into tears of elation and exhaustion. Right then, a photographer from the *Chicago Tribune* snapped a picture of me that ran in the next day's paper. In the picture, I hold a gloved hand to my crying face and next to me stands Callie; her face is not in the frame, but you can see her shoulders. Whenever I look at that picture or think of that marathon, I think of Callie and how she ran me across the finish line. At the time, I had no idea that she'd been nursing a foot injury and had fretted about her ability to run with me up until the night before. She'd spent several therapy sessions troubleshooting how to take care of her body while also showing up for me because she was loath to let me down.

In response to my text, Callie texted me a picture of us dressed up to run the Turkey Trot on a bitterly cold Thanksgiving morning in 2005. We smiled into the camera, our wind-burned faces sticking out of fleece hoodies, our arms folded across our bodies to stay warm. The picture sent me back to that morning and all the miles Callie and I ran together, sorting out our young lives, trying to become adults.

The therapy session offered a rare

chance to revisit our friendship in a formal way, but the texts brought their own magic. I remembered how much love was in our friendship. It remained after all these years.

We had a second and third session with Callie's therapist, which gave us more space to excavate our hurt feelings and misunderstandings. During each hour, we were both weepy when we acknowledged how much the reconnection meant to us. We also recognized how easy it would be to lose another decade to resentment, dishonesty, and miscommunication.

"I'm up for meeting regularly without the therapist," I said at the end of the third session. Three hours of professionally supported excavation was plenty for me. "Could we try?"

Callie nodded and said she was open to it. I sensed a fear in her — a fear that I would disappear once more, requiring her to mourn the friendship all over again.

"I wouldn't do that again," I said. "I wouldn't leave without a full explanation. If you want, I can commit to having another therapy session with you if I feel the urge to bolt. If things go south, we can do a goodbye ceremony."

Callie nodded. "I'm scared, but let's try it."

For a few weeks, she opened our one-on-one conversations with a question: "How is all of this going for you?"

"I enjoy it. I'm glad we're talking again."

"Really? Are you sure? Do you get off the phone and feel angry or upset in any way?"

"No."

Did she think I was hiding some vital information from her? I wasn't. It irked me that she wasn't accepting my honest answers, though I understood that she was afraid I would abandon her again. I felt an old anger and anxiety rush through me, the feeling that nothing I did would be enough for her.

Miraculously, I spoke up.

"I feel angry and put on the spot when you ask me how this is going and don't seem to believe my answers," I said one Friday when we met over Zoom. "Can we *both* share how we feel about these calls? This can't all be about me."

"You're right," she said. "I'm asking you to go out on a limb and talk about your feelings, but I'm not joining you there."

We agreed that this friendship had to work for both of us or why bother?

It's vulnerable, of course, to reconnect in a friendship where there was a previous rupture. Callie knows a dark, unhealed side of me, and I know something about the things that haunt her. I think of the moms at my kids' school with whom I'm friendly — they've known me a few years from our kids' birthday parties and chaperoning field trips together. I imagine they see me as warm, mouthy, slightly irreverent, and maybe quirky. They don't know me as a ghost, as a new mother, as someone skittish around women sometimes because she still sees herself as the lackluster sister with permed bangs and splotchy skin. Callie knows that version of me. And while I don't have an impulse to run from the friendship, I do sometimes feel the impulse to hide from all she knows about me.

At night, when I can't sleep because I'm anxious about the future or the state of the world, I think about my friends, one at a time. It soothes me to think of each of their histories, senses of humor, intelligence, warmth, professions, strengths, challenges, traumas, triumphs, children, signature desserts. It's a cross between a gratitude list and counting sheep. What a privilege to be alive and have friends, right?

Wish you could see and feel all this.

Your friend,
Christie

Dear Meredith,

On the first anniversary of your death, I woke up and realized the date immediately. I felt full of grief — so full that if someone had tipped me over, it would have spilled out of me. I wrote an email to Gage, telling him how much I missed you and that I was remembering you; I didn't want him to face it alone.

Later that morning, I called Anna.

"I want to talk to someone who misses Meredith as much as I do," I said when she picked up.

"Oh, I do," she said, her voice cracking. "I miss her all the time."

As we talked, I paced the floor of my tiny home office, three paces up and three paces back. My nerves calmed after a few moments, and I sank into the armchair by the window.

We talked about you for a few minutes,

how sometimes it seems like you're still here. We can both hear your voice in our heads, calling us "sweetie" and "honey," and insisting that God has a plan for us. I felt really open to Anna — her voice, her sadness, her willingness to connect with me. Her father had recently passed away, and she shared how hard it had been to manage so many layers of grief during a global pandemic.

"Would you be interested in taking a walk some time?" I asked, not as a throwaway *Let's do lunch,* but as a genuine offer for an in-person connection. If we set out on a walk together, would I confess? About the scratch, about how my envy and insecurity became bloodshed? Probably not. At least, not during our first walk. If we were able to resume our old friendship or start up a new one, I might one day tell her how I burned inside over the notion that she would enter my therapy circle and suck up all the love, attention, and airtime. How she represented my shadow side by living a life I couldn't yet accept for myself. I think I could do it: admit how threatened I'd felt, how deeply afraid I was. She was born into a family with three sisters; she'd understand.

More importantly, I realized that I would

react differently if I heard a rumor today that she was joining my group. I wouldn't have to claw my skin; I could breathe through the fear and sit with the discomfort. I could keep my eyes and heart open. I could tolerate sitting next to her and letting it all unfold. I could do it. I no longer hope that it will *never* happen. If she comes to my group, I will be uncomfortable, but I will be okay. I know that. I also know she'd bring many gifts, and part of me would be ready to welcome them. Yes, I could now welcome Anna into my group because of the work I've done around friendship, but also because of changes I've made in my professional life. Remember all those hours I pined for a schedule that allowed more time to write? Well, I took the leap last spring and let go of my law job. Now, I'm a full-time writer, which astounds me every morning I sit down at my desk without having to write a brief, bill my time, or prepare for an oral argument. While letting go of my law job didn't miraculously fix all my problems, it has made space for the creative work I've always wanted to do, the space I'd always envied Anna for having. You were right all along: we could *both* have this.

"I'd love to take a walk," she said.

Confession: we haven't met for a walk, though I think of it every few weeks. I don't know what stops me, other than fear. Plain old fear of intimacy. But I meant the invitation sincerely, and I fully believe that one day I will call her up and make good on it. Time will tell if I'm for real or if this is akin to my failed promise to work on my core strength for fifteen years and counting.

So I'm a work in progress. But there has been a victory.

Last fall, one year and three months after you died, Anna asked if I would be willing to read the college essay written by one of her daughters. Once I got over the shock that her girls were seniors in high school, I responded yes right away. My resistance to Anna melted to soft butter, easy to drag a dull knife through. I felt an incredible surge of tenderness for Lily, whom I'd seen grow up over the years. I didn't know her well, but from the Christmas brunches we spent together, I knew her to be poised, polite, and articulate. I would bring everything I had to her college essay. I had no complicated feelings about Anna's daughter.

When the essay landed in my in-box, I immediately cleared my schedule. I read it three times before making a mark on the page. Lily's voice leaped off the page — she wrote about climate change and all of her impressive lobbying efforts at school. Setting up recycling. Working with the student council. Writing essays for the school paper. Her commitment shined in her pages, and I rolled up my sleeves to offer praise for her punchy dialogue and her insightful final paragraph. I made a few suggestions for places she might expand her story and let herself be even bigger on the page. When I looked up, I saw that I'd spent two and a half hours on Lily's 650-word essay. Editing in Word, I left twenty-seven comments in the margin; more than half of them were praise. I poured my best intentions into Lily's essay, knowing of course that her future success didn't hinge on Christie Tate's editing suggestions. But I didn't do it just for her — I did it for myself, for Anna, and for friendship. I did it in honor of your memory. The time and care I took with Lily's essay were my amends to Anna and myself for being so careless and reactive in our friendship. In some way, it was an amends to my skin and my arm, too, which is weird but maybe also true. You always insisted that I could

419

love more and expand further. The essay was a start.

Miss you every day,
Christie

Dear Meredith,

This one's awkward. I want to skip it and pretend it's not part of my story. But what will I gain from running away from it or hiding the truth of what lives inside me as habit, character defect, pathology — the fumes and shadows of a spirit I cannot fully excise?

Dr. Rosen announced we were getting a new member one day when I was absent — I was in Texas visiting my parents. Other than being annoyed that he made the announcement when I was not present, I didn't have much energy around the new member because I knew it wasn't Anna. And if it wasn't Anna, who cared? I generally welcome new members — they energize and transform the group dynamic.

In my first session with this new member, a woman named Ellery, I felt some sparking negative energy between us the moment she walked in. She seemed to appraise me in a way that felt offensive — think a thorough once-over with a look like, *Who is this chick?* I thought she was judging me, which of course was projection because I was 100 percent judging her. Her tiny feet were stuffed into three-inch Prada heels, and her purse, crafted by a designer so fancy I'd never heard of her, was made of soft navy-blue leather that made me want to brush my cheek against it. I read her as rich and used to being in charge by the way she took a seat, crossed her legs, and stared at all of us, like, *Whatcha got?*

Honestly, I was irritated that she looked to be about my age but more petite (uh-oh), with clear skin, little makeup, and long brown hair. Her fierce gaze made it clear that she was not afraid of any of us and would not politely wait her turn to ask for help. Her demeanor was as taut and sleek as a Doberman's.

I love you, Meredith, but I'm not a dog person. And I'm sure as hell not a Doberman person.

And her voice. Good Lord, Meredith, you should have heard it. When she spoke, the walls shook and windows vibrated in their panes. This voice. Shit. Imagine a sound as loud and piercing as a siren or a doorbell in a million-dollar estate. She was a human exclamation mark. I don't remember what she said, but my spine will never forget the pitch of her voice. I stifled the impulse to plug my ears with my fingers.

We learned that she was in broadcasting — if I watched the local news, I would have recognized her. Local celebrity, big deal. But she was more confident than any other woman I'd ever met. You know the character that Kerry Washington played on primetime TV, where she fixed problems in Washington and slept with the president? That was Ellery's vibe, except she was ten times louder. My thoughts and my voice were wholly swallowed up by her volume, so it shouldn't have surprised me that I snapped halfway into the session.

I can't remember the details. I know that Max and I had a minor tiff — he called me out for being defensive about something, which only made me more defensive. We volleyed jabs back and forth.

"He's trying to help you, and you are having none of it," Ellery said, piercing the room with her pronouncement. Have I mentioned she had a monstrously loud voice?

I turned to stare at her, truly in shock

that this new bitch had swooped into my therapy group feeling perfectly comfortable telling me what's what. The audacity. Oh hell no. Never mind that her assessment was accurate: I *was* defensive and blocking Max's feedback, absolutely, but she'd been around only thirty minutes. My whole body blazed with fury and shame that the newbie with the purse had already busted me.

Then she doubled down.

"You're so defensive — it's like you can't even hear him."

Welp. My rage shot past orange and yellow and reached white hot. I yelled at her. Maybe "Shut up!" or "No!" Maybe it was a nonsense word. Whatever it was, I said it over and over until my throat was ragged. And I scratched my arm. Again. This time, I did it out in the open for everyone to see. There was no bell sleeve, no hiding. I drew blood, though not as much as the time I flipped out over Anna. I got a few good swipes in — maybe four or five. We'll call that progress.

Dr. Rosen stood up and took my wrists in his hands. By then, I was crying and saying "I'm sorry" to him and the group members. He guided me down to the floor and sat behind me, keeping his hands wrapped around my wrists like human handcuffs so I couldn't do any more damage. I kept my head down. The shame made my bones bend to the floor. How had I done this again? Would I always carry this time bomb inside me? This urgent need to hurt myself — the skin, the blood, the scars — because a younger, prettier, more successful woman entered my intimate sphere? Was this defect in me getting worse or getting better?

You can make a case either way, I suspect.

As you can imagine, I spiraled into the whole routine of "I'm so sick, can you believe how fucked up I am?" But despite my bleeding arm and the very obvious reason for my lashing out, I couldn't muster as much self-recrimination as I usually did. Even as I sat on the floor, my breath still ragged, and my therapist holding my wrists like I was a suspect under arrest, I could see how different this was from the time with Anna. That time, my self-harm had been surgical and secretive. That's way worse, right? It's objectively worse to quietly carve myself up for an hour at the mere mention of a name than to pop off at the top of my lungs in the wide-open space of the circle in the

425

presence of the culprit?

Next time, maybe I'll barely break the skin.

I'm not naive enough to think it'll never happen again. It very well might. I'm humbled is what I'm saying, which I imagine looks good on me. How foolish and silly would it be if I walked around saying, "I know *that* will never happen again. I won't let it." As if those other two incidents arose with my permission.

So there I was, slumped on the floor with Dr. Rosen restraining my hands. I avoided everyone's gaze, Ellery's most of all. It was our first meeting, and I'd introduced myself by shredding my skin and screaming myself hoarse. Now she'd know how threatened and afraid I was. Would she lord that power over me?

At the end of the session, probably forty minutes after my outburst, she offered up a second assessment of me. "Christie was so vulnerable and so real. That was" — she paused for a second, and I held my breath waiting for her verdict — "impressive."

She didn't express criticism or an aversion to my over-the-top reaction. She didn't say she was repulsed. I heard a judgment but not the bad kind. Goddamn if her words didn't sound like praise, Meredith.

Everything suddenly flipped upside down — my self-harm now recast as a sort of superpower of the unrepressed? And now this terrifyingly loud woman who repelled me at the top of the hour looked like someone who might become a friend? My backward movement now looked like forward motion. Could that be true? My mind transformed into an M. C. Escher painting — one second the stairs marched upward; the next they descended to a lower floor.

Over the next few weeks in group, I listened to Ellery share about her life — her struggles with her career, parenting, and managing her relationship with her spouse, who'd taken an academic job in Boston. I respected how hard she worked and how much pressure she felt to excel in all areas of her life. Her voice still struck me as three decibels louder than necessary, but I appreciated her insights. When I discussed a work issue in a therapy session — a colleague had promised to help with a project and then went AWOL — she said, "You don't need him. You think you do, but you don't. Find someone else to help you." She's like that: practical, certain, unwavering. She would never let herself be beholden to a male colleague, and she didn't want me to either.

You'd like her. She has her challenges, of course, but she arrived at adulthood with an intact self-esteem. It's a beautiful thing.

Early on, Ellery and I figured out we lived less than a mile from each other. A few months after her entry into my group, she texted me, offering a ride to an early-morning session. When I first read her text, I scrunched up my nose, thinking I wasn't sure I could handle being trapped in a car with her. That voice in such a confined space? Plus, I liked my routine of walking to the train, reading my book, rocking gently side to side next to other commuters on the eight-mile ride down-town. I relished the three-block walk from the train station to Dr. Rosen's office that allowed me to clear my head.

I didn't want to ride with Ellery.

But I said yes. You know why? Because if I stuck to my regular, solitary routine, I would one day look back and say to myself, "Why didn't you take Ellery up on her offer to drive you to group? Why weren't you available for her friendship?" Saying no was ultimately passing up an opportunity to build a friendship. So I stood on the corner and waited for her to scoop me up in her German luxury SUV.

"What's your sister like?" she asked less than two minutes into the ride. There would be no small talk.

"That's an out-of-the-blue question."

"If you have trouble with women, I assume there's stuff with your sister."

I laughed. We hurtled up Lake Shore Drive, Ellery driving well over the speed limit while I traced my friendship struggles back to my golden little sister, blah blah blah.

I liked her. And she kept offering me rides, so I kept saying yes. Driving downtown with her before sessions meant I got to hear more details about her long-distance marriage, her son's college applications, her new side hustle as a media consultant. I didn't miss the train or the other commuters. Last winter we started walking together in the early mornings in Jackson Park before our workdays, each walk another chance to draw closer to her.

This will sound strange, but she reminds me of you. Not on the surface because she's a loud boss-lady who rarely doubts herself. She's never once invoked a Higher Power or suggested she finds any solace in God's will. She would rather burn down her house than attend a twelve-step meeting of any kind, and she'd go naked before stepping foot in a thrift store. But when I return to my house after I've joined her and her dog Ali for a walk, I feel the way I used to feel when you and I would part ways after coffee or breakfast. It feels like being known and cherished and held tightly. It makes me feel weepy, this being chosen as company by someone for whom all I have to do is offer my presence, you know? With guys, I always had to make them love me, fuck them, or let them down easy. It feels different to be chosen as a friend. Ellery, like any of my friends, could hang out with anyone, and yet she chooses me at least one morning a week. And I choose her. These are the most basic of insights, but I feel them deeper than I ever have. Time is limited — I think we can give you full credit for teaching me that — and we all have jobs, families, hobbies, CrossFit classes to hustle to, dinner to prep or order, library books to read, shows to watch, breasts to self-examine, and ill-fitting corduroy leggings to return within thirty days of purchase. None of us *has* to do friendship. Except maybe we do.

I've always thought friendship was in the hands — that's where it lives inside me. The hands that wear the friendship ring, that scratch, that hold the pink rocks, that write these memories.

Like you did, Ellery makes me feel less alone. With Ellery, as it was with you, I feel like someone is always holding my hand, and these days I'm slower to yank mine away just because I feel uncomfortable.

In friendship, I've found connections that make me feel like I'm not the only woman walking the planet with a set of poisonous beliefs or rabid obsessions. Sometimes, I turn to John after a party or some social gathering and say, "I hate myself." He just shakes his head at the darkness I can harbor about myself; he doesn't understand. You always did. So does Ellery. My closest friends get this in a way that my husband never will.

Ellery's funny. Sometimes she worries that my friendship and affection for her is nothing more than a display of southern codependence. On our third walk together, she said, "I don't trust you. I don't trust that you really want to be here and that you really want to be hanging out with me. I think you lie to people because you don't want to say no to them. Don't do that with me."

"I *do* want to be here. You're going to have to trust me."

"Would you tell me if you were lying?"

"Probably not."

Isn't this exactly what any relationship is? The leap into the abyss of another person's words and intentions, even though you can never really know? How can we ever really know if someone truly loves us or just hates to disappoint? We can't. All we can do is put one foot in front of the other and follow the path around the lagoon. That's how you build a friend-ship.

Or at least that's my very best guess.

Christie

Dear Meredith,

I emailed Gage on your wedding anniversary this year. He moved west to Colorado to be near mountains and friends. He said it wasn't a "morbid" escape from the city that reminded him of you; rather, he'd always wanted to be in a beautiful place. He said you knew this plan. I like thinking of him nestled under purple mountains and wide-open skies.

The other morning, I typed your name into my text screen so I could read through them again, but none of our messages loaded. A blank white screen stared back at me. I gasped when I realized all of our texts had disappeared. That blankness felt like a slap. The emails survive, though. The other day, I found one you wrote to me in August 2016. You wrote: *Your path is emerging. Believe it. I do. I believe.* Then, you signed it, *Love, Love, Love.*

I saved six of your voice mails. I love hearing your voice. In one from March 2019, you talked for forty-eight seconds about how you wanted to set a boundary with a friend who called you too often — you needed a break from her rambling, three-times-a-day check-ins but were scared to tell her. You said, "I need more space, you know?" In another message, you must have been responding to some panicked voice mail from me, probably something about how I felt disgusting or ugly or stupid — who knows? For twenty-four seconds you assured me that whatever I was feeling was probably "old stuff" that I needed to share with someone else to release the shame and obsession. You ended the message: "I love you no matter what."

I'm sad as hell you're gone, Meredith. It surprises me how I haven't let you go, even though you're quite unreachable. Death is the ultimate abandonment, and yet, I'm still here. I'm still with you. I'm still in the friendship. I'm still attached to you. Still and always. And the way our friendship changed me altered my life forever. I couldn't hold on to Lia through boyfriends and college; I lost Callie during motherhood; I drifted away from so many people

434

for so much less than death. And yet, I'm still here with you, my sweet friend. And back together with Lia and Callie, and on my way with Anna. You'd call that a miracle, and I would agree.

I'm most proud of our friendship. And I know you would be so proud, too. Of yourself and of me. Me — your messy, good enough friend. I'm fuzzy on the afterlife — whether I believe in it, whether it exists, whether we'll be in the same garden again one day — but I can say in this moment, I have my pink rocks, my memories, and your voice in my head. And I have a circle of friends. I offer them my hands, my friendship. I learned that from you.

Thank you for all you taught me. Thank you for being proof of Good Orderly Direction. Your life and your love have helped me believe in God. I hope you get credit for that wherever you are right now.

I love you.

But mostly thank you.

Your B.F.F.,
Christie

ACKNOWLEDGMENTS

And now for my favorite part: the gratitude.

Thank you to the Avid Reader Press team, a group of people whose unparalleled smarts and humor have graced my life and changed me for good. Jofie Ferrari-Adler, Ben Loehnen, Meredith Vilarello, Jordan Rodman, Amy Guay, Caroline McGregor, Samantha Hoback, Alicia Brancato, Lexy East, Paul O'Halloran, Allison Greene, Wendy Sheanin, Lauren Castern, Leah Hays, Felice Javit, and Leora Bernstein. This book would not exist in any readable form without Lauren Wein's editing, and I'm so grateful for all the ways she helped bring forth the right story in the right words.

For the first eighteen months I was writing this book, I was adamant that it should open with a big dramatic scratch. Several early readers and teachers encouraged me to rethink that decision and give readers a little more context before bloodying the page, including Melissa Febos, Jumi Bello, Janina Atra, and Lesley Provost. Thank you all; you were right.

Also on Team Don't Start with the Scratch was Amy Williams, and this book would not exist if she hadn't spent summer 2021 helping me with the revision process. I'm so grateful for all the direction and loving feedback she offered — regarding all things — about where to let go and where to lean in. It's no small or easy thing to hold writers' hands for a living, and I'm grateful she's holding mine.

Throughout the writing process, I've leaned mightily on the writers from my Wednesday writing group, which actually meets on Tuesdays. They've laughed, cried, cringed, and celebrated with me, and allowed me to do the same for them. Their hearts are bigger than my imagination. Thank you to Carol Claassen, Tanya Friedman, Annie Gudger, Mary Mandeville, and Lois Ruskai Melina.

Thank you to Lidia Yuknavitch for supporting this book and putting together an amazing crew of writers to help me workshop the early pages and shape them into something more than a jumble of memories and micro-scenes. So much gratitude to Anne Falkowski, Emily Falkowski, and Jane

Gregorie.

Thank you to Carinn Jade, my ride or die. I've covered more than a hundred miles walking through my neighborhood while we hashed out our lives and books on the phone. I'm hoping to cover thousands more. None of this happens without a friend like you to hold my hand and cheer me on.

ROBERT SULLIVAN has never gotten proper credit for the friendship he's extended to me for upwards of eighteen years. That ends today. Thank you, dear friend, Robert Sullivan. Our coffee dates are often the highlight of my weekdays. Robert is a friend-brother-father figure. I once sent him a panicked text, and he drove to my house to give me a hug. He once complimented my green suede coat, and now it's my favorite article of clothing. I am grateful for the big and small ways he loves and attends to me.

Dana Edelson is fond of saying she'll hold my hair back whenever I need to puke. While it's a curious offer to make to a former bulimic, she means it both literally and metaphorically. I'm grateful for friends like Dana who aren't afraid of the dirty work or the messy parts. Mostly, I'm grateful I never, ever have to tiptoe around her. What a gift.

Thank you to Shoaib Memon for always insisting on a Wednesday latte break — as long as it fits his schedule, and we stick close to his office. He's taken more than one panicked call from me about writing in general and this book in particular. I'm grateful he picks up the phone and says all the right things most of the time.

Speaking of panicked phone calls (and texts and emails), Joyce Polance has fielded many during her tenure as one of my nearest and dearest. She also read an early copy of this book and provided so much love and support. She was the first to assure me that it was okay to share my story and that I didn't have to dive into codependence as penance (coda-pennance) for telling. This book might exist without her, but I'd be squirreled away in an undisclosed hidey hole, which would complicate the marketing team's efforts on the book's behalf, so I'm grateful she cleared the way for me to stand tall in broad daylight.

Thank you to Cathy Combs for always having my back and encouraging me to let my life expand. I find expansion extremely scary, but she helps me leap forward in all kinds of ways I simply wouldn't and couldn't on my own. Thank you to Tim Landry for joining me on Tuesdays at noon, so I don't have to carry the message alone. I'm grateful for a brother who holds my hand as we trudge the road to happy destiny.

Thank you to J. Ro for continuing to encourage this writing thing. I'm grateful for the years of support, irritation, practice, joy, and challenge you've offered me.

Krista Booth reminded me to keep breathing every step of the way. Whenever I sit down to write, I text Krista and tell her, "I'm going in," like I'm facing a fiery inferno or dark coal mine. Because, honestly, that's how writing feels sometimes — like a place where I could contract a lethal illness or drop dead in a dark shaft. Krista brings the light and helps me get the day's work done.

Debbie South Moss looked me in the eye and told me she believed in me more than once. I always believed that she believed, but I didn't believe myself until about the third time. Thank God for friends who are willing to repeat themselves and to wait for me to get my head out of my ass.

Thank you to Caroline Chambers who always reminded me of novel concepts like abundance, joy, gratitude, and boundaries. Every phone call with Caroline is part pep talk, part bitch sesh, and all girl-boss real-talk. I'm grateful for every single conversation.

Stephanie Smith is a real fucking trouper — she welcomed me back into her life after three decades and loved me just as hard at age forty-seven as she did at seventeen. And she let me write about her in my book. How's that for friendship? Get yourself a Stephanie — you will never stop laughing and you will always have someone available for a genuine heart-to-heart with no bullshit and perfectly placed pop culture references.

Lisa Perkins and Jennifer Saba are also huge fucking troupers. Being welcomed to the Sunday sessions has been one of the most joyful experiences of this weird middle-aged stage of my life. Thank you for the laughs, the memories, the consistency, the parenting advice, and the chance to jump back in the river of your lives.

OSM Beads gets full credit for bringing friendship bracelets back into my life exactly when I needed them. You should order them and give them to your grown-ass B.F.F.s.

My Sisterhood Writing Group also swooped into my life at the perfect moment in 2021, when I left the law and stared at the edge of the new cliff that was my life. I'm so grateful for the loving support from Amanda Churchill, Grace Elliott, and Sara

Cutaia. The inspiration they offer is so strong and shiny that it allows me to forget my bullshit long enough to get busy writing.

We haven't yet settled on a name for the group of writers who gather once a month to process all facets of the writing life, but it's one of the most fulfilling hours of my month. Thank you to Christi Clancy, Wayne Scott, Meg Weber, Tanya Friedman, Grace McNamee, Jonathan Winston Jones, Andrew Neltner, Carinn Jade, Alissa Lee, Celeste Fisher, and Meghan R. Jarvis.

Thank you to Karen Yates for always bringing her A-game to every conversation. I'm so lucky she went to The Workshop and that she bravely wades into the waters of self-expression and exposure every day and generously shares all that wisdom with me. And special thanks to Leslie Darling and Michael Lach for always being the first to pre-order my book, and for all the care and feeding. Our conversations at your kitchen island have bolstered me as a writer more than you know.

Thank you to Javier Ramirez and Kristin Enola Gilbert, Chicago booksellers and book lovers extraordinaire. Their support of my work, books, authors, and readers means so much to me and to Chicago. They've brought so much joy to my life. Thank you!

Thank you to my parents for calmly accepting my memoir career — I promise I'll give fiction a go next.

All love and thanks to Mary Cibelius, whose voice I still hear in my head every single day. I think of her whenever I see quinoa or have an intense friendship experience. And also when I hear a Cher song, which is more often than you might think.

To Jeff, Sadie, and Simon — I'm brimming with gratitude for your patience, your capacity for celebration, and for your ability and willingness to hold me tightly every single day. I can't imagine the hell of living with someone who writes creative nonfiction for a living, but you accept your fate with so much grace and generosity that I can only be humbled and say: Thank you.

ABOUT THE AUTHOR

Christie Tate is the author of the *New York Times* bestseller *Group,* which was a Reese's Book Club selection. She has been published in *The New York Times, The Washington Post, Chicago Tribune, McSweeney's Internet Tendency,* and elsewhere, and she lives in Chicago with her family.

The employees of Thorndike Press hope you have enjoyed this Large Print book. All our Thorndike, Wheeler, and Kennebec Large Print titles are designed for easy reading, and all our books are made to last. Other Thorndike Press Large Print books are available at your library, through selected bookstores, or directly from us.

For information about titles, please call:
(800) 223-1244

or visit our website at:
gale.com/thorndike

To share your comments, please write:
Publisher
Thorndike Press
10 Water St., Suite 310
Waterville, ME 04901